ARDĀS OF THE SIKHS

ARDĀS

OF THE SIKHS

A Distinctive Prayer

JASWANT SINGH NEKI

MANOHAR
2012

First published, 2012

ISBN 978-81-7304-961-3

Published by

Ajay Kumar Jain *for*
Manohar Publishers & Distributors
4753/23 Ansari Road, Daryaganj
New Delhi 110 002

Typeset at

Digigrafics
New Delhi 110 049

Printed at

Salasar Imaging Systems
Delhi 110 035

Contents

Acknowledgements 9

Transcription/Pronunciation Key 11

Glossary 13

A Note Relating the References and Quotations from Sikh Sources 23

Introduction 27

PART I: METAPHYSICAL CONSIDERATIONS

1. What is *Ardās*? 31
2. The Spirit of *Ardās* 35
3. Universality of Prayer 40
4. Metaphysical Perspective on Prayer 45
5. To Whom Should We Pray? 50
6. *Ardās* in the Sikh Faith 53
7. The Evolution of *Ardās* 57
8. Outstanding Features of *Ardās* 62

PART II: FORM OF THE CONGREGATIONAL *ARDĀS*

9. The Text of the Congregational *Ardās* 69
10. The Structure of the Congregational *Ardās* 75
11. Invocation of the Divine Sword 78
12. Pray, Help Us Everywhere 82
13. Spiritual Light of the Ten Gurus 86
14. With Full Attention, Utter *Wāheguru* 90

15. Homage to *Guru Panth* 93
16. The Five Loved Ones 96
17. The Four *Sāhibzādās* of the Master 100
18. The Forty *Muktās* 104
19. Practitioners of *Nām*, Penance and Determination 107
20. Those Who Chanted the *Nām* 111
21. Those Who Shared Their Bread with Others 115
22. Those Who Kept the Cauldron Warm 121
23. Those Who Wielded the Sword 125
24. Who Noticed, Yet Could Overlook 128
25. Those Who Gave Their Lives for Righteousness 132
26. He Who Was Severed Joint by Joint 135
27. The One Who Was Descalped 138
28. Those Who Were Broken on the Wheel 141
29. He Who Was Sawn Through 144
30. Who Cheerfully Accepted the Lord's Will 146
31. Who Upheld the Dignity of the Sikh Faith and the Bestowed Form Until the Last Breath 149
32. The Five High Seats of Authority 152
33. All The *Gurdwārās* 155
34. Let us First Pray on Behalf of the Entire *Khālsā* 158
35. May the *Khālsā* Enshrine *Wāheguru* in Their Heart 160
36. Wheresoever the *Khālsā Jī* Abide 163
37. May Our Rations and Weapons Ensure Victory 166
38. May Our Reputation be Preserved 171
39. May the *Panth* be Victorious 173
40. May the Holy Sword Help Us 176

41. May the Word of the *Khālsā* Ever Prevail 179
42. Beseeching the Right Gift 182
43. The Gift of the Sikh Faith 184
44. Gift of the Holy Hair 187
45. The Gift of Disciplined Life 192
46. The Gift of Discriminating Wisdom 199
47. The Gift of Conviction 202
48. The Gift of Trust 204
49. *Nām* the Gift Above All Other Gifts 207
50. A Dip in the Pool of Immortality 211
51. Long Live Choirs, Banners and Hospices 215
52. Hail Righteousness 221
53. Humble Mind and High Thinking 223
54. From Which the *Panth* has been Separated 225
55. The Will of the Lord Prevails 228
56. Through *Nām* is Attained Resplendent Spirit 230
57. May all Prosper by Your Grace 235
58. The Traditional Way of Performing *Ardās* 238

PART III: PRACTICE OF *ARDĀS*

59. *Ardās:* Personal and Congregational 243
60. Psychological Difficulties 246
61. Philosophical Problems 250
62. Shortcomings in Practice 256
63. The Stages of *Ardās* 259
Bibliography 269
Index of Names 273
Subject Index 277

Acknowledgements

I am deeply indebted to late Professor Harbans Singh, who was chief editor of *The Encyclopedia of Sikhism,* who inspired me to produce an English version of my Punjabi book *Ardās: Darshan, Rūp te Abhiās,* which he thought was an all-time classic in Sikh literature.

I am grateful to my grandson, Hargun Singh, my friend, Dr I.J. Singh, Principal B.S. Rattan and late Sri J.S. Anand for having gone through the manuscript of this book and having made many valuable suggestions.

My sincere appreciation of my friend Dr Mohinder Singh, who impelled me to give priority to producing this book over most of my other literary engagements.

My gratitude to my wife, Kanwerjit, for having spared me from most of my domestic duties to enable me to bring this work to early completion.

My thanks to Sri Ramesh Jain for undertaking the task of publishing this book, and to Sri Naresh Jain for diligent first editing of the text.

JASWANT SINGH NEKI

Transcription/Pronunciation Key for Non-English Words/Phrases

Certain names and terms have been used in the text in their original Punjabi form. In order to facilitate their correct pronunciation, the following key has been used while transcribing the original into the Roman script:

Punjabi phonemes (Gurmukhī script) Letter/Vowel symbol		Hindi/Sanskrit phonemes (Devanāgarī script) Letter/Vowel symbol		Urdu/Persian Arabic phonemes (Persian script) Letter/Vowel symbol		Roman script equivalents
ਅ		अ		اَ	ـَ	a
ਆ	ਾ	आ	ा	آ		ā
ਇ	ਿ	इ	ि	اِ	ـِ	i
ਈ	ੀ	ई	ी	اِ+یِ	ـِی	ī
ਉ	ੁ	उ	ु	اُ	ـُ	u
ਊ	ੂ	ऊ	ू	اُ+وُ	وُ	ū
ਏ	ੇ	ए	े	اِ+ے	ے	e
ਐ	ੈ	ऐ	ै	اَے	ے	ai
ਓ	ੋ	ओ	ो	او	و	o
ਔ	ੌ	औ	ौ	اَوْ	وْ	au
ਸ		स		ث، س، ص		s
ਹ		ह		ح، ہ، ھ		h
ਕ		क		ک		k
ਖ		ख		کھ		kh
ਗ		ग		گ		g
ਘ		घ		گھ		gh
ਙ		ङ		-		ṅ
ਚ		च		چ		ch or c (1)
ਛ		छ		چھ		chh or ch (1)
ਜ		ज		ج		j
ਝ		झ		جھ		jh
ਞ		ञ		-		ñ
ਟ		ट		ٹ		ṭ
ਠ		ठ		ٹھ		ṭh
ਡ		ड		ڈ		ḍ
ਢ		ढ		ڈھ		ḍh
ਣ		ण		-		ṇ

Punjabi phonemes (Gurmukhi script) Letter/Vowel symbol	Hindi/Sanskrit phonemes (Devanāgarī script) Letter/Vowel symbol	Urdu/Persian Arabic phonemes (Persian script) Letter/Vowel symbol	Roman script equivalents
ਤ	त	ت، ط	t
ਥ	थ	تھ	th
ਦ	द	د	d
ਧ	ध	دھ	dh
ਨ	न	ن	n
ਪ	प	پ	p
ਫ	फ	پھ	ph
ਬ	ब	ب	b
ਭ	भ	بھ	bh
ਮ	म	م	m
ਯ	य	ی	y
ਰ	र	ر	r
ਲ	ल	ل	l
ਵ	व	و	v, w (2)
ੜ	ड़	ڑ	ṛ (3)
ੜ੍ਹ	ढ़	ڑھ	ṛh
ਸ਼	श	ش	sh, ś
ਖ਼		خ	<u>kh</u>
ਗ਼		غ	<u>gh</u>
ਜ਼		ذ، ز، ض، ظ	z
ਫ਼		ف	f
	ऋ		ṛ (4)
	ष		ṣ (4)
	क्ष		kṣ
	त्र		tr
	ज्ञ		jñ, gi, gy (5)
		ع	' followed by vowel symbol
		ق	q

Glossary

Ādi Granth	:	vide *Srī Gurū Granth Sāhib.*
ahankār, hankār	:	vain pride, arrogance, haughtiness.
akāl	:	timeless, beyond time, immortal.
Akāl Purakh	:	The One beyond time. God.
akhāṛā	:	lit. arena; meeting place, living quarter.
ahanmat	:	egoistic intellect.
amrit	:	the drink that imparts immortality; nectar used metaphorically.
amritdhārī	:	one who has been initiated into the Order of the *Khālsā* through the *amrit* ceremony.
amrit sanskār	:	the ceremony of administering *amrit.*
anahad shabd	:	lit. unstruck music; mystic sound experienced in deep meditation; the primordial sound *Om.*
ārtī	:	ritual worship with lighted lamps and flowers in a tray moved in circular motion in front of an idol or person; the accompanying hymn of praise.
ardās	:	prayer.
ardāsīā	:	one who leads the congregational prayer, *ardās.*
āsrā	:	support, refuge, haven, protection.
bairāg	:	renunciation, non-attachment with worldly affairs.
bāṇī	:	utterance, speech; see also *gurbāṇī.*
baolī	:	step well.
bhagat	:	devotee, votary, holyman.
bhagautī	:	sword; the goddess of power (*shakti*).
bhakti	:	loving devotion and dedication to God.
bhāṇā	:	divine pleasure.
bhau	:	fear, terror.
bhekhī	:	imposter.
bhram	:	illusion—in particular that material things

		are everlasting and non-realization of God as eternal.
bibek, vivek	:	discriminating intellect.
bārd	:	singer, minstrel.
bharosā	:	confidence, trust.
birhā	:	distressing feeling of separation from the loved one. In *gurmat,* as also in Sūfism, it is considered a sign of spiritual awakening.
brahm	:	the Ultimate Reality; God.
brahmgiānī	:	one who has realized God.
buṅga(h)	:	living quarters.
caṛhdī kalā	:	sublime state of consciousness full of inspired joy and exultation before which anxiety, grief, sinfulness and wicked mentality evaporate and with the resplendent spirit of *nām,* one is inspired for the well-being of all.
caukī	:	a choir of four singers; *bhajan maṇḍalī.*
caur, caurī	:	fly-whisk.
cauthāpad	:	the fourth (highest) state of consciousness; experience of attributeless God; also called *suṅn.*
darvesh	:	Mohammedan hermit, recluse, mendicant.
dastār	:	turban.
dātā, dātār	:	giver.
deg	:	literally, cauldron; figuratively, kitchen, *laṅgar* or *kaṛāh prasād.*
ḍhāḍhī	:	a minstrel, ballad singer.
dharam/dharma	:	a complex of religious and social concepts and practices; also nascent character, faith, righteousness; moral or religious duty.
dharam kalā	:	power of *dharam* (righteousness).
dharmsāl	:	place of worship.
dhāt	:	the way of worldly rat-race.
dhiān	:	inner attention and concentration.
dīdār	:	sight, glimpse—particulary of a holy man.
Divālī	:	the festival of lamps commemorating Lord Rāma's return home after vanquishing Rāvaṇa.
dīwān	:	royal court; religious congregation.

dukh	:	suffering.
dusht̤	:	wicked person.
faqīr	:	one who practices renunciation and austerities.
farmān	:	an order, a royal order, a divine ordinance.
fateh	:	victory.
gāyatrī	:	a verse from *Rigveda* recited by Brahmins as prayer.
ghalūghārā	:	pogrom, genocide.
giān	:	knowledge, insight, religious or spiritual enlightenment.
gurbāṇī	:	guru's word, his utterance or composition.
gurdwārā, gurduārā	:	Sikh place of worship, Sikh temple.
gurmaṅtar	:	The *mantar* given by the *guru*; *nām* or *shabad* given by him.
guru	:	religious or spiritual guide or preceptor.
gurmat	:	*guru's* percepts; teaching of Sikh *gurus*; tenets of the Sikh faith.
gurmattā	:	resolution or consensus arrived at in a Sikh congregation.
gurmukh	:	*guru*-oriented; a model or ideal Sikh.
Gurprasād	:	*guru's* grace.
Gur-shabad	:	*guru's* word.
Gursikh	:	disciple or follower of a *guru*.
hājī	:	one who is going to or has already made a pilgrimage to Meccā.
haṭh	:	pursuing something obstinately; dogged determination.
haṭhī	:	tenacious, obdurate, wilful, one practising renunciation.
haumai	:	the ego; self-centredness; attributing everything to oneself to the exclusion of the Divine Will and Divine Omnipotence.
hukam	:	Divine Will, God's Command.
hukamnāmā	:	a written command, mandatory epistle from a *guru* or other spiritual authority.
īmān	:	faith; belief especially in God; conscience, integrity.

jaikārā : slogan or shouts of victory.

jap : vocal or silent recitation of God's name, mystical *mantra* or prayer.

japī : one regular in *jap,* worshipper.

jhaṅḍā : flag; standard, banner; ensign.

jīvan-mukt : emancipated, liberated while still alive, i.e. in the present life itself.

jīvan-muktī : liberation in life; state of being *jīvan-mukt.*

janam sākhī : biography, especially of a holy man or *guru.*

jogī : practitioner of *yoga;* an ascetic sect or its member.

jot : light, flash, flame, fig. soul

jugat : manner, method, skill, knack, device, plan, scheme.

kachehrā : underwear, shorts.

Kaliyuga : Age of darkness; the last of the four eons in Indian thought.

kalimā : confession of faith in Islam, the saying : there is no God but Allah, and Muhammad is the messenger of God.

kām : passion, lust, sexual appetite, sexual instinct, libido, lechery.

kaṅghā : comb.

kaṛā : metallic bangle, steel bangle worn by Sikhs as a religious symbol.

kaṛāh prasād : special consecrated pudding distributed in *gurdwārās.*

karm : act, action, deed, occupation, business, activity.

karm-kāṅḍ : ritualism, rituals.

kartā, kartār : doer, creator; God as Creator.

kathā : sermon, religious discourse, oral exegesis.

kes : hair.

Khālsā : commonwealth of baptized Sikhs; crown land.

Khālsā, Bandaī : section of the *Khālsā* that followed Baṅdā Siṅgh Bahādur.

Khālsā, Sarbat : plenary meeting of representatives of all baptized Sikhs; the entire Sikh community.

Khālsā, Tat : the essential *Khālsā* directly connected with the *guru* without intervention by Baṅdā or anyone else.

khaṅḍ : one of the nine regions of the world.

khaṅḍā : a type of double-edged sword.

kirpā : kindness, compassion, benignity, benevolence.

kirpān : curved sword, sabre, scimitar; sword carried by baptized Sikhs as their religious symbol.

kirt karnī : to work, toil, or labour.

kirtam nām : names of God related to His attributes such as creator, preserver, destroyer.

kīrtan : singing hymns; devotional singing in praise of deity.

krodh : anger, ire, rage.

kvāo : sentence, command.

laṅgar : the free open kitchen in a Sikh *gurdwārā.*

liv : concentration or contemplation imbued with feelings of love.

lobh : greed, avarice.

Lochan Dhūm : a demon from whose eyes come out smoke and fire.

lok : world, universe, any of the metaphysical regions of creation.

mahaṅt : priest, head of a temple or monastery.

manmukh : self-oriented (in contrast to *guru*-oriented), wilful, irreligious, atheist.

maṅtar : mystic formula, holy hymn, text or word; spell, charm.

māyā : goddess of wealth, Lakshmi; wealth, riches; illusory world of senses, material world; illusion, illusory phenomena; phantasmagoria.

Mehkhāsur : a demon wild as a he-buffalo.

mīrī : temporal authority.

misl : anyone of the eighteenth-century Sikh confederacies.

moha : attachment, infatuation, love, affection, fondness; ignorance causing such behaviour.

muktā : liberated person; (in Sikh history) any of the martyrs of Camkaur or Muktsar.

muktī : freedom, liberation, emancipation, salvation, redemption, end of transmigration.

nād : sound, music; conch, horn.

nadar : sight, a kind glance, grace (an important attribute of God).

Nām : the name, the name of God; the transcendent and immanent God; the *guru's* word.

Nām, dān, ishnān: Guru Nanak's formulation for the Sikh way of life - worship through the *Nām*, honest earning and sharing with others and physical and moral purity.

Nām japnā : to recite or repeat the name of God.

Nām mārg : the spiritual path entirely linked with the *Nām*.

Nām simrin : remembrance of God's name, meditation on the name.

nihāl : delighted; exalted, elevated.

nihaṅg : a sect of baptized Sikhs, any of its members; pure, untainted.

niṅdak : slanderer.

nirbhau : fearless, undaunted.

nirguṇ : without attributes, transcendent aspect of reality.

nirmal : unpolluted, pure, unsullied, clean.

nirvair : without rancour, malice or animosity; amiable, friendly.

nirvāṇa : salvation, emancipation, liberation (Buddhist term for *mukti*).

Nishān Sāhib : an honoured flag, a national flag.

nivritī : indifference to worldly affairs, non-attachment, renunciation.

Oaṅkār : the formless yet manifest one God.

pāhul : consecrated drink administered during initiation rite of the *Khālsā*; *amrit.*

paij : honour, dignity.

paṅc : a member of a committee of five (*paṅcāyat*).

paṅḍit : Brahmin, scholar, learned person.

paṅgat	:	line, row especially in *laṅgar* hall.
Paṅj Piāre	:	the Five Loved Ones of Guru Gobiṅd Siṅgh who offered their head to him.
parbrahm	:	the transcendental one, God.
parikarmā	:	circumambulation.
parmeshwar	:	the supreme Lord, God.
param-pad	:	the ultimate state of spiritual progress.
parupkār	:	act performed for others' good, benevolence, benefaction.
pātshāhī	:	kingship, kingdom, empire,
patit	:	fallen (in religious or moral sense), apostate, degraded, sinner.
pauṛī	:	ladder, staircase; rung of a ladder, step of stairs; stanza of a ballad or ode.
pīrī	:	religious/spiritual authority.
prakriti	:	nature, disposition, inherent tendency.
pravritī	:	proclivity, propensity, natural/instinctive tendency.
prāṇāyām	:	a system of breathing exercises and regulation of respiration.
prāṇsaṅglī	:	method of regulating *jāp* with inspiration and expiration of breath.
prasād	:	grace, favour, kindness; also sacred food.
qāzī	:	an important official for administration of justice under Muslim rule.
qudrat	:	power; divine power behind creation and behind all that happens.
rahīm	:	one who shows mercy; God.
rahit	:	the conduct of life prescribed by the *gurus*.
rāj	:	rule, rulership; metaphor for the temporal concerns of the *gurus* as essential for regeneration.
rājā	:	king, ruler.
Rakt Bīj	:	a demon from whose every drop of spilt blood, another demon like him arises.
Rām-nām	:	the name of God.
ras	:	juice; relish, flavour, savour, aesthetic pleasure, delight in spiritual pusuits.
razā	:	wish; divine pleasure, God's will.

sādhsaṅgat	:	holy congregation.
sādhū	:	saint, holyman, mystic; also used for the *guru.*
sahaj	:	an absolutely placid state without tension or hurry; the state of liberation and bliss.
sahibzāde	:	the offspring of a dignitary; the sons of the *gurus*.
sākhī	:	story, anecdote usually connected with a holy person; evidence, testimony.
samādhi	:	deep meditation as a mystic exercise or experience, trance.
saṅgat	:	congregation.
saṅjam	:	temperance, continence, self-control, discipline, restraint.
saṅt	:	virtuous man, saintly individual.
sanyāsī	:	a renunciate, ascetic.
sarab loh	:	all-steel, pure steel; strong as steel.
sarab kāl	:	eternity.
sarguṇ	:	endowed with attributes; immanent aspect of God as against transcendent.
Satguru	:	the true *guru,* used for God as well as for Guru Nānak and his successors.
Sat-nām	:	the true name; God in His transcendent state for whom the only appropriate epithet is *sat* which means 'true' as well as 'existent'.
satsaṅgat	:	the true association; the Sikh congregation.
savayīyā	:	a eulogy in a specific poetic mode consisting of a four-line stanza.
sevā	:	free and voluntary service; attending upon, looking after; worship.
Sevāpaṅthī	:	a Sikh sect dedicated to humanitarian service activities.
shabad	:	the word; divine self-revelation; a composition of the *guru.*
shahādat	:	martyrdom.
shahīd	:	a martyr.
shalok/slok	:	a couplet or, occasionally, longer verse composition.

shāṅti	:	peace, generally characteristic of the state of *mukti.*
Shivālā	:	a temple dedicated to the worship of Lord Shiva.
Srī Guru Graṅth Sāhib	:	the principal scripture of the Sikhs, considered to be their perpetually living guide.
Srī sāhib	:	The holy sword.
suṅn samādhī	:	the highest *samādhī.*
ta<u>kh</u>t	:	lit. throne; royal seat; the Sikh seats that take decisions on mundane affairs.
tan<u>kh</u>āh	:	salary, emoluments; (in Sikh parlance) punishment.
tap	:	austerity, penance, self-mortification.
tapī	:	an ascetic, recluse, hermit.
taquia	:	hermitage.
teg	:	sword.
Thakurdwārā	:	a Hindu temple.
turīāvasthā	:	fourth and final stage of spiritual quietude, bliss, beatitude.
udāsī	:	sadness, sorrow; any of the long travels of Guru Nānak; a religious sect of Sikh or Hindu monks.
uddam	:	impulse to exert oneself, endeavour, readiness to make effort.
upāran	:	uprooting.
vāk	:	oral; sentence, utterance.
vāk laiṇā	:	to recite the first hymn on the left page when *Guru Graṅth Sāhib* is randomly opened.
vaṅḍ chakṇā	:	sharing one's (honestly earned) bread with others.
visāh	:	trust, faith, reliance.
vismād	:	wonder, awe, bliss, ecstasy, rapture.
Wāheguru	:	Sikh name for ultimate reality or God, lit. wondorous enlightener.

A Note Relating the References and Quotations from Sikh Sources

The original quotations from these sources have been translated into English by the present author. However, he has taken care to consult *Tīkā* by Giāni Badan Siṅgh and *Saṅthyā* by Bhāī Vīr Siṅgh as well as taken into consideration the extant translations by M.A. Macauliffe, Dr. Gopal Singh, Gurbachan Singh Talib and the International Institute of Gurmat Studies.

The sources from which quotations have been brought into the present work are as under:

1. *Srī Guru Graṅth Sāhib* also known as *Ādi Graṅth*, this is the principal source of the Sikh *gurus*' message. The following have made contribution to it:

I. THE GURUS

Name	Lifetime	No. of hymns	Comments
Guru Nānak Dev	1469-1539	974	First Guru. Founder of Sikh faith
Guru Aṅgad Dev	1504-52	62	2nd Guru. Adopted Gurmukhi script.
Guru Amar Dās	1479-1574	907	3rd Guru, Made *laṅgar* compulsory.
Guru Rām Dās	1534-81	679	4th Guru. Founded Amritsar.
Guru Arjan Dev	1563-1606	2,218	5th Guru. Compiled *Srī Ādi Graṅth.*
Guru Tegh Bahādur	1621-75	115	9th Guru. Sacrificed himself for the freedom of faith.

II. THE SAINTS

Name & Comments	Lifetime	Religion	Domicile	No. of hymns
Sheikh Farīd (Sufi fakīr)	1173-1265	Muslim	Puṅjāb	134

Jai Dev (Brahmin)	12th century	Hiṅdū	Beṅgāl	2
Trilocan (Vaishya)	1267-1335	Hiṅdū	Mahārāshṭra	4
Nāmdev (Calico-printer)	1269-1344	Hiṅdū	Mahārāshṭra	60
Sadhnā (Butcher)	13th century	Muslim	Siṅdh	1
Beṇī (?)	14th century	Hiṅdū	Bihar	3
Rāmānaṅd (Brahmin)	1340-1430	Hiṅdū	U.P.	1
Parmānaṅd (Brahmin)	15th century	Hiṅdū	Mahārāshṭra	1
Dhaṅnā (Farmer)	1415-1513	Hiṅdū	Rājasthān	4
Sain (Barber)	1390-1440	Hiṅdū	M.P.	1
Pīpā (Prince)	1408-68	Hiṅdū	Rājasthān	1
Ravidās (Cobler)	1399-1514?	Hiṅdū	U.P.	41
Kabīr (Weaver)	1380-1460	Muslim	U.P.	541
Bhīkhan (Sufi fakīr)	1480-1573	Muslim	U.P.	2
Mardānā (Companion of Guru Nānak)	1460-1530	Muslim	Puṅjāb	3
Sattā & Balvaṅḍ (Bards)	16th century	Muslim	Puṅjāb	8
Suṅder (Great-grandson of Guru Amardas)	1560-1610		Punjab	1
Sūrdās (Brahmin)	1528-85	Hiṅdū	Haryana	2

In addition to the above, 11 bard-poets of Guru Arjan Dev's court contributed variable number of hymns—Kalashār, 54; Nalh, 16; Mathurā, 14; Gyaṅd, 13; Kīrat, 8; Jalap and Bal, 5 each; Salh, 3; Bhīkhā and Harbaṅs, 2 each; and Bhal, 1.

The *gurus* seldom, if ever, sermonized. They generally sang their songs of the Lord's praise that are called *shabads* in Sikh terminology. When the works of the *gurus* were compiled into *Guru Graṅth Sāhib,* they were arranged in accord with the modes of music (*rāgas*) in which those are supposed to be sung. There are 31 *rāgas* in *Guru Graṅth Sāhib.* These are: 1. Srī; 2. Mājh; 3. Gauṛī; 4. Āsā; 5. Gujarī; 6. Dev Gaṅdhārī; 7. Bihāgṛa; 8. Wadhaṅs; 9. Soraṭh; 10. Dhanāsarī; 11. Jaitsarī; 12. Toḍī; 13. Bhairavī; 14. Tilaṅg; 15. Sūhī; 16. Bilāwal; 17. Gauṅd; 18. Rāmkalī; 19. Nat Nārāiṇ; 20. Māli Gauṛā; 21. Mārū; 22. Tukhārī; 23. Kedārā; 24. Bhairo; 25. Basaṅt; 26. Sāraṅg; 27. Malār; 28. Kānṛā; 29. Kalyāṇ; 30. Prabhātī; 31. Jai Jaiwaṅtī.

All quotations out of *Guru Graṅth Sāhib* that find a place in our text begin with the name of the *rāga* under which they occur in the source *Graṅth.* After the *rāga* comes the author. All the *gurus,* considered themselves as embodiments of the spirit of Nānak, and employed the eponym Nānak in their works. Therefore they are indicated in our references as m1, m2, m3, m4, m5 or m9—'m' denoting *mehla* meaning embodiment. For our purpose, we may even take it to mean 'master'.

m 1 stands for Guru Nānak Dev,
m 2 for Guru Aṅgad Dev,
m 3 for Guru Amar Dās,
m 4 for Guru Rām Dās,
m 5 for Guru Arjan Dev
m 9 for Guru Tegh Bahādur

(masters 6, 7, 8 and 10 made no contribution to *Srī Guru Graṅth Sāhib*)

Besides the *gurus*, there also are 18 saints some of whose works also find a place in the holy *Graṅth Sāhib*, they are mentioned by their names after the *rāga*. Finally, comes the page number of the holy *Graṅth Sāhib* (of the standard edition of 1,430 pages). In the case of references out of larger texts than hymns, the title of that text follows the indication of the *rāga*. Thus is completed the reference to a quotation from *Srī Guru Graṅth Sāhib*.

2. *Dasam Graṅth* is the book of the Tenth Master, Guru Gobiṅd Siṅgh. It encompasses his spiritual as well as mundane poetic works. Being stylistically distinct from *Srī Guru Graṅth Sāhib*, it was compiled as a separate volume. Quotations from it have been referred to as *DG* followed by the name of its section from which the quotation comes—*Akāl Ustat, Bacitra Nāṭak, Jāp, Krishnāvtār, Ukt Bilās, Zafar Nāmā*. Thereafter comes the specific verse number in that section.

3. Bhāī Gurdās has been a renowned Sikh scholar of the times of Guru Arjan Dev, who (the *guru*) engaged him as the chief scribe when the *Ādi Graṅth* was compiled.

His work of personal composition has been designated as the 'key' to *Srī Guru Graṅth Sāhib*. Quite a few quotations from his work *vārāṅ* (ballads) find a place in our work. Reference to these start with the author's name, followed by the *vār* (ballad) number and its verse number.

4. *Rahit Nāmās* embody the code of conduct for the Sikhs. They

have been compiled by some devout Sikhs such as Campā Siṅgh, Devā Siṅgh, Bhāī Naṅd Lāl, etc. References to the material quoted from these has been identified by the name of the compiler and the title of the *Rahit Nāmā.*

5. *Janam Sākhīs* are biographies of Guru Nānak Dev. There are quite a few of them, but the one referred to in the present work is that by Bhāī Bālā, who is said to have been a companion of Guru Nānak. References provided are to the respective *sākhī* number in that work.

6. Bhāī Manī Siṅgh, though elder to Guru Gobiṅd Siṅgh in age, was his lifetime companion. He authored some important works such as: *Sikhāṅ dī Bhagat Mālā.* These have been referred to by name of the author as well as of the work.

Introduction

Who has not prayed? Someone might pretend that he hasn't; but almost everyone who finds himself in a state of utter helplessness during threatening or trying times, tends to turn to prayer. That is why, prayer has been perennial as well as universal. However, historians have always chosen to keep quiet about them.They talk at length about emperors and potentates, invaders and conquerors, autocrats and despots, tyrant dictators and paranoid proprietors, but say little about those who suffered at the hands of such personages. Undoubtedly, millions in distress must have prayed. In spite of the negligent silence of history, there yet exists an important document that has sought to fill this gap. It is the congregational prayer of the Sikhs popularly known as the *ARDĀS.*

To pray without words, one needs to be on top of spiritual form. However, spiritually accomplished souls might occasionally have uttered a phrase or two that history gets compelled to preserve. The *Ardās* is a remarkable album of such spiritually charged phrases that have come to be incorporated into it over a long series of generations. Occasionally a half-baked phrase also managed to sneak into it, but soon such phrases got weeded out. Thus the *ardās* became an ever evolving creative work of great significance.

The phrases that got incorporated into the *ardās* were no ordinary ones. Lives had actually been lived according to them before they found their place in the *ardās.* Divine Presence had actually been experienced. His Holy Name had verily been meditated upon. Bread had been shared with the needy, even with 'enemies'. Holy cauldrons had been continually kept warm. The sacred sword had been plied to save the oppressed from the oppressors. Faults of others had actually been overlooked. Divine Will had been accepted without demur. Thus every phrase in the *ardās* became an epitome of a truly lived faith.

Multiple dimensions seem to characterize the structure of the *ardās.* It is at once an invocation, a laudation, an inspiration, a dedication, an affirmation of faith and a supplication. Every supplication is on behalf of the entire congregation. In its first part, it speaks for the entire commonwealth of those who have pledged to be the Lord's saint-soldiers, the *Khālsā.* It reinforces the fraternity of the *Khālsā* by awakening their pride in the lofty traditions of the religious fraternity to which they belong, and praying for the fulfilment of their collective aspirations. The next supplication is for those who claim themselves as belonging to the Sikh faith.

Then there is space for supplication on behalf of an individual or individuals for any specified purpose. The penultimate supplication in *ardās* is: 'Grant us, O Lord, company of such lovely souls, meeting whom we may automatically remember Your Name'. The *ardās* does not conclude without an ardent supplication for the welfare of the entire mankind under the Lord's Benevolent Will. Thus it becomes the prayer for all mankind for all times, transcending both time and space. It is a prayer that is held in utmost reverence, almost at par with *gurbāṇī* (the *gurus*' word), even though it is the composition of the *panth* (the entire Sikh fraternity).

This hermeneutic study of the *ardās* aims at providing a faithful exposition of every section of this delightful piece of poetic prose, the like of which, it is said, is hard to come by anywhere else.

PART I
METAPHYSICAL CONSIDERATIONS

CHAPTER 1

What is *Ardās*?

There is a wonderful legend from the Persian mystic Rūmī that reveals the essence of *ardās.*

One day, a shepherd left his flock grazing in the forest and sat down meditating under the shade of a tree. His face lit up, his lips quivered, and he began to murmur, "O God, if you ever meet me, I'll serve you the milk of my goats, launder your clothes, give you a decent bath and scrub you dirt-free".

By chance, Prophet Moses was passing by. He heard what the shepherd was saying and took offence at the way he was caricaturing God. He shook the shepherd by his shoulder and said, "What are you saying, O fool? What need has the Master of the universe for the milk of your goats? How dare you propose to cleanse Him who can purify all the sinful? What you are saying is sheer insolence."

It is said that a voice was heard from the heavens, "Moses! You have been sent to unite people with me and not to tear them apart from me. You have been unjustly enraged over the words of the shepherd, you have scarcely appreciated his sentiments. He has in no way been insolent. You have been!" Moses felt ashamed and suddenly realized that Divine Light shines not only atop Mount Sinai; it also radiates from the depths of a prayerful heart.[1]

Prayer indeed does not rest in the rhetoric employed. It lives in the simple and chastened outpourings of an anguished soul. Words spoken can hardly reach the ceiling, how then can they reach the heavens? Prayer is the song of the spirit, and like a song, it transcends words. It is the anguish of apartness from God that cries out from the innermost core of one's being and goes out to tug at His hem. It is not a mere ritual of kneeling or lying prostrate; it is, rather, the soul bowing in reverence. Folded hands and lowered head are only external signs of inner feelings

[1]Mevlānā Rūmī: *Masnavī.*

of absolute dedication, for if one's mind has not surrendered, bowing the head has little meaning.

Human history, as taught in schools, is lopsided. It tells us only distorted truth. It informs us mostly about kings, emperors, rulers, potentates, tyrants, invaders, rebels and traitors, but little about those innumerable men and women who fell a prey to oppression at the hands of despots and tyrants. It does not say a word about the wailing and mourning of multitudes. Though history is cruelly silent about this, we can be sure that the grief-stricken hearts of those unfortunate millions must have cried out to some higher Being for help. They must have implored Him and sought His intervention. Their imploring was nothing but *ardās*. Indeed, human history has been an ever recurring tale of prayer, and that is why a prayerful heart is never alone. It is linked with the immemorial continuity of mankind's sufferings. In this way, *ardās* embraces within its narrative, the all-pervasive suffering of the human race.

Pain and suffering are the fate of all humans. Our needs are enormous, but our abilities are small. Our existence is an endless tale of privations. However, when we cry out for help in moments of helplessness, we are in an *ardās*. The *ardās* invokes the Supreme Power of God to fulfil our wants and needs. Who can be better aware of our wants and privations than our Creator? That is why He has given us the right of calling upon Him for help. *Ardās* is this right of ours to call out to Him. Whenever a helpless soul cries out, 'O my Father!' it always gets the loving response, 'Yes, my child!'

Two different etymological sources have been suggested for the term *ardās*. According to one,[2] it is an abbreviation of the Persian word *arzdāsht* that means 'a petition'. According to the other source,[3] *ardās* is compounded from two Sanskrit roots: *ardan* (to ask) and *ās* (desire), thus meaning 'to ask for what one desires'. Both these roots appear equally relevant. The ingenuity of the originator of this term lay in that he made it accord with

[2]Bhāī Kāhn Siṅgh Nābhā: *Mahān Kosh,* Delhi: National Book Shop, 1990.

[3]Kapur Singh: Personal Communication.

Islamic as well as Hindu expressions—therefore giving it the ring of universality.

The term *ardās* has acquired special theological connotations in the Sikh spiritual lore as well. Sprung from the collective consciousness of the entire *Paṅth*, it became a powerful spiritual vehicle for communicating the collective longings of the entire fraternity as well as the desires of any individual soul to *Wah-e-guru* (the Wonderful Lord). It is through the Divine Grace of *Wah-e-guru* that the welfare of one and all is invoked.

Some scholars ascribe the following meaningful significance to each phoneme of the term *ardās:*

A = *Antaryāmī*: The One who resides within us and so knows all about us from inside.
R = *Rākhā:* The One who is our protector.
Da = *Dātār:* Benevolent Giver.
S = *Sahārā:* Great support.

It follows that *ardās* means invoking the benevolent Giver, who dwells within us, for His help and support.

Ardās is one of the major Sikh practices of worship. It is 'knocking at the portal of the Lord's Court'. It is also 'the key to the door of one's own heart'. Only one whose prayers have been answered can realize that the door of one's own heart and the portal of the Divine Court are one and the same.

Ridden by our needs, we pray for the fulfilment of our desires. However, supplicatory prayers are of rudimentary spiritual significance only. Sublime prayers beg for higher spiritual attainments. Indeed, the loftiest prayers seek oneness with the Lord, and nothing else.

The *ardās* is thus many things simultaneously: first, it is an acknowledgement of being a creature of God. It is affirmation of our own helplessness. And finally, it is inviting the Infinite to come and pervade the confines of our finitude. A prayerful heart soon realizes that Divine Grace does not merely respond to our yearnings, it actually even antedates them and even shapes the very yearnings that we think are ours. Thus every *ardās,* ensues indeed from the Grace of God.

The *ardās* has many dimensions. It may be a supplication, a thanksgiving, a laudatory exclamation, an expression of love and devotion, or a declaration of self-surrender. It may be soaked in tears of remorse or clothed in confident hope of redemption. An unending variety of sentiments can find expression in it.

Language seems to have a peculiar relationship with it, for it often serves as its medium of expression. The men of faith who chiselled the hallowed phrases of the *ardās* were indeed spiritual giants. They had actually put into practice in their own lives the spirit of these phrases that reflect their spiritual stature. Every letter of the *ardās* illustrates the beauty of their mind and grandeur of their spirit.

In the higher ranges of *ardās*, one experiences Divine benevolence uninterruptedly. All one's worldly demands seem to vanish; even words tend to come to a standstill. At this stage, one does not perform *ardās*; rather, one becomes *ardās*—a living *ardās*.

A prayerful soul always obeys the Divine Will. If one's supplication is accepted, it is considered to be God's gift; if it is not accepted, it is considered to be His wisdom. In either case, Divine Grace is seen to be at work. In this way, the prayerful heart feels blessed under all circumstances.

CHAPTER 2

The Spirit of *Ardās*

All that happens and all that'll happen is by His Will.
Aught if we could, we would have done.
Nothing by our own will ever come to happen.
As it pleases Him, us He preserves.
Dear Lord!
All your beings are under your sway
We, your creatures, have little say.
Lord! Forgive us through Your Grace.
You gave us a body; You gave us a soul,
And yoked us to such tasks as You chose.
The way You command us, so we act.
Whatever we do is per Your writ.
Out o' five elements You shaped everything.
Is there one who can fashion a sixth?
Some, through the Guru, Your mysteries grasp.
Self-centred others, but only grieve.
Who can describe the glory of the Lord?
I'm but the lowliest thoughtless fool.
Forgive me, prays Nānak, Your bonded slave.
The ignorant, I, Your refuge crave.

—Sūhī m 4, p. 736

The above quotation from *Srī Guru Granth Sāhib* represents in every way many verses that express the spirit of prayer. Reflecting on this verse, one can identify three main sentiments of prayer. The first is the feeling of one's own frailty, lack of power, and the state of helplessness; the second is that of trusting faith in God's greatness, omnipotence and grace; and the third comprises intense desire to receive that grace by taking refuge with God. The feeling of helplessness engenders *humility*; *faith* sprouts from the assurance of God's trustworthiness; and *self-surrender* results from the desire to take refuge with Him. Humility, faith and self-surrender, then, are the three fundamental sentiments involved in prayer.

HUMILITY

In a *janam-sākhī* (biography) of Guru Nānak Dev, the Guru says, 'The desires of the Sikhs who'll pray in utter humility shall be fulfilled'.[1] The humility of *ardās* is of a special kind—it arises from helplessness. When frail human clay cries out to God out of the feeling of land sliding underneath the feet, that cry is nothing short of *ardās*. We must never despair of our helplessness as it is this that inspires us to pray and prevents us from going astray. *Prayer is the special prerogative of the meek and the humble.* Those proud of their own intellect are simply unable to pray. The greater our humility, the greater the approval our prayers receive. We cannot get admittance to the Lord's abode as long as our ego continues to hold its ground. 'The portal of grace opens only when the ego is dismembered'.[2]

In the gracious kingdom of God, love is the only legal tender. Those who with the utmost humility take refuge with the loving God receive His ready care. One who has no one to look after him receives God's protection. Divine nature favours the humble and protects the unprotected. Out of compassion, God becomes the haven for the destitute. He reveals His mysteries only to an unassuming mind. The more one bows before Him, the higher He elevates him. During his dialogue with Sheikh Brahm, Guru Nānak Dev said, 'the deeper the water of a fountain sinks, the higher does it rise. Likewise, those who practice humility rise to sublime divinity'.[3]

Humility, besides being the fundamental sentiment of the *ardās*, is also the basis of our relationship with God. When we realize our utter impotence before His absolute omnipotence, we have no option but to humbly bare our helplessness before Him, saying:

[1] *Janam-sākhī Bhāī Bālā*, Amritsar: Catar Siṅgh Jīvan Siṅgh, 1978, sākhī 94.

[2] *Vār Āsā* m 1, p. 466.

[3] *Janam-sākhī Bhāī Bālā*, sākhī 94.

Poor and meek, we are but Yours,
Save us, pray, O Greatest of the great.
—*Gauṛī Pūrbī* m 4, p. 171

In humility rests the mystery of ardās.

FAITH

Faith implies sincere devotion to, confidence in, and reliance upon God. There can be no faith without sincerity and candour, and there can be no prayer without confidence or trust.

If faith is absent, helplessness turns into hopelessness. Losing hope is tantamount to turning one's face away from the portal of grace. Faith lends us strength and sustains us even during absolute helplessness. A faithful heart proclaims thus:

While some might have others to support them,
Poor and humble, I, have only You.
—*Vār Sūhī* m 3 sl. m 2, p. 791

Thereafter, he leaves his concerns to God. The faithful consider their God not just their support, but also their power, fortune, and intellect.

The following event in Sikh history is a fine example of unflinching faith.

Sulhī Khān, a Pathān military officer, set out to mount an attack on Guru Arjan Dev. The news caused much concern in the Guru's court. Some made the suggestion that a letter be sent to the Emperor asking him to order Sulhī to desist from his evil design. A few others proposed that a deputation of a couple of men be sent to wait upon the Emperor and beseech Him to forbid Sulhī from attacking the Guru. There were some others who counselled 'prompt action ourselves to stem Sulhi's march'. The Guru, however, simply prayed and had faith in divine intervention. The prayer was answered. Sulhī met with a fatal accident while still on his way.[4]

A man of faith never loses his poise even under the most adverse circumstances. He advances his begging bowl with absolute hopefulness and awaits His gift with calm patience. *Faith, hope*

[4]Based on *Āsā* m 5, p. 371.

and patience are the essential ingredients of ardās. A man of faith fears nothing because wherever he casts his glance, he finds his Lord present to take care of him.

One whose faith is not resolute is often in two minds and cannot focus single-pointedly on God. However, *ardās* is essentially the function of a single-minded focus. One, in two minds, is in doubt about whether or not his prayers shall be answered. This doubt erupts in him even before he begins his prayer, continues to be present while he is praying, and remains alive even after he has said his prayer. This is a pity; to pray to God, and yet be doubtful about the outcome of the prayer. It is both blasphemy and hypocrisy.

How may this doubt and skepticism, that can muddle our mind, be dispelled? Guru Amar Dās instructs us thus:

> The mind gets polluted with skepticism.
> How may it be cleansed?
> Wash your mind with (the precept of) the Word,
> And keep your thought focused on God.
>
> —*Rāmkalī* m 3, p. 919

Doubt does not mean that faith is absent. Rather, it signifies that faith has not yet matured. Even rudimentary faith is helpful because it can cause one to pray for relief from doubt. 'O Lord! Doubt and double-mindedness do not let my mind be focused on you. You have always helped your devotees get rid of these. Pray, help poor me as well.'[5] God first dispels the doubt and double-mindedness of those unto whom he decides to reveal His mystery. Then the devotee, rid of skepticism, focuses on God with redoubled faith and love.

SELF-SURRENDER

The *ardās* must contain nothing apart from prayer. If anything else is attempted during *ardās,* it is bound to interfere with its sentiment. Lest his prayers should go unanswered, a skeptical person tends to supplement his *ardās* with many other practices. He might consult an astrologer or a soothsayer. He might even

[5] *Bilāwal* m 3, p. 796.

practise austerities or penance. There can be no prayer when the self is engaged in such efforts. Prayer reveals one's powerlessness to God, and *when there is less of the self, there is more of God.*

O Lord! I know not what to ask of you. You are aware of my needs more than I can ever be. You love me intensely. O Father, give your child that which he cannot even ask for. Whether you keep me alive or let me perish, give me pleasure or expose me to pain, please keep me under your Will. I do not know your ways. I can only surrender myself before you. That I do! Teach me how to pray. Pervade in my prayerful outpourings.

Such prayer can be a prayer of self-surrender.

I hereby surrender my mind, my body, my soul unto You,
Pray, keep me, as You Will. —*Prabhātī* m 1, p. 1345

Whenever a person surrenders his self before God and seeks refuge with Him, God provides him His custody with pleasure. This is His eternal covenant with us.

Lovingly the Lord embraces him whoever comes to His sanctuary.
This, indeed, is His covenant. —*Bihāgṛā* m 5, p. 544

CHAPTER 3

Universality of Prayer

Hold not the Vedas and the Semitic scriptures as false,
False is he who ponders not over them.

—*Bibhās Prabhātī* Kabīr, p. 1350

Prayer is the most universal sentiment of the human race. Every human being must, some time, have invoked some supernatural power for aid and assistance. Is it possible then to have a religion that would not include prayer in its spiritual armour?

In every faith, prayer is expressive of the inmost yearnings of the soul. Prayer points to the unity that binds diverse faiths together as it is one outstanding feature that is common to all active religions.

The Vedic *Sandhyā-Upāsanā,* the Muslim *namāz,* the Christian 'prayer', and the Sikh *ardās* are all varying forms of the same sentiment—a sentiment that finds expression differently in different places, at different times, and in different tongues. A shared intent pervades them all. Indeed, in certain places, even the form of expression is also almost identical.

To pray is to bathe in the holy waters of faith and then to look into the mirror of the cleansed soul. Whosoever, takes this spiritual bath daily without fail, finds his soul getting more and more lustrous day by day.

Faith is not subservient to routine. Hence no specific time can be prescribed for prayer. For the faithful, all times are prayer-times. Spiritual yearnings have always transcended time and space. Those who begin their days with the blessings of prayer and bid them farewell with its benediction find their lives sanctified. They who never cleanse their souls with prayer find nothing but darkness within. Their souls remain in slumber and need to be awakened. The practice of prayer is essential for such awakening. One's soul becomes more alert as one proceeds with this practice, and one's spiritual yearnings become sharper and stronger. One's soul then reflects an ever-fresh resplendence.

In many religions, practising prayer is prescribed at least twice a day: before daybreak and after sunset. During these two most beautiful times when we are about to leave for work or return from it to rest, the soul is imbued with greater spiritual sensitivity and so has a greater inclination for prayer. It has been said, *'Prayer should be the key to our days and the lock to our nights'.*

The *Rigveda* affirms:

Pray when the sun rises,
Pray also when it sets.

Zarathushtra says

This morning, this noon, this dusk,
They are all creations of someone,
They remind the yearning soul
These are the hours for praying.[1]

One whose day starts with prayer spends his entire day in the presence of God. One whose night begins with prayer reposes his soul in the loving grace of God. Divine light shines all the time on those who dip their life in prayer. With prayer, we extend an invitation to Divine Light to irradiate the inner recesses of our being.

Om!
O my Father, who pervades the three states and the three worlds,
Light our heart with your resplendent visage
And inspire us.
We bare our wits to catch the glimpses of your resplendence.
—Vedic Gāyatrī

It is recorded that whenever Prophet Mohammed faced a problem, he began to pray tearfully and invoked God to show him the right path. While in prayer, his body would begin to tremble and even convulse. Without eating or drinking, he would spend many days at a stretch in that state. He would rise only when the

[1] I.J.S. Taraporewala, *Chants of Zarathushtra,* Bombay: Treasure House of Books, 1951.

Divine Light began to shine within him. Then, whatever he uttered was accepted as the revealed Word. The Holy Qur'ān is the collection of such revelatory sayings. This scripture makes it obligatory for the believers to pray five times a day. The prayer, or *namāz* as it is called, begins with the following invocation or *kalimā:*

O Lord of the Creation, kind and merciful *Allāh,*
We sing Your praises.
O reckoner of the day of reckoning,
We seek Your refuge and help,
Show us the path treading which
We receive Your blessing.
Keep us on the path You approve,
Keep us away from the one You disapprove,
And which can make us
Fall from Your Grace. —The Holy Qur'ān

There is also a Parsee prayer that illustrates the same intent:

O Ye *Ahurmazdā,*
Bless us with that intellect
That may help us to consciously fulfil our obligation.
Bless me with that virtue from which
All treasures emanate.
Bless me with forbearance.
Show me the right path—
That is Yours and leads to You.

Whenever desire for prayer arises in any heart, it affirms assurance of safety under the protectorate of the One to whom the prayers are addressed. This may be illustrated with a Jain prayer:

O You, the transcendent one, beyond the entire world,
You, the Highest Gnosis,
Who are of the nature of reflective ideation,
Attainable through the highest reaches of *samādhī,*
O the Soul Supreme,
Come and enter my heart.
... ...

Whoever seeks the refuge of this Resplendent Supreme Soul,

And contemplates on it,
Can attain the highest spiritual state.
—*Amit Gati Samyak Recitation*

Seeking refuge in the Supreme Soul, man feels at one with all the holy souls. He adores the Presence whose refuge he has sought and adores the company with whom he has become one. An authentic Buddhist prayer illustrates this.

I seek refuge with the Buddha.
I seek refuge with the Dharma.
I seek refuge with the Holy Congregation.

In the traditional Jewish prayer *Amidāh,* God has been addressed as the source of life and all the living beings, and thanks are offered Him for His enormous benediction towards His creatures. In the concluding part of this prayer, peace and protection are sought for all. The seeker is advised, 'whosoever desires to get absorbed in prayer, let him keep his eyes lowered and mind elevated'. God ordained Israel thus:

You should pray in the temple of your town.
If not there, pray in the field.
If not there even, pray in your bed.
If not even there, then remember me in your heart
And be blessed with peace.

Every man of faith knows that God's grace rains equally on all His creatures.

His sun rises for both the good and the evil
And His rain falls equally on both the virtuous and the sinful.
—The Bible

In Christianity, prayer has been called 'breath of the soul'. None can live without breathing; likewise, none can remain spiritually alive without prayer. In the Christian faith, prayer is an important institution.

In the Sikh faith also the *ardās* is a spiritual activity of tremendous significance. The three main pillars of the Sikh worship are *simran* (remembering God), *sevā* (selfless service), and *ardās* (prayer). *Sevā* generates humility that aids *ardās. Simran,* in turn, is aided by *ardās.* Thus, *ardās* has a pivotal position in Sikh worship.

The above is a bird's-eye view of prayer in various active religions. It underscores the fact that faith and prayer are universal features of spiritual yearning. Language varies and idioms differ, but the sentiment remains the same.

CHAPTER 4

Metaphysical Perspective on Prayer

Man seems to be the meeting point of time and eternity. Prayer is the principal means by which such a meeting can be actualized because it is a call to the eternal to come and pervade the time-bound destiny of man. It is a *kairos* for man's finite consciousness to get in tune with the infinite. Prayer may be considered a dialogue between mortality and immortality. It enables one to demolish the wall of falsehood and let the light of truth enter the heart. It is, in essence, the mode by which the presence of God can be experienced. If the ultimate goal of the individual *ātman* (soul) is to reach the Lord's Court, then it is the *ardās* that makes a knock on His door. All the above metaphors testify to the fact that prayer occupies a central position in a man's spiritual life.

Religion has two fundamental aspects: experiential and moral. Prayer is intimately connected with both.

EXPERIENTIAL ASPECT

This aspect of prayer pertains to recognizing the presence of a Supreme Being behind all external phenomena as well as every inner experience. Philosophy seems to be related to the laws of the empirical world as well as to the personality that experiences it. It makes a search for the fundamental laws that govern them both. It can therefore be said that religion and philosophy—each from its distinctive viewpoint—explores the same ground. The approach of philosophy is intellectual, while that of religion, experiential. Prayer combines the immanent and the transcendent. Intellect works primarily on the basis of data provided by imperfect and limit-bound sense organs. Therefore it has only finite reach. It cannot fathom the Infinite. It can only raise questions about it, but cannot answer them. In contrast, spiritual experience does not depend on sense organs. In fact, it is only when the functions of sense organs are suspended, that spiritual experiential observations come to be facilitated.

For a spiritual experience to take place, attention has to be withdrawn from outside and focused on a point inside in a sustained way. The din of the sense perceptions does not permit the peaceful quietude required for the single-pointed attention. Hence sense organs have to be trained to observe silence. This is the method that *Pañcāṅga Yoga* advocates.

An alternative method is that of *bhakti* (devotion). According to this, one is expected to arouse one's devotional longings to such a high pitch that the noise of sense perceptions is no longer able to interfere with one's single-pointed attentivity. *Bhakti* is the approach of love and devotion toward the Divine. Prayer is therefore prominent as a mode of worship in those religions in which love for the Divine is the mainstay. This is because *it is through prayer that one can make a communication in love with the deity.*

Love is not a philosophy, nor does it rest on any particular philosophy. However, with whatever philosophy it may establish its relationship, it turns that into poetry. It is no wonder then that most Indian *bhaktas* as well as Sufi *dervishes* have been adept poets. The Sikh religion is also a love-based faith, and the Sikh *gurus* produced their lofty mystical-lyrical works in rich poetic genres.

The basic premise of a religion of love is that God Himself is love. *'Here, there, and everywhere He pervades as love.'*[1] Love only gives. It expects nothing in return. 'The Giver goes on giving; it is the receivers who tire out receiving.'[2] 'He never repents after giving.'[3] All this shows that His Heart is ever over- brimming with love.

According to the Sikh belief, God, before Creation, was in an intent-less *samādhi* (trance). Something stirred within Him that impelled Him to create. What stirred in Him was nothing but His

[1] *DG Jāp*: 80.
[2] *Jap(u)* p. 2.
[3] *Vār Soraṭh* m 4 sl. m 3, p. 653.

love that welled up. As a result, He created the universe in order to shower His loving grace upon it.

His grace did not stop with the act of Creation. He continued to shower His love on His Creation. Prayer is the human response to the unceasing divine grace. *God's glance of love arouses faith in human hearts, and ardās is the tongue of that faith.* It speaks thankfully to Divine benediction and acknowledges having received Divine grace.

Prayer can be addressed only to a God—a loving God. In atheistic religions, the tradition of prayer cannot be expected to be present since there is no God who may answer prayers. Even so, prayer-like activity does seem to take place even in them—as, for instance, in Buddhism and Jainism. In polytheistic religions, ritualistic worship, offering and sacrifice preponderate rather than prayer. It is in monotheistic religions that the tradition of prayer flowers *par excellence.*

Prayer conveys the longing of the finite human love for merger with the infinite divine love. *Human love finds its expression in devotion, while divine love finds its expression in grace. In prayer, both these come together.* Prayer brings about their natural confluence.

Man cannot deserve divine grace through merit. He can only pray for it from his state of incompetence and sinfulness and yearn for God's compassion and forgiveness.[4] Prayer can be our recourse for deliverance from a sinful life. The quality of life is then not a matter of entitlement but of grace that falls like manna from heaven?

> Annul my million sins and teach me in various ways.
> My ignorance is great and intellect puny,
> Pray, Lord, comply with Your covenant (of forgiveness).
>
> —*Dhanāsrī* m 5, p. 674

MORAL ASPECT

Religion has been the main source of moral guidance for mankind. Ethics, a branch of philosophy, is also concerned with morality

[4] Like the ocean full of water, full of faults are we.
Show us your compassion through your grace, O Lord,
For You can make even sinking rocks float.
—*Gauṛī Cetī* m 1, p. 156

and studies the laws governing moral behaviour. However, it has not been able to inspire moral conduct. In contrast, adherents of a religion readily accept the rules of good conduct that their religion prescribes. This is because ethical philosophies are emotionally cold, while religion is emotionally warm.

Love appears to be the prime source of human morality. Man is capable of loving only because God teaches him to love, and it is our obligation to return the love that we receive from God. This obligation engenders the general sense of duty that develops in the heart of man. Without such a sense of duty, one is not morally alive. That is why one who does not love God remains morally dead.[5]

They who love God, love even strangers and serve them as if they were their kin. This they do because service is in the nature of love. Human love, thus, is simply an echo of God's love.

One who receives love ought to deserve it. *One who continues to receive love must continue to deserve it.* It should be our unceasing obligation to deserve the incessant and infinite love that we receive from God. That should be our test. Since divine love never dries up, our life must be a continual test. The more we are blessed, the harder does the test become for us. And yet God's love continues to flow unstinted. The human predicament is great: God is invisible; the world is chaotic; and our consciousness turbid. However, in such a predicament lies the secret of man's moral sensibility. There could not have been the possibility of discriminating good from evil if God could be seen, if the world was in perfect order and if our consciousness was clear and free of any illusion or delusion. The freedom that we enjoy—to do good or evil—becomes our test.

At every step, life poses some questions to us and challenges our love. If we give inappropriate answers to these questions, we make our lives meaningless. We may not be materially deprived, but spiritually we definitely fall. On the other hand, if we give suitable answers to these questions, our spiritual life evolves,

[5] Even if one is a real beauty, of lineage high,
Endowed with intellect, learning and wealth,
If he loves not God, says Nānak,
Reckon him as dead. —*Gauṛī* m 5, p. 253

mysteries unfold themselves unto us, and our life becomes meaningful.

There is a common misconception concerning the relation between work and prayer. It is generally believed that work is of primary importance and prayer is required to assist it to achieve results. Actually, the true position is that prayer is of primary importance, and its effectiveness can be witnessed in work.

> Offer your prayer to the Guru
> No obstacle you shall confront.
> —*Bilāval* m 5, p. 816

Since God is Truth, the test of our *karma* is also truth. Evil from this angle is not disobedience or transgression of any kind; it is simply deviation from truth, i.e. being untrue to one's source. Since God is Love, the test of our *karma* is also love. Whenever we are alienated from our source, in truth or in love, it begins to reflect in our conduct as evil.

Ardās is the prime approach for reestablishing our contact with our source. A life charged with prayerfulness is automatically imbued with truthfulness.

CHAPTER 5

To Whom Should We Pray?

We only need to pray to the One who can grant our prayers. God Almighty is the only one who is able to do so. He gives us benevolently, seldom withdraws his hand and never repents after giving. Therefore,

The One alone I shall serve,
The One alone I shall contemplate,
To that One alone shall I pray.
—*Jaitsarī* m 5, p. 710

Our needs are enormous but vision is narrow. We know how to beg but hardly know of whom. We have heard of God, but we have never seen him. We cannot bring ourselves to rely on one we have not even seen. Humans we have seen, so it is only humans we approach. But as soon as we spread our hand before a human being, we come to sense its futility.

To whomsoever I supplicate,
Him too I find in misery.
—*Gūjarī* m 5, p. 497

How, then, can any man be worthy of our prayers? Many are need-ridden themselves. Many may be miserly, and therefore disinclined to give. Many would repent after giving. Again, many would put the receiver to shame. All are limited in their resource to give. So

I feel ashamed to beg of another
When my Master is the greatest monarch,
And none equals Him. —*Āsā* m 5, p. 401

Begging from humans is fishing in air. God alone is truly benevolent. Everyone else is a beggar at His door; even kings and potentates beg of Him.

An event from the life of Mahārājā Raṇjīt Siṅgh, the well-known Sikh monarch readily comes to our mind here.

It took place in 1813 AD, that he set out to mount an attack on the Fort of Jamrod. On the way, he stopped at a shrine, and requested the holy man there to pray for his victory. The holy man obliged him. The Mahārājā, on his return after victory, again halted at that shrine and contacted the holy man.

"I have come to thank you", the Mahārājā said, "and would like to make a grant to your shrine." "What can you grant, Mahārājā?" the holy man asked. "I can grant anything! I am the monarch, can grant you whatever you may ask." The holy man smiled and said, "When you came here last, you had come only as a beggar at this door. How have you now become a giver?" The Mahārājā got the message. Humbled, he lowered his eyes.

There is only the One giver whose gifts everyone receives. He does not stop giving *and never suspends his charity*.

During his encounter with Guru Nānak at Eminābād, Emperor Bābur asked him, 'Ask me for whatever you may want, and I'll grant you that'. The Guru replied, 'I depend only on the One Supreme Lord. He gives me all I need without my asking for it'.

When even kings are beggars at His door, why must we go to beg elsewhere? Our worldly supports are all short-lived. How can such a one vouch support to another who is himself unsure even of his next breath?

> Him alone, O my mind invoke—
> Who always was, still is, and shall always be.
> —*DG* 33 Sawayīye, 16: 24

However, out of sheer habit, we look toward other people for help whenever we are in distress. All human beings together can, at best, avert some minor problem. A real catastrophe like death defies even our collective might. The only one who can raise man above the fear of death is one who himself is beyond the grip of fear. Only He who has no fear (*bhau*) can inspire fearlessness in others.

> Meditate on the one fearless, and be freed from fear.
> —*Gauṛī* m 5, p. 293

Gods and goddesses are all afflicted with fear. They are all jealous and afraid of one another. Even Dharma Rāja, the god of reckoning, one who has the whole world under his sway, suffers from fear himself. How can such gods and goddesses protect us from fear? The deity that the Sikhs believe in is a non-jealous, universal God. He loves all—the sinners as well as the virtuous. Indeed, saving the sinner is his special covenant.

> Purifying sinners is his very nature, the Law of His Grace.
>
> —*Sūhī* m 5, p. 784

Good or bad, we are all His children. He provides us all His fatherly care and protection. It behoves us to ask only of Him whatever we need.

> All belong to You, You also belong to all,
> Everyday, they supplicate unto You.
>
> —*Vār Srirāg* m 4, p. 86

To Him alone we owe our gratitude throughout our lives for He is the one from whom we ever continue to receive His benediction.

> Hail! to Him whose benediction sustains us.
> How dare we command him?
> With Him only prayers work.
>
> —*Vār Āsā* m 1, p. 474

CHAPTER 6

Ardās in the Sikh Faith

Prayer as an instrument of worship is a living part of every religion. However, in the Sikh faith it is a vital institution. Whenever a Sikh faces a problem in life or is in any predicament, he is enjoined upon to pray and seek divine intervention:

> Whenever one is in distress and none gives him support,
> When enemies gather in upon him and kinsfolk him desert,
> When all the props one loses, and none doth him sustain,
> Then, should he remember the Lord, hot winds will scorch him not.
>
> —*Srīrāg* m 5, p. 70

Anyone who is in privation, pain or agony, grief or bereavement may call out to the Almighty for help. A Sikh does not pray merely at times of predicament but, in fact, relies on the *ardās* at every stage of life and for every task or venture that he has to undertake.

The traditional *ardās* of the Sikhs is their congregational prayer. Since it is a great storehouse of spiritual inspiration, it has become popular even as a vehicle of personal petitions as well. As an unsavory result of it, the purely personal prayer has become less prevalent among the Sikhs. In fact, the congregational *ardās* has become so popular that it has come to be employed even as personal prayer. Nonetheless, *spiritual seekers know that it is just not possible to do without personal prayer.* In fact, the whole of *Srī Guru Granth Sāhib* is a great compilation of personal prayers. An uninterrupted stream of the sentiments of prayer flows in this holy book. In it prayer has spread its wings over multiple spheres of meditation.

The *ardās* has a special place in the daily life of the Sikhs. Personal prayer has no specifications. If a soldier while mounting his horse says just this: 'O Lord of the Blue Steed, be my protector', it is a complete prayer. Before setting out on a journey, celebrating a house warming, or undertaking a new enterprise, a Sikh would invoke the Lord's blessings prayerfully. Even before taking his meals, he thankfully remembers his Lord. The *ardās* marks every rite of passage: the birth of a child, giving the child a name, sending the child to school, engagement for marriage, or entering wedlock. No rite or ceremony up to and including death can be completed without the *ardās*.

If the *ardās* complements the mundane occasions cited above, naturally, it becomes obligatory for all religious occasions also. After the daily liturgical services in the *gurdwārās*, and after the conclusion of *kīrtan* (liturgical music) and *kathā* (exposition of the scripture), the *ardās* is invariably performed. The *amrit saṅskār* (baptismal ceremony) has to begin as well as conclude with *ardās*.

The *ardās* is a prerequisite for launching any collective undertaking or struggle by the community.

> Call upon the Lord if anything you want to be done.
> Your task shall be accomplished is the Guru's assurance.
> —*Vār Srīrāg* m 4, p. 91

The *ardās* thus presides over every aspect and occasion of Sikh life; it is what connects the individual mind to the universal mind that lies within it.

A Sikh would not consult an astrologer or soothsayer as he does not believe in omens and portents. Yet, he knows that any occasion can be sanctified and made auspicious by saying *ardās*:

> Learned Sikhs reckon not omens and stars.
> Their sole refuge is the Lord.
> 'Auspicious occasions' they seek not,
> But *ardās* they would perform.
> —*Gur Bilās Pātshāhi Chevīṅ*, ch. VI, pp. 139-40

In the *Rahitnāmās* (Codes of conduct), *ardās* has been prescribed as obligatory before undertaking any task. Bhāī Naṅd Lāl, in *Sākhī Rahit kī* says:

> In the morning, a Sikh must visit a place where the holy Word is being recited, should make his obeisance there, listen or himself recite the holy Word, perform his *ardās* and only thereafter should he attend to his daily chores.

The same author in his work *Tankhāh Nāmāh* observes:

If a Sikh starts any undertaking of his without performing *ardās*, the Guru would not approve of it.

Bhāī Caupā Siṅgh in his *Rahit Nāmā* says,

One, who turns his back upon *ardās*, deserves to be penalized.

A Sikh's heart and soul ought to be in it whenever he performs *ardās*. An event from the life of Guru Nānak well illustrates the point:

As his first proclamation as Guru, Nanak declared, 'There is no Hindu, nor any Muslim'. He presumably meant thereby that all are but one. The Qāzī of the town asked him, in that case, would he join him in saying his *namāz*.[1] The Guru readily gave his assent. However, while the Qāzī was saying his prayer, and making the customary moves of obeisance, the Guru only stood by smiling. After his *namāz*, the Qāzī remonstrated with the Guru for not having joined him in his prayer. The Guru replied, 'You did not say your prayer. Your mind was elsewhere. You were thinking all the while of your new born foal and worrying lest it should fall in the well in your courtyard. How could I join you in your *namāz*?'

It can easily be understood that if *namāz* requires single-minded attention, so does the *ardās*.

Faith and belief are gifts of God, and without these, no genuine *ardās* can be performed. God's grace is required even to get into the mood of *ardās*.

Through your grace alone I pray, O my Creator!
I can utter only what you command.
—*Vadhaṅs* m 1, p. 566

The sentiment of thankfulness is an important constituent of *ardās*. Thankfulness to God ought to sprout at every step in our life. In his epistle to Emperor Auraṅgzeb, Guru Gobiṅd Siṅgh wrote:

You eye your riches and your forces,
I thankfully look toward my Almighty Lord.
—*DG: Zafar Nāmā*: 102

[1] *Namāz* is the Muslim liturgical prayer.

Ardās need not employ long-winded rhetoric. It should be sincere. The greater the verbosity, the less meaningful it becomes. Hypocrisy often steals into a long-winded *ardās*.

The traditional Sikh congregational *ardās* is a unique prayer. It is the living archive of the Sikh faith, a capsule of spiritual inspiration and a testament to the moral beauty that has shaped the Sikh lives.

CHAPTER 7

The Evolution of *Ardās*

The practice of *ardās* apparently began during the times of Guru Nānak. Once he was on the eve of leaving his village Talvaṅḍī. Rāe Bulār, the alderman of the town, invited him over for a communion meal. Before the Guru bade him 'good bye', the Rāe addressed him, 'Revered Nānak, God alone knows when we would meet again. Pray, give me some spiritual counsel before you leave'. The Guru said, 'Dear Rāe, whenever you feel that your own powers have betrayed you, and rendered you despondent, take refuge with the Lord and pray before Him'.

In the *Janam-sākhīs*,[1] several events are reported wherein individuals like Bebe Nānakī, Rāe Bulār and others are described as praying to the Guru, and the latter as responding to their *ardās*.

In one of the *sākhīs*,[2] it is reported that 'the *ardāsīā*[3] stood up before the Guru and prayed with folded hands invoking him to cast his benevolent glance over the Sikhs who had made offerings and to bless their undertakings with success'. It is clear that the practice of congregational *ardās* had begun to evolve within the lifetime of Guru Nānak himself.

The tradition of *ardās* developed further with successive Gurus. Gobiṅd, a Sikh of Guru Aṅgad Dev (Guru Nānak's immediate successor), made plans to develop a new town that he wanted to name after the Guru. However, in the middle of the night, some troublemakers from the neighbourhood would pull down the structure erected during the day. Gobiṅd brought this to the Guru's notice. The Guru asked Srī Amar Dās to take charge of the project and deal with the situation. Srī Amar Dās said nothing to anyone. He simply prayed, 'O Lord Almighty, pray make ill-will and hatred

[1] *Janam-sākhīs* are biographies of Guru Nānak Dev.

[2] A *sākhī* is an event in the Guru's biography.

[3] An *ardāsīā* is one who offers *ardās* to the Guru on behalf of the congregation.

vanish from all hearts and let compassion and fellow-feeling prevail'. There was no trouble after that. Thus, *ardās* became a vehicle for promoting fellow feeling.

Guru Rām Dās specified *simran* (remembering God), *kīrtan* (singing His praises) and *ardās* (prayer) as the trilogy of Sikh worship. He stressed *ardās* as a prime means of achieving spiritual heights.

When Guru Arjan Dev compiled the *Pothī Sāhib*[4] and installed it in the Harmaṅdar, he gave up his own special seat and just sat in attendance on the holy book. He would even offer his *ardās* in its presence. It is likely that from then on the practice of offering *ardās* in the presence of the holy book became prevalent. Additionally, the concept of the eternally living *shabad guru* (the Word as Guru) had come to be established.

Guru Arjan Dev's own life is replete with prayers of thanksgiving. At every crucial occasion when he received providential help, he said his thanks to the Lord and preserved those prayers for us in *Srī Guru Granth Sāhib*. The Guru offered a special prayer of thanksgiving even on the completion of Harmaṅdar.

During the time of the fifth Guru, *gurdwārās*[5] began to be established in various places with copies of *Pothī Sāhib* installed therein. By the time of the sixth Guru, Hargobiṅd, *ardās* began to be performed in the *gurdwārās* regularly—even though its textual form was then quite rudimentary compared with what is now current. Guru Hargobiṅd paid special attention to congregational prayer. Mohsin Fānī, a historian who was his contemporary, has recorded: 'Whenever a Sikh wished for the fulfilment of his desires, he would go to a congregation and request it to supplicate for him. At times, Guru Hargobiṅd himself requested the assembly to pray for him.'[6]

History testifies that on several occasions when a Sikh fervently prayed to see the Guru, the Guru responded to his *ardās* and reached him.

During the time of the tenth Guru, Gobiṅd Siṅgh, *ardās* began

[4] *Srī Guru Granth Sāhib*, as first compiled by Guru Arjan Dev was called *Pothī Sāhib* (the Revered Book) by him.

[5] A *gurdwārā* is the Sikh public place of worship.

[6] Mobad, *Dabistān-e-Mazāhib*, p. 289.

to be performed in the presence of the *Pañj Piāre* (the Five Beloved ones) and addressed to *Srī Guru Granth Sāhib*. When the Guru dispatched Baṅdā Siṅgh from Naṅder towards the Puṅjāb, the Guru counselled him to 'take five Sikhs along and offer *ardās* if ever you get into a problem'.

The *Hukamnāmās* (epistles issued by the Guru) testify that wherever there were Sikh congregations, their offerings vowed for the Guru were retained and *mevṛās* (collectors appointed by the Guru) would gather them and present them to the Guru.

Perhaps, an early version of the present form of the congregational *ardās* was compiled by Bhāī Manī Siṅgh.[7] Certain manuscripts, however, do indicate that something like the current *ardās* had started taking shape even during the days of Guru Gobiṅd Siṅgh. One such manuscript records the text of *ardās* as follows:

> The One Lord, Master of victories!
> May we receive the aid and assistance of the Divine Sword.
>
> *The Ballad of the Divine Sword* by the tenth Guru.
> Invoke we the Divine Sword that Guru Nānak meditated on,
> That rendered help to Aṅgad Guru, Amar Dās and Rām Dās.
> Arjan, Hargobiṅd and Har Rāe remembered it,
> Invoked it was by Srī Harkishan, seeing whom miseries depart.
> Remembered also Tegh Bahādur, to whom all nine treasures flock.
> Everywhere may it be of help to us.
> O Thou Khālsā of the Timeless Lord, utter '*Wāheguru!*'
>
> Meditate thou on Guru Granth, and utter '*Wāheguru!*'
> Remember thou Srī Amritsar, Srī Taran Tāran, Dūkh Nivāran and utter '*Wāheguru*'.
>
> This *Ardās* dedicates to you the *Shabad Caukī* of *Rahirās*,[8]
> May who recited it and who lent their ear to it, all benefit.
> May they remember the Lord's Nām so that they receive every comfort.
>
> The Khālsā belong to the Lord who is Master of victories!

The current text of *ardās* has largely evolved from this. One specific section of the *ardās* in vogue nowadays commemorates

---

[7] As per Bhāī Kāhn Siṅgh Nābhā: *Mahān Kosh*.
[8] It is the designation of the evening liturgical service.

Sikh martyrs. They include those who were 'hacked joint by joint', 'broken on the wheel', 'descalped' or 'sawn through'. They are considered martyrs because they gave up their lives but kept their faith intact.

Out of shared calamity emerged shared sympathy. When a price had been placed on the heads of the K̲h̲ālsā and they were being hunted like wild animals, the hearts of the K̲h̲ālsā began to throb for every single member of the brotherhood. Every morning and evening, Sikh congregations wherever they could assemble began to pray for *rachiā riāyat* (protection and favour) for the K̲h̲ālsā 'wherever they may be'. Such prayers not only augmented their fellow feeling, but also strengthened their fortitude, buttressed their hope and reinforced their morale. Whether they were in the woods of Kāhnuvān, the hills of Shivālik or the desert of Bīkāner, the *ardās* being performed almost everywhere began to infuse *Caṛhdī Kalā* (spiritual strength) in them.

Ardās thus became a source of spiritual inspiration for the Sikhs. It also assumed the significance of a sacred pledge. Many historic events bear testimony to it. Men of faith would not let their determination for it falter after they had said their *ardās* and invoked the Lord's help for an undertaking. Here is an example: Mahārājā Rañjīt Siṅgh had set out to mount an attack on Naushehra, when he was informed that the adversary forces far outnumbered his. While he considered that the attack be postponed, the Mahārājā parleyed about it with Akālī Phūlā Siṅgh, who was in command of the vanguard. The Akālī said, 'Mahārājā! we have already said our *ardās*; now under no circumstance can we change our mind. Victory, after all, has to be bestowed by the Master of victories, and Him we have already invoked.' They decided to move on and were victorious. This event illustrates the faith that the Sikhs reposed in *ardās*.

It was after saying their *ardās* that Mehtāb Siṅgh and Sukhā Siṅgh headed for Harmaṅdar Sāhib to do away with Massā Raṅghaṛ who was perpetrating sacrilege of the *sanctum sanctorum* there.

It was again after saying the *ardās* that a band of the Sikhs set out to rescue a Brahmin girl abducted by the Muslim ruler of Loharī Jalālābād. They rescued her and restored her dignity by designating her 'daughter of the Paṅth'.

Those who reposed their full faith in *ardās* found their obstacles removed. Jassā Siṅgh Rāmgaṛhiā, as a result of his differences with the Ahlūwāliā *misl* (confederacy), left the Puṅjāb and sought safety in Bāṅgar. In the alien land, he ran into financial difficulty. He said his *ardās* to invoke divine intervention. After that he peeped into a well, as he wanted to draw water from it, and found a treasure lying in it.

Many other events also testify to the Sikh faith in the efficacy of the *ardās*. The Sikh forces under the command of Mahārājā Raṅjīt Siṅgh came to a place where they had to cross the Attock (Indus) River that was then in high spate. Crossing it looked well-nigh impossible but the Mahārājā alighted from his horseback, said his *ardās* and announced:

> Whoso harbours hesitation within his mind,
> For him alone will Attock be an obstacle.

Thereafter, his forces plunged into the river and waded across safely. It was such faith that enabled the Sikhs to rely on *ardās*.

The sacred memory of their martyrs made the Sikhs ready to offer sacrifices themselves if an occasion arose. During the third decade of the twentieth century, thousands of Sikhs laid down their lives for restoring the sanctity of their *gurdwārās* that were being desecrated by *mahaṅts* (priests).[9] The *Paṅth* has since incorporated their memory into the *ardās*.

After the Partition of India into Bhārat and Pākistān, the Sikh people had to abandon not only their hearths and homes in Pākistān, but also their important holy shrines such as those in Nanakāṇā Sāhib in Shekhūpurā, Ḍehrā Sāhib in Lāhore and Paṅjā Sāhib in Eminābād. The pangs of deprivation of those shrines became incorporated in their *ardās*:

> Ever-protector of the Paṅth, O Lord, let the Khālsā again be granted unhindered visits to, and care of, such *gurdwārās* as Nanakāṇā Sāhib from which the *Paṅth* has been separated.

Thus *ardās* has all along, preserved the traditions and faith of the Sikh people along with the memories of their struggle and aspiration. *Ardās* is thus an evolving testimonial of the *Paṅth* and will continue to evolve in the future as well.

[9]This struggle by the Sikh people was called 'Gurdwārā Reform Movement'.

CHAPTER 8

Outstanding Features of *Ardās*

Ardās is a creative work of great historic significance. Generations of great souls have created it phrase by phrase. God has actually been meditated upon and his presence practised. Honestly earned funds have been shared with the needy. Holy cauldrons have ever been kept warm. The sacred sword has actually been plied to save the oppressed. Faults of others have generously been overlooked. God's will has unhesitatingly been accepted and most willingly carried out. Thus *ardās* is a reflection of a truly lived faith.

Multiple dimensions characterize its structure. It is at once a laudation, a supplication, an inspiration, an affirmation of faith, and a dedication. It begins with laudation and only afterwards enters the phase of supplication. Even its supplication is collective first and personal later. While the collective part is compulsory, the personal part is optional.

The principal Sikh scripture, *Srī Guru Granth Sāhib,* opens with a statement of *uncompromising monotheism.* The numeral '1' (one) placed before *Oaṅkār* (The Transcendent-Immanent God) testifies to this.

Ardās opens with the following affirmation of faith:

The One Lord is the Master of victories.

In *Ardās,* the invocatory part opens with the imploration of the One Almighty, followed by that of the ten Gurus and then by that of the *Shabad Guru* (the Word as Guru) or *Srī Guru Granth Sāhib.* The following command follows the section of invocations as well as subsequent sections:

O Khālsā, utter with rapt attention, *Wāheguru* (Wonderful Lord!).

The supplication that follows the invocations begins with a collective entreaty on behalf of the entire Order of the Khālsā.

"May the K͟hālsā ever remember Wāheguru, Wāheguru, Wāheguru".

Ardās contains the following penultimate supplication:

Grant us, O Lord, company of such lovely souls, meeting whom we may effortlessly remember Your Name.

Thus *ardās* not only repetitively reminds us of our monotheistic faith, but also prompts us to remain in tune with *Wāheguru* throughout our *ardās*.

Ardās generates a sense of belongingness among the faithful. It reinforces their fraternal ties by reawakening their pride in the lofty traditions and achievements of the Order of the K͟hālsā to which they belong. By praying for the fulfilment of collective aspirations of the community, every Sikh reaffirms his feelings of solidarity with his brethren in faith.

A Sikh delights in collective establishments by being reminded of the outstanding institutions of the community: *takhts*,[1] *gurdwārās*, *caukīs*,[2] *jhaṅḍās*,[3] and *buṅgāhs*.[4] Thus the *ardās becomes a vehicle of collective unity* for the Sikhs.

Ardās is also the Zafar Nāmāh[5] of the Sikhs. It glorifies the martyrs, salutes the swordsmen and venerates the heroes of the community. The Holy Sword is invoked for the protection of the men of faith. Glory of the K͟hālsā is sought. Victory for the K͟hālsā is affirmed. A pledge is taken to keep the spirit of the congregation high. Begun with 'Victory for the Lord', the *ardās* also concludes with 'Victory for the Lord'. No prayer in the world has been made with so much suffering and fortitude nor does any other prayer glorify altruistic heroism in such a fashion. The 'victory' envisaged in the *ardās* is moral victory, the victory of *dharma*.

Ardās is also the K͟hālsā's *declaration of collective pledge*. It vouches to consider all mankind as one when it craves for *sarbat kā bhalā*

---

[1] *Tak͟ht* (throne): a seat of temporal authority.
[2] *Caukī:* a singing party. Not every singing party can be a *caukī*. We need a clearer translation here. A party of Irish drinking songs cannot be one. A *caukī* sings *gurbāṇī*, the Guru's word.
[3] *Jhaṅḍā*: a national flag.
[4] *Buṅgāh*: a lodging house for pilgrims.
[5] *Zafar Nāmāh*: an epistle of victory.

(the welfare of one and all). It supplicates for protection and security of the downtrodden and the oppressed. In it, a Sikh pledges himself to lay down his life to defend righteousness and honour. He vows to defend the sanctity of the holy places and maintain the perpetuity of religious institutions. It makes a Sikh take a vow to be true as well as to be true to his word. At Harmaṅdar at the end a line also asks for *Sikh paṛhde suṇde sarbat lāhevaṅd hovan*, i.e. 'The Sikhs who peruse (the holy Word), and those who hearken it, may benefit therefrom'.

It is a *declaration of ever-readiness—tiār bar tiār* (readier than ready). It glorifies discipline and does not ask for an easy life; rather, it supplicates for courage and fortitude to brave any hardship.

In addition to all that we have considered above, the *ardās* is rightfully *a petition-paper* asking for divine support in the fulfilment of the pledges taken. It supplicates for ever-renewing faith and trust, for high spirits and a life of disciplined spontaneity. It is a prayer for the perpetuity of Sikh traditions and institutions. It gives expression to the Sikh's yearning for a visit to Amritsar, their spiritual capital, and for a dip in the holy pool there. It petitions for protection and favour for the entire Khālsā wherever they be. For the individual self, it supplicates for a humble mind and a lofty intellect, the latter to be guided by divine wisdom. Last, but not least, it voices yearning for the 'supreme gift'—the Lord's Holy *Nām*. While the *ardās* supplicates the desire for remembering God, it also serves as a medium for its practice—time and again asking the supplicant to utter '*Wāheguru*'.

Ardās seems to spread its mighty spiritual wings over space and time. By encapsulating within itself the historical *raison* of the community, it folds up time. With its vision of 'wherever the Khālsā may be', it brings the entire world into its gamut. It scarcely remains the prayer of any single individual, nor does it pertain to any specific place or time. Supplicating for 'the welfare of all', it becomes the prayer for all mankind through all times.

... ...

Ardās has tremendous literary significance. Some scholars consider it the *bāṇī* (sacred composition) of the Guru Paṅth. It enjoys the same reverence as do the Gurus' own hymns in the hearts of the Sikhs. A true Sikh would not consider any ceremony, religious or secular, complete without the *ardās.*

Ardās is a delightful piece of poetic prose—powerful, lyrical and inspiring. It is no exaggeration to say that it is a distinctively unique composition. It is at once superbly delicate and robustly vigorous; it is self-effacing, yet bubbling with confidence; its form is brief, but its message brings time as well space into its fold. Unarguably, no single prose piece in the literature of the entire world matches its vigour or its inclusiveness. It embraces together both the Divine Truth and the worldly truth. It beats the kettledrum of victory while yearning for submission of the ego. Such paradoxes inhere in the *ardās* and weave a superb matrix for spiritual experience. It appears that the *ardās* leads one through the humble experience of worldliness to the experience of sublime divinity.

Ardās has a clear folkloric style. It brims with folk images and is a true folk genre created by folk wisdom. Such a splendid example of spiritual folk literature is not easy to come by elsewhere.

Like folk literature, it has continued to evolve over time—now admitting an expression, later pruning it out or replacing it by a more apt one. Thus it has enhanced its vigour and intensity all the time, and it can never be considered final. As long as the spiritual life of the Sikhs remains active and intense, the *ardās* will continue to evolve because it is the mirror of the similarly evolving spiritual life of the Sikhs.

PART II

FORM OF THE CONGREGATIONAL *ARDĀS*

CHAPTER 9

The Text of the Congregational *Ardās*

1. THE ORIGINAL IN GURMUKHĪ SCRIPT

ਅਰਦਾਸ ਦਾ ਪਰਵਾਣਿਤ ਰੂਪ

ਅਰਦਾਸ

ੴ ਵਾਹਿਗੁਰੂ ਜੀ ਕੀ ਫ਼ਤਹ ।
ਸ੍ਰੀ ਭਗਉਤੀ ਜੀ ਸਹਾਇ ।
ਵਾਰ ਸ੍ਰੀ ਭਗਉਤੀ ਜੀ ਕੀ ਪਾਤਸ਼ਾਹੀ ੧੦ ।
ਪ੍ਰਿਥਮ ਭਗਉਤੀ ਸਿਮਰ ਕੈ ਗੁਰ ਨਾਨਕ ਲਈ ਧਿਆਇ ।
ਫਿਰ ਅੰਗਦ ਗੁਰ ਤੇ ਅਮਰਦਾਸੁ ਰਾਮਦਾਸੈ ਹੋਈ ਸਹਾਇ ।
ਅਰਜਨ ਹਰਿਗੋਬਿੰਦ ਨੋ ਸਿਮਰੌ ਸ੍ਰੀ ਹਰਿ ਰਾਇ ।
ਸ੍ਰੀ ਹਰਿ ਕ੍ਰਿਸ਼ਨ ਧਿਆਈਐ ਜਿਸ ਡਿਠੈ ਸਭਿ ਦੁਖ ਜਾਇ ।
ਤੇਗ ਬਹਾਦਰ ਸਿਮਰੀਐ ਘਰ ਨਉ ਨਿਧਿ ਆਵੈ ਧਾਇ ।
ਸਭ ਥਾਈਂ ਹੋਇ ਸਹਾਇ ।
ਦਸਵਾਂ ਪਾਤਸ਼ਾਹ ਸ੍ਰੀ ਗੁਰੂ ਗੋਬਿੰਦ ਸਿੰਘ ਜੀ
ਸਭ ਥਾਈਂ ਹੋਇ ਸਹਾਇ ।
ਦਸਾਂ ਪਾਤਸ਼ਾਹੀਆਂ ਦੀ ਜੋਤਿ ਸ੍ਰੀ ਗੁਰੂ ਗ੍ਰੰਥ ਸਾਹਿਬ ਜੀ ਦੇ
ਪਾਠ ਦੀਦਾਰ ਦਾ ਧਿਆਨ ਧਰ ਕੇ
ਬੋਲੋ ਜੀ ਵਾਹਿਗੁਰੂ !
ਪੰਜਾਂ ਪਿਆਰਿਆਂ, ਚੌਹਾਂ ਸਾਹਿਬਜ਼ਾਦਿਆਂ, ਚਾਲੀ ਮੁਕਤਿਆਂ,
ਹਠੀਆਂ, ਜਪੀਆਂ, ਤਪੀਆਂ, ਜਿਨ੍ਹਾਂ ਨਾਮ ਜਪਿਆ,
ਵੰਡ ਛਕਿਆ, ਦੇਗ ਚਲਾਈ, ਤੇਗ ਵਾਹੀ,
ਦੇਖ ਕੇ ਅਨਡਿੱਠ ਕੀਤਾ,
ਤਿਨ੍ਹਾਂ ਪਿਆਰਿਆਂ ਸਚਿਆਰਿਆਂ ਦੀ ਕਮਾਈ ਦਾ ਧਿਆਨ ਧਰ ਕੇ
ਬੋਲੋ ਜੀ ਵਾਹਿਗੁਰੂ !
ਜਿਨ੍ਹਾਂ ਸਿੰਘਾਂ ਸਿੰਘਣੀਆਂ ਨੇ ਧਰਮ ਹੇਤ ਸੀਸ ਦਿੱਤੇ,
ਬੰਦ ਬੰਦ ਕਟਾਏ, ਖੋਪਰੀਆਂ ਲੁਹਾਈਆਂ, ਚਰਖੜੀਆਂ ਤੇ ਚੜ੍ਹੇ,
ਆਰਿਆਂ ਨਾਲ ਚਿਰਾਏ ਗਏ,
ਗੁਰਦੁਆਰਿਆਂ ਦੀ ਸੇਵਾ ਲਈ ਕੁਰਬਾਨੀਆਂ ਕੀਤੀਆਂ,

ਸਿੱਖੀ ਕੇਸਾਂ ਸੁਆਸਾਂ ਨਾਲ ਨਿਬਾਹੀ,
ਤਿਨ੍ਹਾਂ ਦੀ ਕਮਾਈ ਦਾ ਧਿਆਨ ਧਰ ਕੇ,
ਬੋਲੋ ਜੀ ਵਾਹਿਗੁਰੂ !
ਪੰਜਾਂ ਤਖ਼ਤਾਂ, ਸਰਬੱਤ ਗੁਰਦੁਆਰਿਆਂ ਦਾ ਧਿਆਨ ਧਰ ਕੇ
ਬੋਲੋ ਜੀ ਵਾਹਿਗੁਰੂ !
ਪ੍ਰਿਥਮੈ ਸਰਬਤ ਖ਼ਾਲਸਾ ਜੀ ਕੀ ਅਰਦਾਸ ਹੈ ਜੀ,
ਸਰਬੱਤ ਖ਼ਾਲਸਾ ਜੀ ਕੋ
ਵਾਹਿਗੁਰ, ਵਾਹਿਗੁਰੂ, ਵਾਹਿਗੁਰੂ
ਚਿਤ ਆਵੈ
ਚਿਤ ਆਵਨ ਕਾ ਸਦਕਾ ਸਰਬ ਸੁੱਖ ਹੋਵੈ ।
ਜਹਾਂ ਜਹਾਂ ਖ਼ਾਲਸਾ ਜੀ ਸਾਹਿਬ, ਤਹਾਂ ਤਹਾਂ ਰਛਿਆ ਰਿਆਇਤ
ਦੇਗ ਤੇਗ ਫ਼ਤਹ, ਬਿਰਦ ਕੀ ਪੈਜ, ਪੰਥ ਕੀ ਜੀਤ, ਸ੍ਰੀ ਸਾਹਿਬ ਜੀ ਸਹਾਇ,
ਖ਼ਾਲਸਾ ਜੀ ਕੇ ਬੋਲ ਬਾਲੇ,
ਬੋਲੋ ਜੀ ਵਾਹਿਗੁਰੂ !
ਸਿੱਖਾਂ ਨੂੰ ਸਿੱਖੀ ਦਾਨ, ਕੇਸ ਦਾਨ, ਰਹਿਤ ਦਾਨ, ਭਰੋਸਾ ਦਾਨ,
ਦਾਨਾਂ ਸਿਰ ਦਾਨ ਨਾਮ ਦਾਨ, ਸ੍ਰੀ ਅੰਮ੍ਰਿਤਸਰ ਜੀ ਦੇ ਇਸ਼ਨਾਨ,
ਚੌਕੀਆਂ, ਝੰਡੇ, ਬੁੰਗੇ ਜੁਗੋ ਜੁਗੋ ਅਟੱਲ,
ਧਰਮ ਕਾ ਜੈਕਾਰ,
ਬੋਲੋ ਜੀ ਵਾਹਿਗੁਰੂ !
ਸਿੱਖਾਂ ਦਾ ਮਨ ਨੀਵਾਂ, ਮਤਿ ਉੱਚੀ, ਮਤਿ ਦਾ ਰਾਖਾ ਆਪ ਵਾਹਿਗੁਰੂ !
ਹੇ ਅਕਾਲ ਪੁਰਖ, ਆਪਣੇ ਪੰਥ ਦੇ ਸਦਾ ਸਹਾਈ ਦਾਤਾਰ ਜੀਓ,
ਸ੍ਰੀ ਨਨਕਾਣਾ ਸਾਹਿਬ ਤੇ ਹੋਰ ਗੁਰਦੁਆਰਿਆਂ ਗੁਰਧਾਮਾਂ ਦੇ
ਜਿਨ੍ਹਾਂ ਤੋਂ ਪੰਥ ਨੂੰ ਵਿਛੋੜਿਆ ਗਿਆ ਹੈ,
ਖੁਲ੍ਹੇ ਦਰਸ਼ਨ ਦੀਦਾਰ ਤੇ ਸੇਵਾ ਸੰਭਾਲ ਦਾ ਦਾਨ
ਖ਼ਾਲਸਾ ਜੀ ਨੂੰ ਬਖ਼ਸ਼ੋ ।
ਹੇ ਨਿਮਾਣਿਆਂ ਦੇ ਮਾਣ, ਨਿਤਾਣਿਆਂ ਦੇ ਤਾਣ, ਨਿਓਟਿਆਂ ਦੀ ਓਟ
ਸੱਚੇ ਪਿਤਾ ਵਾਹਿਗੁਰੂ ਜੀ,
ਆਪ ਜੀ ਦੇ ਹਜ਼ੂਰ......[1]..........ਦੀ ਅਰਦਾਸ ਹੈ ਜੀ ।
ਅੱਖਰ ਵਾਧਾ ਘਾਟਾ ਭੁਲ ਚੁਕ ਮਾਫ਼ ਕਰਨੀ ।
ਸੇਈ ਪਿਆਰੇ ਮੇਲ, ਜਿਨ੍ਹਾਂ ਮਿਲਿਆਂ
ਆਪ ਦਾ ਨਾਮ ਚਿੱਤ ਆਵੇ ।
ਨਾਨਕ ਨਾਮ ਚੜ੍ਹਦੀ ਕਲਾ, ਤੇਰੇ ਭਾਣੇ ਸਰਬਤ ਕਾ ਭਲਾ ।

[1]ਇਥੇ ਉਸ ਬਾਣੀ ਦਾ ਨਾਮ ਲਉ ਜਿਸ ਦਾ ਪਾਠ ਕੀਤਾ ਹੈ, ਜਾਂ ਉਸ ਕਾਰਜ ਲਈ ਪ੍ਰਾਰਥਨਾ ਕਰੋ ਜਿਸ ਲਈ ਅਰਦਾਸ ਕੀਤੀ ਹੈ ।

2. TRANSLITERATION IN ROMAN SCRIPT

ARDĀS

Ik Oaṅkār Wāheguru jī kī Fateh
Srī Bhagautī jī sahāe
Vār Srī Bhagautī jī kī Pātshāhī 10.
Pritham Bhagautī simar ke Gur Nānak laī dhiāe.
Phir Aṅgad Gur te Amardās Rāmdase hoī sahāe.
Arjan Hargobiṅd noṅ simro Srī Har Rae.
Srī Harkrishan dhiāīe, jis ḍiṭhe sabh dukh jāe.
Tegh Bahādar simrīe ghar nau nidh Āve dhāe.
Sabh thāīṅ hoe sahāe.
Dasvāṅ Pātshāh S̄rī Gurū Gobiṅd Siṅgh jī
sabh thāīṅ hoe sahāe.
Dasāṅ Pātshāhīāṅ dī jot Srī Guru Graṅth Sāhib jī de
Pāṭh dīdār dā dhiān dhar ke
Bolo jī Wāheguru !
Paṅjaṅ Piāriāṅ, Cauhāṅ Sāhibzādiāṅ,
Cālī Muktiāṅ
Haṭhīāṅ, japīāṅ, tapīāṅ, jinhāṅ Nām japiā,
vaṅḍ chakiā, deg calāī, teg vāhī,
dekh ke aṇḍiṭh kītā,
tinhāṅ piāriān saciāriāṅ dī kamāī dā dhiān dhar ke
Bolo jī Wāheguru !
jinhāṅ siṅghāṅ siṅghaṇīāṅ ne dharam het sīs ditte,
baṅd baṅd kaṭāe, khoparīāṅ utarvāīāṅ, carkhaṛīāṅ te caṛhe,
āriāṅ nal cirae gae,
gurduāriāṅ dī sevā laī kurbānīāṅ kītīāṅ,
Sikhī kesāṅ suāsāṅ nāl nibhāī,
tinhāṅ dī kamāī dā dhiān dhar ke
Bolo jī Wāheguru !
paṅjāṅ takhtāṅ, sarbat gurduāriāṅ da dhiān dhar ke
Bolo jī Wāheguru !
Prithme Sarbat Khālsā jī kī Ardās hai jī,
Sarbat Khālsā jī ko
Wāheguru, Wāheguru, Waheguru cit āvai,
cit āvan kā sadkā sarab sukh havai.
Jahāṅ jahāṅ Khālsā jī Sāhib,tahāṅ tahāṅ rachiā riāit,

deg teg fateh, bird kī paij, Panth kī jīt, Sirī Sāhib jī sahāe,
Khālsā jī ke bol bāle,
Bolo jī Wāheguru !
Sikhāṅ nuṅ sikhī dān, kes dān, rahit dān, bharosā dān,
dānāṅ sir dān Nām dān, Srī Amritsar jī ke ishnān,
caukīāṅ, jhaṅde, buṅge jugo jug aṭal,
dharam kā jaikār
Bolo jī Wāheguru !
Sikhāṅ dā man nīvāṅ, mat uccī,
mat dā rākhā āp Wāheguru.
He Akāl Purakh, āpṇe Paṅth de sadā sahāī dātār jīo,
Srī Nankāṇā Sāhib
te hor gurduāriāṅ, gurdhāmāṅ de
jinhāṅ toṅ Paṅth nūṅ vichoṛiā giā hai,
khule darshan dīdār te sevā sambhāl dā dān
Khālsā jī nūṅ bakhsho.
He nimāṇiāṅ de māṇ, nitāṅiāṅ de tāṇ, nioṭiāṅ dī ot,
sace pitā Wāheguru jī,
āp de hazūr . . .[2]*. . . dī ardās hai jī,*
akhar vadh ghaṭ bhul cuk māf karnī,
seī piāre mel, jinhāṅ miliāṅ
āp dā Nām cit āvai.
Nānak nām caṛhdī kalā,
Tere bhāṇe sarbat ka bhalā.

[2]Here may be named the *gurbāṇī* that has been recited, or mentioned the reason for which supplication has to be made.

3. ENGLISH TRANSLATION OF *ARDĀS*

God is one; victory to Him!
May the Divine Sword ever be of assistance.

We begin by remembering the Almighty Sword,
And think of Guru Nānak.
May the Gurus Aṅgad, Amar Dās and Rām Dās give us help.
Let us also remember Arjan, Hargobiṅd and holy Har Rāe
And think of holy Harkrishan whose sight dispels sorrows.
Let us keep in our thoughts Tegh Bahādur—may he grant us all the nine treasures.
May they all support us everywhere.
May our Tenth Lord, Guru Gobiṅd Siṅgh, also help us everywhere.
Turn your thoughts, O Khālsā, to the holy *Guru Graṅth Sāhib,*
That brings together the spirit of all the ten Gurus—and
chant: *Wāheguru!*

Remind yourselves of the noble deeds of the Five Loved Ones, the Four Princes,[3] the Forty Saved Ones, and the many other steadfast devotees who practised the presence of God, shared their earnings with others, carried out charity, wielded the holy sword, and overlooked others' faults. While you think of them,
chant: *Wāheguru!*

All those who laid down their lives for the faith—had their bodies severed joint by joint, the scalp removed, were torn on the toothed wheel, or sawn alive, but until their last breath, did not let their holy hair be harmed—remember them and
chant: *Wāheguru!*

Think of the Five Sacred Thrones and all the *gurdwārās* and
chant: *Wāheguru!*

We pray, first, on behalf of the entire *Khālsā.*
May the *Khālsā* ever keep *Wāheguru* in their mind—and, in turn, be blessed with peace.
May the *Khālsā,* wherever they are, receive God's protection, and concessions of His grace.

[3]The sons of Guru Gobiṅd Siṅgh.

May their rations and their weapons ensure victory.
May their honour be upheld,
May they ever be victorious,
May they be aided by the holy Sword,
May the word of the *Khālsā* ever prevail. So
chant: *Wāhegurū!*

May the Sikhs, O Lord, receive from You the spirit of the Sikh faith,
May their unshorn hair shine forever!
Grant them the gift of disciplined life, faith and confidence,
Grant them Wisdom that can discriminate between good and evil,
Grant them the supreme gift of the Holy *Nām.*
Grant them a dip in the Sacred Pool of Amritsar.

May their choirs, banners and hospices survive forever.
May righteousness ever give calls of victory.
chant: *Wāheguru!*

May the conduct of the Sikhs be humble, and their thinking high.
May the Lord preserve their wisdom.

O Lord, the protector of Your *Panth*, pray, grant the *Khālsā* free, unhindered approach to, and care of, such shrines as Nankāṇā Sāhib, from which the Sikhs have been torn apart.

O Real King! You are the honour of the humble, the protector of the helpless, the shelter of the unsheltered, we pray to dedicate to You our recitation of . . . .[4]
Forgive us for our errors during our reading and bless us so that our recitation is always clear and correct.

We pray that tasks of one and all be accomplished.
Let us, Lord, meet such noble souls, as would make us remember You.

May through Your *Nām*, says Nānak, our morale be ever ascendant, and may one and all prosper by Your grace.

[4]Here name the holy text recited, or the reason for any other supplication that is to be made.

CHAPTER 10

The Structure of the Congregational *Ardās*

Sikhism is a prayer-centred religion. It provides for both personal and congregational prayers. While examples of personal prayer abound in the principal scripture *Srī Guru Granth Sāhib,* their beautiful congregational prayer *ardās* is the gift of the devout Sikhs to the world.

For convenience of understanding, the *ardās* can be divided into the following sections:

1. From *Ek Oaṅkār Wāheguru jī kī fateh*	to	*Srī Bhagautī jī sahāe*
2. From *Pritham Bhagautī simar kai*	to	*Sabh thāīṅ hoe sahāe*
3. From *Dasveṅ Pātshāh Srī Guru Gobiṅd Siṅgh*	to	*Pāṭh dīdār dā dhiān*
4. From *Paṅjāṅ piyāriāṅ*	to	*Tinhāṅ dī kamāī dā*
5. From *Paṅjāṅ Takhtāṅ sarbat gurduāriāṅ*	to	*Dhiān dhar ke*
6. From *Prithmai sarbat Khālsā jī kī*	to	*Khālsā jī ke bol bāle*
7. From *Sikhāṅ nūṅ Sikhī dān*	to	*Dharm kā jaikār*
8. From *Sikhāṅ dā man nīvāṅ*	to	*Sevā sambhāl dā dān*
9. From *Hey nimāṇiāṅ de māṇ*	to	*. . . dī ardās hai*
10. From *Nānak nām caṛhdī kalā*	to	*Sarbat kā bhalā*

The first five sections are *maṅgalācharan* or invocation addressed serially to:

The Supreme Lord *Wāheguru,*
His Divine Power *Srī Bhagautī jī,*

The Ten Gurus—from Guru Nānak Dev to Guru Gobiṅd Siṅgh,
The Divine Word as Guru—*Srī Guru Granth Sāhib,* and
The Holy Community as Guru—*Guru Paṅth.*

Ardās does not begin by asking for the fulfilment of any desires. Rather, it first affirms one's faith in the Lord Almighty and the Gurus, whom the devotee reverently invokes for their grace. Supplication follows only after this.

One's first supplication is not for oneself, but on behalf of the entire Khālsā and for the entire Order of the Khālsā (section 6). In this section, a Sikh first asks for the gift of *Nām* or God's holy Name. This is repeated three times to remind a Sikh of the Gurus' advice for its practice. This is followed by a prayer for 'favour and protection for the Khālsā wherever they are'. This collective supplication makes every individual Sikh feel that he is an inseparable part of the Khālsā brotherhood. Even before his personal safety, therefore, he supplicates for the collective safety of the entire Khālsā fraternity.

In the next supplicatory section (section 7), a Sikh prays for all his co-religionists and requests for them the gift of the Sikh way of life. That includes the Sikh faith, the Sikh conduct, the Sikh character, and a discerning intellect. With the desire for uniting with his religious capital, he prays for the grant of a visit to Amritsar and a dip in the holy tank there. He tops these prayers with a yearning for *Nām,* the holy Name, calling it the loftiest of all gifts. Closing this section, he utters 'Hail Dharma!'—laying stress, once again, on spiritual victory.

After the two sections of collective supplication, the Sikh now addresses *Wāheguru,* addressing Him as 'the Honour of the humble and the Strength of the despirited'. Then he dedicates his works to Him and asks for the grant of any favour for oneself or one's dear ones. In this section, the practitioner of *ardās* may give full vent to whatever his personal yearnings may be. One may submit one's plans to *Wāheguru* and invoke His divine guidance. The devotee may thank God for the grace and the gifts that he has received. At this point, one may also make a vow for the realization of his ideals and seek the Lord's benevolence for the fulfilment of such a vow. One may seek forgiveness for any transgressions of divine commands that one might have committed, particularly for faults and slips during the recitation of the holy texts

This section is climaxed by a yearning for meeting persons in whose company one may remember the Lord.

In the final section, the Sikh ideals are pithily recapitulated as follows:

> May through Your *Nām*, says Nānak, our morale be ever in the ascendance,
> May one and all prosper by Your grace.

Ardās that begins with 'the One Lord to whom all victory belongs' ends with the same utterance. In other words, what begins with 'victory' also ends in 'victory'.

CHAPTER 11

Invocation of the Divine Sword

Ik Oaṅkār, Wāheguru jī kī Fateh!
Srī Bhagautī jī sahāe.

God is one; victory to Him!
May the Divine Sword help us.

Let us begin by remembering the Almighty Sword,
And think of Guru Nānak.
May the Gurus Aṅgad, Amar Dās and Rām Dās help us.
Let us also remember Arjan, Hargobiṅd and holy Har Rāe,
And think of holy Harkrishan whose sight dispels all sorrows.
Let us keep in our thoughts Tegh Bahādur—may he grant us all treasures.
May they all support us everywhere.
May our Tenth Lord, Guru Gobiṅd Siṅgh, also help us everywhere.
Turn your thoughts O Khālsā, to the holy *Guru Graṅth Sāhib* that brings together the spirit of all the ten Gurus, and chant: *Wāheguru!*

The above verse marks the opening of *ardās*. It was taken out of *Vār Srī Bhagautī jī kī* (The Ballad of the Divine Sword), a work of Guru Gobiṅd Siṅgh. This work is a free translation of *Durgā Pāṭh*[1] into Paṅjabī verse. This ballad narrates the war that Goddess Durgā waged against the demons who had usurped the throne of Indra, the king of gods. The Guru translated this work in the popular tongue of his people because it inspires valour and courage. He also translated many other mythological tales with the same motive.

This ballad is a wonderful poetic piece that yields multiple layers of meaning. Contrary to the fixed definitions of the

[1] *Durgā Pāṭh* is the name given to a specified section of the 4th chapter of *Mārkaṅḍeya Purāṇa*, the work of Mārkaṅḍeya Rishi. It consists of 700 verses.

Vār Srī Bhagautī jī kī is its abbreviated translation in 55 verses.

discipline of philosophy, good poetry invariably yields multiple layers of meaning and this ballad does that so very well.

Although some scholars contend that this ballad is in praise of Bhagvatī or Durgā, thoughtful perusal of its content makes clear that the ode is in praise of the Divine Sword. Within that ballad, a verse affirms:

> Durgā took into her hands the benevolent *Bhagautī*,
> Struck Rājā Sumbh with it, and so drank his blood.
> —*Caṅḍī dī Vār* 53: 2

It is obvious that the *Bhagautī* that Durgā took into her hands was the Divine Sword. This ballad therefore pertains to the holy sword rather than to Goddess Durgā.

To remember God with symbols of weaponry is the unique style of Guru Gobiṅd Siṅgh as he believed that one became the like of the one whom one worshipped. Some of his repetitive phrases that pertain to God are, 'We invoke the protection of All-Steel',[2] 'Protect us O One with The Sword-Banner',[3] 'Salute to the Supreme Sword'[4] and 'Supreme over all is the Sacred Sword'.[5] The Guru had himself undertaken the task of awakening a slumbering nation and inspiring it with renascent valour and heroic spirit.

The Sword that he conceived was 'the cause of the Creation', 'bestowing boons upon His devotees' and 'striking lightning on those who molest others'. Such an omnipotent Sabre is the Sword of Divine Justice, the Scimitar of His covenant, the instrument of His creativity and the emblem of His own nature.[6] So the ballad refers to that Mighty Sword and to none else.

[2] *DG: Akāl Ustat.*
[3] *DG: Benatī Chaupaī.*
[4] *DG: Bacitra Nāṭak.*
[5] *DG: Akāl Ustat.*
[6] Cf. Phillip Brooks' sermon *The Sword Bathed in Heaven* wherein he says, 'Everywhere . . . throughout the perplexed universe, He can see the flashing of His Sword. 'His Sword!' we say, and that must mean His nature uttering itself in His own form of force. Nothing can be in His Sword which is not in His nature. And so the Sword of God in heavenly region (Is xxxv.5) must mean perfect thoroughness and perfect justice contending against evil and self-will and bringing about everywhere the ultimate victory of righteousness and truth.'

The Lord, whose inevitable victory was to be the watchword of the Gurus' followers, was conceived as follows:

The Sword Supreme that can slice the universe,
Decimate the hordes of fools,
Wage a fierce war, and distribute blessings;
Whose arms are unbreakable like a bar,
Whose flame is lambent, dazzling, blinding,
And glory like the sun;
Who comforts His devotees,
Destroys evil-mindedness,
Conquers sin, and provides refuge;
Hail the Creator of the world, sustainer of the Creation,
Provider of raiment, O, hail the Sword!

— *DG: Bacitra Nāṭak* 7:2

The Sword referred to in the above verse whose attributes are creator and sustainer of the universe is not a mere weapon of steel, but emblem of the awesome Power of God Almighty. This becomes amply clear in the second verse of the ballad:

Having created the two-edged Sword who shaped the world, created He Brahmā, Vishnu and Mahesh and spread out His Mighty Game,
Who fashioned oceans, mountains and earth, and without pillars sustained the sky,
Who created gods and demons and engaged them in mutual strife.
You created Durgā to destroy the demons,
From You did Rāma derive power to destroy the ten-headed monster.
From You did Krishna derive power to smash the demon Kaṅsa.
For your pleasure, hermits and saints observed penance,
But none could fathom Thy Might.

—*DG: Vār Srī Bhagautī jī kī:* 2

The above verse makes clear that the attributes of the Sword illustrated therein belong to none but God Almighty.

In this ballad, the Goddess Durgā, with the help of *Bhagautī* (the supreme Sword) killed the great demons who caused distress to the gods. If we ponder over the names of those demons, we find that they have real symbolic significance.

Rakt Bīj was one such demon, every drop of whose spilt blood would turn into a new demon like himself. *Lochan Dhūm* was one from whose eyes smoke and fire emanated (which signifies intense anger). *Mehkhāsur* means one whose temperament is like that of a he-buffalo: a hardy, stubborn temperament. The bevy of the three demons signifies three major vices of human character. Invoking the Sacred Sword to decimate these deadly vices establishes the *ardās* at the sublime ethical level.

In his *Mūlmantra,* Guru Nānak described the Lord *inter alia* as 'Fearless'. The same value is concretized as *Bhagautī* in this ballad, and it serves to provide a logo for the Sikh identity.

CHAPTER 12

Pray, Help Us Everywhere

The Sikhs are ordained to address their *ardās* to their Guru.[1] God is pervasive everywhere but invisible to us. We cannot therefore readily relate to him. For us to be able to generate relationship with Him, He gave us the Guru. The institution of the Guruship was established by the express pleasure of the Lord. *Janam Sākhīs* bear ample testimony to this:

When Guru Nānak did not emerge from the river Veyīṅ, he found himself in a mystical trance in the presence of the Lord. God presented him a cup of ambrosia to drink. Nānak quaffed it. Then God said, 'Nānak I am with you. I hereby bless you. Go and ever remember my *Nām* and make others remember it too. Go and do as I bid. Those who receive your grace will receive mine too. Those who receive your benevolence, will receive my benevolence as well. My name is *Pārbrahm Parmeshvar*, yours *Guru Parmeshvar*.'

That is how Nānak became commissioned as the Guru, connected on the one hand with God and with people on the other. God was to address the people through him. It is said:

He (the Lord) installed Himself in the Guru
to become manifest to the world.
—*Vār Malār* m 1, p. 1279

That is why, if we turn our face towards the Guru, we come face to face with God; and prayer before the Guru is prayer before God Himself. *Gurbāṇī* testifies:

Reckon the Guru and God as one.
—*Gauṅḍ* m 5, p. 864

[1] Offer your *ardās* to him whom the Creator caused you meet
The true Guru who gifted you *Nām* has an overflowing treasure.
—*Srīrāg* m 5, p. 49

In the *Bhakti Mārga*, many indulgent bhaktas preferred the Guru over God. Sahjobāī, in one of her popular verses eulogized Guru as the manifest form of God and said:

God created the world and caused us to be born therein.
It was the Guru who freed us from the bonds of birth and death.
God put us into the throes of vices like passion, avarice and anger,
It was the Guru who rescued us from that helplessness.
God tied us with attachment to our kin.
It was the Guru who severed the strings of that attachment.
God let us suffer sickness and grief,
It was the Guru who made us transcend over these.
God put us into the bondage of rituals and religions,
It was the Guru who made us cognize our true selves.
God concealed Himself from us,
It was the Guru who lit the lamp of enlightenment to let us behold Him.
God put us into the conflicting state of bondage and salvation,
It was the Guru who caused these delusions to disappear.

That is why she said:

I shall not forsake the Guru, even if I forsake God.

Such an extreme statement would not be acceptable in Sikhism. Here, even the Guru is believed to manifest himself through the grace of God.

He, in His Mercy, made His benevolence manifest
And we met with our great friend, the Guru.
—*Sl.* m 5, p. 1429

It was indeed God's love that became manifest as Guru. His *prasād* (benevolence) became the Guru for us. That is the meaning of *gurprasād.* The Guru embodies God's grace; hence, he is not apart from God.

What laudation may I make of the Guru?
He is the source of Truth and Wisdom.
From the very beginning, and through all the ages,
The guru has been God Himself perfectly.
—*Āsā* m 5, p. 397

If anyone seeks refuge with the Guru, God Himself rushes to protect him:

Those who take the Guru's refuge, get firmly established.
To protect them God Himself rushes forth.
—*Kānṛā* m 4, p. 1311

That is why in the opening verse of *ardās,* not only are the Gurus invoked, they are to be remembered and to be the focus of our devotion. There is also supplication addressed to the Guru for our protection and help everywhere. Here is the Guru's covenant:

The Guru looks after the Sikh with all his heart.
—*Gauṛī* m 5, p. 286

Not only is Guru one with God, he is also one with the other Gurus. Guru Gobiṅd Siṅgh provides testimony to it thus:

I would like you to believe that Guru Nānak became Guru Aṅgad.
And that Aṅgad should be recognized as Amar Dās.
Amar Dās himself came to be known as Rām Dās.
This, the saints recognized, the fools understood not.
When Rām Dās ascended to God,
He enthroned Arjan transforming himself into him.
As Arjan was leaving this world, he installed Hargobiṅd in his place.
When Hargobiṅd ascended to God, Har Rāe took his place.
He was followed by his son, Harkrishan,
Who was further followed by Tegh Bahādur.
Most people thought one Guru different from the other.
Rare ones alone reckoned them as one.
They alone, who saw them as one, attained perfection.
Those who couldn't, perfection evaded them.
—*DG: Bacitra Nāṭak,* Ch. 5

The same Light was manifest in all of them, and their mode of work was also the same.

The selfsame Light, the selfsame stratagem,
Only the physical frame was different.
—*Vār Rāmkalī,* Balvaṅd-Sattā, p. 966

That is why when you focus on one Guru, you are actually focusing on all of them; when you remember any one of them, you remember all of them. Vision of one is the vision of all, and help from one is help from all.

From what has been said so far, three main characteristics of the Guru stand out:

1. that he is established by Divine Grace,
2. that there is identity of light and stratagem between all the Gurus, and
3. that a Guru is supra-corporeal.[2]

Guru Nānak affirmed that the real Guru is his Word, not his body. When the *siddhas* asked him, 'Who is your Guru, whose disciple are you?' His reply simply was:

The Word is the (real) Guru and constantly receptive consciousness the (actual) disciple. —*Sidh Goshti Rāmkalī* m 1, p. 943

[2]Everyone in this world beholds the Guru
Seeing alone doesn't yield salvation, unless his Word is pondered upon. —*Vār Vaḍhaṅs* m 4, p. 594

CHAPTER 13

Spiritual Light of the Ten Gurus

In the *ardās* after the invocation to the ten Gurus, the *Guru Granth Sāhib*, the spiritual light of all the Gurus, is revered and invoked. 'Spiritual light' means divine enlightenment that alighted in the hearts of the Gurus and emerged from their hearts as Word. Such manifest form of the Divine Word is called *gurbāṇī*, and it was held dearer by the Gurus than their own life as evidenced by the careful measures they took to preserve it.

The chronicles of Guru Nānak's life show that when he visited Mecca, he was carrying a book with him under his armpit. In all likelihood, it was the volume of his works. The *hājīs* there pointed to that book when they asked him, 'Pray, open your book and tell us who, according to you, is superior—a Hindu or Muslim?'[1]

According to the *Janam-sākhī* of Bhāī Bālā, Guru Nānak passed that book on into the personal custody of Guru Aṅgad Dev. The latter, along with his own compositions, entrusted it to Guru Amar Dās. After Guru Amar Dās passed away, the two volumes containing the content of compositions of the previous two Gurus as well as his own passed into the hands of his elder son Bābā Mohan.

During the time of Guru Amar Dās, apocryphal versions of *gurbāṇī* had begun to appear. He called them *kacī bāṇī,* or counterfeit *bāṇī.* Measures were therefore required to put together the genuine *bāṇī* into an authentic volume.

Guru Arjan Dev undertook that task. He acquired the two volumes that Bābā Mohan possessed, and reviewed them. Additionally, he had with him his father Guru Rām Dās's compositions as well as his own. He also added the compositions of like-minded Hindu and Muslim holy men and prepared one composite volume out of all that material. His scribe was Bhāī

[1] *Bhāī Gurdās Vār* 1:33.

Gurdās, a great scholar of Sikh learning. The resulting volume was designated as *Pothī Sāhib* or the Revered Book. Upon completion, it was installed in Harmaṅdar Sāhib, and Bābā Budḣā was appointed as its caretaker. The same day, Guru Arjan Dev made an exposition of some verses out of the book, and the additional important message he gave that day was as follows:

> My physical self at any one time can be in one place only. Elsewhere one cannot behold it. I, therefore, call upon you to consider this Book as the heart of the Guru. Revere it to the utmost. This Guru is eternal. Reposing full faith in it is your proper duty. Consider it higher than my physical form. I myself hold it in high reverence.[2]

Thereafter, as long as the Guru stayed in this world, he would install the Book on a pedestal while he slept on the floor by its side. In an informal way, Guruship had been bestowed on the Holy Book.

However, the tenth Guru, Guru Gobiṅd Siṅgh, reassembled the volume from his memory and added to it the compositions of his father, Guru Tegh Bahādur. Before his ascension to God, he brought an end to the tradition of personal Guruship by formally installing that Book as his perpetual successor and designating it *Srī Guru Graṅth Sāhib.* There is overwhelming and reliable contemporary evidence of the closure of personal Guruship and conferring perpetual Guruship on the Holy Book.

Notwithstanding irrefutable evidence regarding bestowal of Guruship on *Srī Guru Graṅth Sāhib,* some traditions (such as Nāmdhārī and Niraṅkārī) regard a personal living Guru a necessity and do not accept the closure of personal Guruship after Guru Gobiṅd Siṅgh.

The evidence in Bhatt *Vahīs*[3] is considered very reliable as it is contemporary evidence. A Bhatt, Narbud Siṅgh, son of Keso Siṅgh and descendant of Bhāī Bhikā, a Sikh of Guru Amar Dās, recorded in his *Vahī* the transfer of Guruship to *Guru Graṅth Sāhib.*

[2] Bhāī Santokh Siṅgh, *Gurpratāp Sūraj,* Amritsar: Office of Khalsa Samachar, 1936.

[3] Bhaṭṭs were ancestral minstrels. They also maintained genealogical records of the families they served. Their records are called *vahīs.* The discovery and research of these records we owe to Giānī Garjā Siṅgh.

He was present in the final congregation addressed by Guru Gobiṅd Siṅgh and records in his *Vahī* the following:

> Guru Gobiṅd Siṅgh, the 10th Master, son of Guru Teg͟h Bahādur, grandson of Guru Hargobiṅd, great grandson of Guru Arjan Dev and a descendant of Guru Rām Dās, of Surajbaṅsī Gosal gotra, Soḍhī Khatrī, resident of Ānaṅdpur, Pragnā Kehlūr, at Naṅder on the bank of Godāwarī in the South of the land, in Samvat 1765 Kārtik 4th of the bright half of the lunar month, the Wednesday, asked Bhāī Dayā Siṅgh to bring over to him *Srī Guru Graṅth Sāhib*. The Guru then placed five paisę and a cocoanut fruit in front of it and made an obeisance before it. Then addressed the congregation and said, 'It is my command that in my place, you shall consider *Srī Guru Graṅth Sāhib* as your Guru. Whoso will do so, his spiritual effort will bear fruit. The Guru will always come to his rescue. Believe this as true!

Apart from Bhaṭṭ *Vahīs*, evidence of conferment of Guruship on *Srī Guru Graṅth Sāhib* is available from other reliable sources as well. A *Hukamnāmā*[4] issued by Mātā Suṅdrī jī (the wife of Guru Gobiṅd Siṅgh) says thus:

> Ek Oaṅkār, Wāheguru jī kī Fateh. O 'molten-pot' K͟hālsā jī of the Timeless Lord, by seeing you one should remember the Lord. Let the entire K͟hālsā accept my salutation 'Wāheguru jī kā K͟hālsā, Wāheguru jī kī Fateh'. May you be blessed by ever remembering the Timeless Lord. May the K͟hālsā's word be ever in the ascendancy. . . . Remember the Guru and Wāheguru will always be by you. You will be protected by His benevolence. . . . It behoves you to be awake and alert so that the discriminating intellect of the K͟hālsā does not worship anyone but the Timeless Lord. They should reckon as Guru, the ten living Gurus only. Having faith in eleventh or twelfth—Baṅdā, Caubaṅdā, Ajītā, etc,—is a grave sin. Other sins can be forgiven, considering any currently living man a Guru after the ten Gurus is not pardonable. K͟hālsā jī! do not rest your faith on anyone except the Timeless One. . . . Whoso searches through the Word will find the Lord's true abode. . . . The Guru resides in the Word. God installed Himself in the Guru and through him manifested Himself as the Word. Wāheguru jī kī Fateh.

Even *Rahit Nāmās* and an almost contemporary Sanskrit work

---

[4]This *Hukamnāmā* is available with Bhāī Cet Siṅgh of village Bhāī Rūpā, Distt. Bhaṭiṅḍā, Puṅjāb.

Nānak Chāṅdogya Mahākāvyam by Dev Rāj Sharmā support this transition. Such overwhelming evidence just cannot be ignored.

Compared with other scriptures of the world, *Guru Graṅth Sāhib* has the following distinctive features:

1. This is perhaps the only scripture in which compositions of a bevy of holy men—Hindus as well as Muslim—beside those of the Sikh Gurus have been preserved.
2. The contents of this holy book consist of original hymns in praise of the One Universal God. It is not a historical document, a biographical document, a manual of instructions or a law book.
3. Ultimate spiritual progress is possible through it because it is fully consonant with divine intent.
4. It is a book that represents the core of all religions and everyone, not just the Sikhs, may bow before it.
5. Anyone who bows before it would not be able to entertain pride of caste, class, creed or colour.

Its contributors did not hail from the Puṅjāb alone. They were from many places representing the length and breadth of India and they were not just contemporaries of the Gurus; rather, they represented full five centuries of spiritual renaissance—from the birth of Sheikh Farīd (1231 Bi) to the ascension of Guru Tegh Bahādur to God Lord (1732 Bi). Thus this holy book represents remarkable spiritual outpourings extending over considerable space and time.

In the *gurduārās*, the *ardās* is addressed to *Guru Graṅth Sāhib*, and after the *ardās*, the message for the day is randomly read from the Holy Book.

This Holy Book, which is the eternal living Guru of the Sikhs, reigns over the Sikh minds. Recitation from the *Graṅth Sāhib* is considered equivalent to having a vision of the Guru.

In *ardās*, the *Shabad Guru* is paid homage, and while focusing on the spiritual sublimity of its message, the congregation utters '*Wāheguru*!'.

CHAPTER 14

With Full Attention, Utter *Wāheguru*

To offer *ardās* on behalf of the congregation, a devout Sikh steps forward facing *Guru Granth Sāhib* and recites *ardās.* The rest of the congregation stands behind him participating in the recitation with solemn attention. Periodically, the *ardāsīā* (one who is uttering the *ardās*) raises his voice and exhorts 'with full attention utter *Wāheguru* !'. The entire congregation in one voice echoes back *Wāheguru* ! after him. This process, that is repeated a number of times during the course of the *ardās,* is of considerable spiritual significance.

First of all it is a call for alertness and attention. *Ardās* is a spiritual performance entirely contingent upon attention, and one who is inattentive during the *ardās* is absent from it. Being mentally aware is the foremost requirement for participation in the *ardās.* That is one of the reasons why the *ardāsīā,* time and again, calls upon the congregation to utter *Wāheguru* ! *Ardās* is best performed when one is linked mind and soul with *Akāl Purakh.*

In the Sikh *ardās,* we unite not only with *Akāl Purakh,* but also with the Guru's Word, with virtuous men and women who have earned spiritual merit, with the martyrs, with religious institutions, and with the entire community of the faithful. Therefore, the call for uttering *Wāheguru* is effectively a call to unite with all these sources of faith.

Before making the call to utter *Wāheguru,* the *ardāsīā* emphatically says 'pray! focus your attention'. Thus, he impresses on us that the *ardās* is essentially a function of an attentive mind. Attention (*dhyān*) is the basis of devotional activity. It is focusing our mind with soulful *liv.* In the Sikh parlance, *liv* is single-pointed, uninterrupted and love-intoxicated attention. In Sikhism, two ways of living are identified: the way of *liv* and the way of *dhāt.* The latter is the path of *māyā*, the cosmic illusion. *Liv* is the path of *Nām*, the Divine Essence. *Dhāt* is materialistic, *liv* is awareness of eternal values. The call to 'focus your attention and say *Wāheguru* is to participate in *ardās* with *liv*.

Says Nānak, through the Guru's grace,
They who achieved *liv* realized the Lord
even while living within *Māyā*.
—*Rāmkalī* m 3, p. 921

The call to utter *Wāheguru* also invites us to practice the presence of God. *Wāheguru* is our *gurmantra* and reminds us of our Creator. A Sikh is required to repeat this *gurmantra* verbally or mentally all the time.[1] During the *ardās* one says:

First, we pray to You, O Lord,
On behalf of *Sarbat Khālsā;*
(The Commonwealth of the Pure ones),
May the Khālsā ever remember
Wāheguru! Wāheguru!!, Wāheguru!!!
By virtue of remembering it, bestow on them every comfort.

Repeating *Wāheguru* three times in the above-mentioned supplication, one practises the presence of God. The yearning before it is not just for oneself but for the entire Khālsā commonwealth.

In the *ardās*, we do not merely supplicate God for the gift of *Nām*, we actually practise it[2] by repeating it three times at a stretch.

During the *ardās*, we remember the lofty achievements of our community. We are astonished at the firm determination and devotion of those who laid down their lives to uphold righteousness. By uttering *Wāheguru* we acknowledge the sublime wonder we feel towards the strength of their moral conviction. When we say *Wāheguru*, we say *Wāh*, meaning 'bravo!' to the Guru through whose grace ordinary lives attained such lofty spiritual heights.

[1]The Guru's Sikh while following his vocation, buying or selling wares, should repeat *Wāheguru*. —*Rahit Nāmā* of Caupā Singh

[2]A similar practice also obtains in *Janam Sākhīs* wherein at the end of every *sākhī* (story), a call is given to utter *Wāheguru!*

When we remember the *Pañj Piāre,* the Five Loved Ones, we are inspired to the sentiment of self-dedication. When we remember the *Cār Sāhibzāde,* the four little sons of Guru Gobiṅd Siṅgh, the firmness of their faith surprises us. *Cālī Mukte,* the Forty Saved Ones, inspire us to reestablish our own bonds with the Guru. When we remember those who had been severed joint by joint, or who were mercilessly descalped but did not wince at all, our hearts melt with compassion as well as admiration. When we then utter *Wāheguru,* it is the cry of a ruthful heart.

When we realize that we are members of a community that produced men of such high spiritual attainments, our hearts are filled with pride and thankfulness. When we utter *Wāheguru,* we admire as well as laud our creator. Doing so, we also take a pledge to live up to the reputation of our forefathers.

By uttering *Wāheguru* we invite the Lord's grace into our *ardās,* as also His mercy to rain on our lives. We invoke His benevolence to spread its wings over our faith. By uttering *Wāheguru,* we not only fix our own attention on the Lord, we also invite His attention to our supplications.

The utterance of *Wāheguru* by the entire congregation generates feelings of spiritual unity among the devotees, between every individual and the whole congregation and between prayerful minds and the Lord to whom the *ardās* is addressed. Whoever utters *Wāheguru* at the calls during the *ardās* should be able to enter the realm of spiritual ecstasy.

'Focus your attention and utter *Wāheguru*' is thus premier among the key phrases of the *ardās.* It should be important for every participant in the congregational *ardās* to respond respectfully and wholeheartedly to this command with full faith and sincerity. Those who keep silent and do not appropriately respond to the call to utter *Wāheguru* neglect their duty and deprive themselves of the enormous spiritual benefits that are likely to accrue from the utterance. To them, the Guru says:

> Speak up O man of Righteousness;
> On what count are you mum?
> —*Bihāgṛā* m 5, p. 547

CHAPTER 15

Homage to *Guru Panth*

Following the invocation to *Guru Granth Sāhib*, the *ardās* pays homage to *Guru Panth*—the *Gurmukh Panth* which stands uniquely at variance with the other religions of the world. Sikhism is a faith that inspires an undaunted spirit coupled with the lack of malevolence. It values moral *ahimsā*, or non-violence, but not one that becomes culpable for inaction against grave injustice and the armed aggression against the meek, the helpless and the down-trodden. It values valour and courage to hold out against aggression, yet never attacks anyone first.

The gallantry taught by the Gurus has two aspects: inner and outer. The former pertains to facing and subduing the inner enemies such as lust, anger, avarice, worldly attachment and pride.[1] The latter pertains to the valour that destroys tyranny, savagery and other inhuman behaviour in order to protect the meek, the poor and the unprivileged.[2] This bi-modal gallantry is a hard task, for martyrdom is its pledge and sacrifices its vow.[3] This has an appropriate connection with the two swords of *mīrī* and *pīrī*.

Ardās inspires readiness for martyrdom. The Sikh *Panth* has carved its history through high moral courage. History has not carved its ideals, its ideals have carved its history. *Ardās* remembers the eternal heroes not by their names but by their acts. The Sikh heroes carved history by living their ideals and by

[1] Says Nānak, really brave is he who has slain the evil pride within.
—*Vār Srīrāg* m 4, p. 86

[2] Recognize him as valourous who fights for the meek.
Even if cut into bits, he does not desert the field.
—*Mārū* Kabīr, p. 1125

[3] The one who is a real hero accepts death unflinchingly.
Anyone who deserts the field gets into the cycle of birth and death.
—*Mārū* m 5, p. 1019

dying for them. They were the ones who remembered the Lord, shared their resources with fellow brethren, kept the 'temple of bread' active, wielded the sacred sword when time came, overlooked the shortcomings and faults of others, never gave up righteousness but gave up their lives instead, preserved the sanctity of their *keshas* (unshorn hair) until their last breath, had themselves severed joint by joint, boiled in cauldrons, sawn alive and suffered the cruellest labour. It pays homage to the spiritual fortitude of those mothers whose infant offspring were cut into pieces and thrown back into their laps, but they did not flinch from their faith. Great homage is paid in the *ardās* unto such martyrs, disciples of faith, and the Guru's loved ones.

Such valourous morality relied on the concept of *Guru Paṅth*—the collectivity of great souls. It is to them that adequate homage has been paid in the *ardās*. Guru Gobiṅd Siṅgh alluded to the loftiest traditions of the Paṅth when he said, 'The Khālsā is my own special form'[4] and acknowledge that:

> Through their (the Khālsā's) benevolence have I been decked,
> Else, there exist a million wrecks like me.
>
> —*DG: Keshodās Prabodh* 2-4

The concept of *Guru Paṅth* is a sublime concept that mirrors the lofty spiritual achievements of the Khālsā. It is a unique contribution of the Sikh faith to the religious thought of the world. No other religion is known to have transformed the community to the status of a prophet, a community where the spirit of His Word percolated so admirably into the collective consciousness of the community.

It is important to identify the characteristics of the Khālsā as Guru. It is nothing but single-pointed undaunted sublime consciousness which has become one with supernal spiritual inspiration provided by the Gurus' Word. Guru Gobiṅd Siṅgh bowed in reverence before this type of Khālsā and obediently carried out their command given in the fortress of Camkaur. Those five Sikhs to whom Guru Gobiṅd Siṅgh thus submitted were imbued with *liv*. It is the collectivity of the followers of the path

[4]Bābā Saṅtā Siṅgh, *Sarabloh Graṅth,* Amritsar: Bhai Catar Siṅgh & Co., 2000.

of *liv* that can be considered *Guru Paṅth.* The K͟hālsā with whom Guru Gobiṅd Siṅgh entered into such a covenant were no other than men of great spiritual endowment. What follows is the word that Guru Gobiṅd Siṅgh gave the K͟hālsā:

> As long as the K͟hālsā preserve their uniqueness,
> I shall bestow on them all glory.
> If they begin to follow the Brahmanical ways,
> From them will I withdraw my trust.

In other words, the Guru meant that as long as the K͟hālsā preserve their unique identity and their lofty conduct, he will continue to bless them with the benediction from which they originally sprouted.

Such is the K͟hālsā of Guru Gobiṅd Siṅgh whom he created out of the fullness of spiritual awareness, beauty of conduct, and sheer dauntlessness. On the altar of Time, it manifested itself as *Guru Paṅth.* Every time one remembers the unprecedented achievements of *Guru Paṅth,* one is spontaneously impelled to utter *Wāheguru.* In doing so, every Sikh heart, drenched in Guru-consciousness, renews its faith and determination.

CHAPTER 16

The Five Loved Ones

From the time of Guru Nānak, five spiritually accomplished Sikhs have constituted a sort of advisory body for the Guru.[1] However, history has not preserved the names of all of them and only a few names are available.[2]

The five Loved Ones attained an eminently important status by offering supreme sacrifice at Guru Gobiṅd Siṅgh's call and are especially remembered in the *ardās.*

On Baisākhī day on 30 March 1699 AD in Ānaṅdpur (where at present stands *Takht Srī Kesgaṛh Sāhib*) a mighty congregation was convened under the instructions of Guru Gobiṅd Siṅgh. Historical records indicate that around eighty thousand individuals had gathered there. When the gathering was at its maximum, Guru Gobiṅd Siṅgh, in his glory, came and ascended the decorated platform and stood there in resplendent dignity. He cast a glance over the vast gathering with unusual affection and recited the following verse of his:

O Holy Sword! With love and devotion
I bow to you heartily
Assist me that I may bring this task to conclusion.
You are the conqueror of countries,

[1]The five companions who accept the Guru's precept
are brethren in faith —*Mārū* m 1, p. 1041

The five, shorn of falsehood and drenched in unstruck melody
as well as the Divine Word,
Such brethren-in-faith decked the congregation.
—*Bhāī Gurdās Vār* 29.6

The *five* is the tradition of the Guru's house.
—Bhāī Saṅtokh Siṅgh, *Gur Pratāp Sūraj* 5.41

[2]The five advisors of Guru Arjan Dev were Bhāīs Bidhī Caṅd, Jethā, Laṅgāhā, Pirāṇā and Paiṛā; those of Guru Tegh Bahādur were Bhāīs Matī Dās, Gurdittā, Dyālā, Uḍā and Jaitā.

Destroyer of the armies of the wicked in the battlefield
You adorn the valourous with awards and rewards.
Your arm is infrangible and brilliance refulgent.
Your radiant splendour is dazzling as the sun.
—*DG: Bacitra Nāṭak* 1.1

After having saluted the Sword thus, he made a stimulating appeal in the name of the country and the nation. He emphasized the necessity of subverting the tyrannous Mughal rule and building a new nation. He presented the picture of a new class of men and women who are ready to sacrifice everything for freedom, even their own life. He emphasized that the time for action was now or never!

After this speech, he drew his sword from its scabbard, raised it up and in a resolute voice and elevated tone addressed the congregation, 'Today my sword is in need of a head. Would any of my dear Sikhs come forward and make the requisite offering?'

Astonished but dignified silence spread throughout the congregation. It appeared that the occasion for testing the dauntlessness of the worshippers of the Great Fearless Lord had arrived. This was the historic *kairos* for which the whole Sikh nation had been preparing for over a century. The *gurmukh* heroism was on the anvil. The condition of 'accepting death first' had been prescribed as necessary[3] for whoever desired to be one with the Guru and this was the time for the fulfilment of that condition. The grace of the Guru was to be obtained from the edge of his sword, and he alone would receive it who was able to offer his head carrying it on his palm. The one who rose first was Dayā Rām, a Khatrī of Lāhore. He approached the Guru's platform and said, 'I offer my head unto you my Master. What better luck can I have than dying under your sacred Sword?' The Guru led him into a tent in the rear. After a while, the Guru returned with his sword dripping blood and asked for another head. Dharm Caṅd, a Jāṭ of Hastināpur advanced and offered his head. He was also led to the tent and again the Guru reappeared with his sword dripping blood. The Guru made three

[3] *Vār Mārū* m 5, p. 1102.

additional calls and Mohkam Cand of Dwarkā, Himmat Dās of Jagganāth and Sāhib Cand of Bidar came forth by turns. They were likewise taken to that tent. The last time when the Guru reappeared, he brought out behind him all those five Sikhs robed in identical bright blue. He led the five on to the platform and introduced them as his *Pañj Piāre*—the Five Loved Ones. All of them had turned their own lives over to the Guru at his call.

During the time of the earlier Gurus, the *Pañches* were selected on the basis of their *bhakti*; this time they had been selected on the basis of both *bhakti* and *shakti*. This was not an election by vote but selection by the sword.[4]

The Guru then prepared *amrit* (the ambrosia) in an all-steel bowl. Sitting in *Bīr Āsan* (heroic posture), he began stirring the water in that bowl with a *khaṇḍā* (double-edged sword) while reciting five liturgical texts.[5] Mātā Sāhib Kaur, the Guru's wife, in utter compassion, added to the consecrated water some sugar pellets while it was being stirred. Thus was *amrit* prepared. The Guru then conferred this celestial gift on his 'Five Loved Ones'.

Then he again addressed the congregation, 'These my Loved Ones, Bhāī Dayā Siṅgh, Bhāī Dharam Siṅgh, Bhāī Sāhib Siṅgh, Bhāī Himmat Siṅgh and Bhāī Mohkam Siṅgh, have now become one with the Guru. Now I pray to them to bestow on me the gift of this *amrit*.' The loved ones, obeying his command, prepared *amrit* in the same way as the Master had done, and the Guru received it from his 'Loved Ones' in the presence of the entire congregation. Just as the Guru had added the title 'Siṅgh' after their first names, so did they to the Guru, and Guru Gobind Rae became Guru Gobind Siṅgh.

The status that these Loved Ones received from the Master has been described by Bhāī Santokh Siṅgh thus:

I shall reside in these five Sikhs;
And shall fulfil whatever they may desire from me.

—*Gur Pratāp Sūraj* 2.123

[4]Through a popular electorate only the spiritually weak can get elected because the weaklings are always in a majority. The spiritually agile can be discovered only through the tough tests of devotion and faith.

[5]These texts were *Jap(u) ji*, *Jāp Sāhib*, *Sudhā Sawayīye*, *Benatī Caupāī*, and *Ānand Sāhib.*

There is ample evidence in Sikh chronicles to suggest that the *Paṅj Piārās* were considered adequate to represent the 'Guru Paṅth'. Moreover, the tradition of the Guru 'being at once Master as well as Disciple' was taken to unprecedented heights. After Guru Nānak had installed Guru Aṅgad on the pontific throne, he spent the rest of his life as an attendant of Guru Aṅgad's court. That is how the tradition of the Guru himself becoming the disciple started. Lehnā alone out of the entire congregation had been selected as the next Guru. Guru Gobiṅd Siṅgh accepted his 'Loved Ones' as his equal, conceding them the right to represent the entire Paṅth. Thus he consecrated his entire following as 'Guru Paṅth'.

This rendered the Paṅth future-oriented. For all its newly emerging problems, the community did not have to look back for guidance, but could focus the entire collective spiritual force in the Five Loved Ones and could pass any resolution relating to the problem while still staying within the suzerainty of the holy Word.

The special importance of the Five Loved Ones had been established from that point on. When the *deg* was to be distributed among the congregation presided over by Guru Gobiṅd Siṅgh, it was first doled out to the Five Loved Ones and thereafter to the rest of the congregation. This tradition is preserved as homage to the *Five Loved Ones* even today.

CHAPTER 17

The Four *Sāhibzādās* of the Master

In Sikh parlance, the term *sāhibzādā,* means the son of a revered person. Here it refers to the sons of the Guru. Being the progeny of the Guru, all of them should have deserved the same respect from the Sikhs. However, some of them did not fulfil the word of their father and lost that privilege. Those who could pass the test of faith remained worthy of respect.

Guru Nānak had two sons: Bābā Srī Caṅd and Bābā Lakhmī Dās. The former was an ascetic *sādhu* who started the *Udāsī* tradition. This celibate tradition, however, is not in consonance with that of Guru Nānak and that son could not get the approval of his father. Bābā Lakhmī Dās was an entirely worldly man and had little interest in spiritual affairs. The Guru's legacy, therefore, went to neither of them but to a disciple Bhāī Lehnā who succeeded Guru Nānak as Guru Aṅgad.

Guru Aṅgad also had two sons: Srī Dātū jī and Srī Dāsū jī, but overlooking them both, Guru Aṅgad installed Srī Amar Dās as his successor. Srī Dātū one day rushed to the Guru's congregation and kicked Guru Amar Dās contemptuously. The Guru did not make any remonstration, but in utter humility, said, 'I am extremely sorry, my old hardened bones may have hurt your foot', and then lovingly began to press the offending foot.

Guru Amar Dās also had two sons: Bābā Mohan and Bābā Mohrī. They too were bypassed by Guru Amar Dās, and Bhāī Jethā was installed the next Guru as Guru Rām Dās. Bābā Mohan protested and said, 'The Guru's seat is not the right of Rām Dās. He is only a son-in-law. I am the son, and it should be my right.' Guru Amar Dās replied, 'This throne cannot be claimed by anyone. It is a Divine gift. It belongs to one who has spiritual right to it.'

Guru Rām Dās had three sons: Srī Prithī Caṅd, Srī Mahā Dev and Srī Arjan Dev. Srī Prithī Chaṅd had been a competent worldly man but with little spiritual insight. Srī Mahādev was an ascetic who had severed almost all worldly relations. Srī Arjan Dev was not only obedient but also spiritually most accomplished and he was enthroned. Prithī Caṅd was stricken with jealousy and tried to belittle and torment Guru Arjan Dev, but the Guru never remonstrated.

Guru Hargobiṅd was the only son of Guru Arjan Dev and became his successor by virtue of his qualities as a leader—spiritual as well as mundane. He, in turn, had five sons: Bābā Gurdittā, Bābā Suraj Mal, Bābā Tyāg Mal and Bābā Atal Rāe. Bābā Gurdittā became an *Udāsī*. Bābā Suraj Mal and Bābā Anī Rāe were of worldly disposition. Bābā Atal Rāe gave away his life for having displeased his father because he had worked the miracle of reviving his dead playmate. Bābā Tyāg Mal, who had received the title *Tegh Bahādur*, on account of his valorous fighting against the offending Mughal forces later became the ninth Guru. But after Guru Hargobiṅd his grandson (son of Bābā Gurdittā) Har Rāe became the Guru.

Guru Har Rāe had two sons, Bābā Rām Rāe and Srī Harkishan. The former, in order to please the Emperor Auraṅgzeb, made an alteration in one of the verses of the Holy Book. That caused Guru Har Rāe to disown him and turn the pontific throne over to his five-year old son, making him Guru Harkrishan. Guru Harkrishan fell mortally ill after three years but declared Guru Tegh Bahādur as his successor.

Guru Tegh Bahādur had only one issue, Gobiṅd Rāe, who later became Gurū Gobiṅd Siṅgh. Guru Gobiṅd Siṅgh had four sons: Bābā Ajīt Siṅgh, Bābā Jujhār Siṅgh, Bābā Zorāvar Siṅgh and Bābā Fateh Siṅgh. They all laid down their lives with unmatched courage and valour for the glory of the Khālsā. In the *ardās*, they are reverently remembered by the whole *Paṅth.*

In the Fortress of Camkaur, Guru Gobiṅd Siṅgh and a meagre forty men were surrounded by Mughal forces numbering a hundred thousand men. The Sikhs prayed to the Guru, 'We shall all die fighting but you and your sons must escape.' The Guru said, 'Which sons are you talking about? Aren't all of you my sons?' Then his eldest son, Ajīt Siṅgh, aged eighteen, stepped forward and sought the Guru's permission to leave the fortress and engage the enemy. The Guru was intensely pleased and sent his son forward along with a band of five Sikhs. Bābā Ajīt Siṅgh leapt into the enemy ranks slaying them left and right. At last, all of his arsenal was finished, and he fell fighting. Guru Gobiṅd Siṅgh, who was watching his valour from on high, shouted the cry of Divine Victory and said, 'O Lord! Your trust has been restored to you.'

Then, his second son, Bābā Jujhār Siṅgh, aged fourteen, after getting his father's permission, jumped into the field and fought until sunset, demonstrating his courage and bravery to his foes. As the sun was setting, he too fell fighting.

... ...

The two younger sons of the Guru, Zorāvar Siṅgh and Fateh Siṅgh, accompanied by the Guru's mother, Mātā Gujrī, were arrested and interned in a minaret of Sirhiṅd by Wazīr Khān, the Nawāb of that place. The next day, the young children were summoned to the court. Throughout the previous night, their grandmother kept reminding them that they were the children of Guru Gobiṅd Siṅgh, grandchildren of Guru Tegh Bahādur and followers of Guru Nānak Dev. She called on them to uphold their dignity at all cost.

In the court, the two young children of the Guru were given various incentives to accept conversion to Islam, but they withstood all temptations. When all efforts to make them comply failed, an order was given to wall them alive. The two innocent children embraced martyrdom but did not yield.

... ...

The unparalleled courage, undaunted gallantry and peerless martyrdom of the four sons of Guru Gobiṅd Siṅgh are a source of inspiration for the entire *Paṅth.*

The exemplary valorous conduct of these *sāhibzādās* makes it patently clear that age has no relationship with spiritual achievement. The same phenomenon is visible in Guru Harkrishan assuming guruship at the age of five and Guru Gobiṅd Siṅgh at the age of nine.

All this firmly establishes that guruship was not hereditary.

After having been born in the Gurus' family, many of the *sāhibzādās* remained without it.

In the *ardās* the *Panth* remembers only those who were either bestowed with guruship or the four *sāhibzādās* of Guru Gobind Singh who raised the tradition of martyrdom to new heights. Those *sāhibzādas* who cultivated enmity and jealousy within the Gurus' house were ostracized by the *Panth.*[1]

[1] Rāmrayye, Dhīrmalīe, Mīne, Prithiye, all are in this category 'Even though they are Gurus' relations, they, on account of calumnious behaviour, are considered evil.—*Rahit Nāmā Bhāī Caupā Singh.* Quoted in Piārā Singh Padam, *Rahitname.*

CHAPTER 18

The Forty *Muktās*

Muktā in the Indian tradition, is one who is free from existential bondage. The bonds linked with human existence are those of birth and death, attachment and illusion, pleasure and pain, etc. Freedom from these is called *mukti*, and one who has attained it is designated as *muktā*.

According to the Sikh view, the major device for attaining the state of *mukti* is total self-surrender: which in Sikh parlance is called 'dying to oneself.[1] Self-surrender can manifest in a number of ways: always remembering God, devoted practice of the Guru's Word, arousing love and compassion within oneself, practising humility and eradicating self-centrism. Total self-surrender requires all of these together. It might manifest itself as penitence followed by re-dedication.

The 40 *muktās* to whom homage is paid in the *ardās* are those who had touched the summit of self-surrender by laying down their lives for the sake of their Guru, the bestower of *mukti*.

There have been two sets of 40 *muktās*. The first were the 40 who gave their lives fighting the innumerable Mughal hordes in Camkaur. Like ocean waves, the invading hordes would attack their mud fortress, but facing grave resistance would retreat again. In between, the Sikhs in small groups would come out of the fortress, fight valorously, destroy enemy ranks and eventually drink the nectarine potion of martyrdom. Both the elder sons of Guru Gobiṅd Siṅgh, Bābā Ajīt Siṅgh and Bābā Jujhār Siṅgh (the account of whose martyrdom we have already discussed) laid down their lives the same way. After their martyrdom, very few Sikhs were left in the fortress. Five of them, as the Five *amritdhārī* Sikhs, decided to 'command' Guru Gobiṅd Siṅgh to leave the fortress and escape. The Guru had no option but to comply with

[1]He also finds the gate of salvation who gives away his self from within himself.—*Malār* m 3, p. 1276

their command. He left, accompanied by three Sikhs. Thereafter, one by one, the remaining Sikhs laid down their lives fighting.[2] They are remembered as *muktās*.

There were another 40 from Central Puṅjab who had on an earlier occasion during the siege of Anaṅdpur disclaimed Guru Gobiṅd Siṅgh as their Guru and deserted him. Perhaps they could no longer endure the prolonged hunger of many days or they had got tired fighting relentlessly for months on end. In a weak moment they wrote their disclaimer and left the Guru.

When they reached home, their folks did not let them in. 'How on earth could you come here after deserting your Guru?' their women asked them. 'You sit at home and do the domestic chores and we shall go to give away our lives for the sake of the Guru. How long will your lives last which you think you have saved now?' They were so much cursed by their own people that Māī Bhāg Bharī was moved into compassion for them. She gathered them from their respective homes and led them back to unite them with the Guru.

At that point in time, Guru Gobiṅd Siṅgh had left Mācchīvāṛā forest and was moving towards Ferozpur via Jaṭpurā while the imperial forces were on his trail. The disclaimers came to know of this. On the banks of lake Khidrāṇā, they decided to intercept and engage the enemy force. They spread sheets of cloth over the trees to create an impression from a distance of an army camp. They took up positions from where they could attack the approaching hordes with advantage. When the enemy forces drew near, they were disarmed by sudden and unexpected attack on them. Some of them were killed, others dispersed, but all these 40 Sikhs laid down their lives and embraced martyrdom.

Guru Gobiṅd Siṅgh was informed of this battle. He went at the

[2]The names of these forty *muktās* are: Samīr Siṅgh, Sarjā Siṅgh, Sādhū Siṅgh, Suhel Siṅgh, Sultān Siṅgh, Sobhā Siṅgh, Saṅt Siṅgh, Harsā Siṅgh, Hari Siṅgh, Karan Siṅgh, Karam Siṅgh, Kālhā Siṅgh, Kīrat Siṅgh, Kirpāl Siṅgh, Khushāl Siṅgh, Gulāb Siṅgh, Gaṅgā Siṅgh, Gaṅdā Siṅgh, Gharbārā Siṅgh, Caṅbā Siṅgh, Jādo Siṅgh, Jogā Siṅgh, Jaṅg Siṅgh, Dayāl Siṅgh, Darbārā Siṅgh, Dilbāgh Siṅgh, Dharam Siṅgh, Dhannā Siṅgh, Nihāl Siṅgh, Nidhān Siṅgh, Būṛ Siṅgh, Bhāg Siṅgh, Bholā Siṅgh, Bhaṅgā Siṅgh, Mahāṅ Siṅgh, Majjā Siṅgh, Mān Siṅgh, Maiyā Siṅgh, Rāe Siṅgh, and Lachman Siṅgh.—Kahn Siṅgh, *Mahān Kosh*

location where the battle had taken place and was deeply touched by the valour and sacrifice of all of them. He sat by the side of each of them, one by one, took their heads into his own lap and blessed them copiously. When he approached their leader Mahāṅ Siṅgh, he found him still breathing. His head he took into his lap and splashed some water on his face to make him regain consciousness. The Guru lovingly patted his brow and called out his name with great compassion. When Mahāṅ Siṅgh heard his name, he burst into tears. Very tenderly, the Gurū said, 'Ask me for anything you like and I would be pleased to grant you that.' With innocent gratitude, Mahāṅ Siṅgh said, 'O my True Lord, I pray you reunite us, the foolish disclaimers, with yourself'. The Guru took out from his girdle the paper on which that disclaimer had been written, tore it up and scattered its pieces in the wind. Mahāṅ Siṅgh, in utter gratitude, kissed the feet of the Guru and breathed his last. The Guru bestowed the title of *muktās* on the entire band of these 40 Sikhs who had thus attained martyrdom.[3]

Māī Bhāg Bharī was the only one who survived, became a part of the Guru's forces. She accompanied him during his march to Nāndeṛ. Sometimes it is asked, 'Who are the 40 *muktās* that are remembered in the *ardās*—those of Camkaur or those of Muktasar?' The answer is simple. Whether one set of *muktās* comes to one's mind or the other, the praying mind shall be equally blessed. If both come to one's mind, one would be doubly blessed.

[3]The names of these forty *muktās* are: Sahaj Siṅgh, Sardūl Siṅgh, Sarūp Siṅgh, Sāhib Siṅgh, Sujān Siṅgh, Sevā Siṅgh, Sher Siṅgh, Sant Siṅgh, Hardās Siṅgh, Himmat Siṅgh, Karam Siṅgh, Kirpāl Siṅgh, Kharaj Siṅgh, Gurdev Siṅgh, Gurdit Siṅgh, Gulāb Siṅgh, Gaṅgā Siṅgh, Gaṅḍā Siṅgh, Charat Siṅgh, Jawahār Siṅgh, Jaimal Siṅgh, Jwālā Siṅgh, Jhaṅḍā Siṅgh, Tek Siṅgh, Thākur Siṅgh, Trilok Siṅgh, Dyāl Siṅgh, Damodar Siṅgh, Naraiṇ Siṅgh, Nihāl Siṅgh, Panjāb Siṅgh, Prem Siṅgh, Basāvā Siṅgh, Bishan Siṅgh, Bhagwān Siṅgh, Mahā Siṅgh, Mohkam Siṅgh, Ram Siṅgh, Raṅjīt Siṅgh, and Rattan Siṅgh. —Kāhan Siṅgh, *Mahān Kosh*

CHAPTER 19

Practitioners of *Nām*, Penance and Determination

Jap is continually repeating the Lord's Name or some holy text. One may utter it loudly, or speak it in whispers or even ponder over it mentally. *Japī* is one who makes *jap* his regular practice.

Tap means penance, contrition, etc., and *tapī* is one who practices *tap*. *Haṭh* is unflinching determination. *Haṭhī* is one who practices *haṭh*.

A variety of *japīs*, *tapīs* and *haṭhīs* only resort to external actions which have little relationship with spiritual life. They seem to engage in superfluous actions not conducive to the life of devotion. Such actions are taboo according to the tenets of Sikh faith.

Another set of *japīs*, *tapīs* and *haṭhīs* desire to attain power to work miracles. That is their chief objective. Even these have been considered as people of an 'alien taste'[1] by Guru Nānak. These do not lead to the attainment of God and are considered equally irrelevant.

There is yet another variety whose sole objective is union with God. The practice of it involves keeping the Lord continually in one's mind, enduring His Will without a demur or reserve, and following the path of righteousness without compromise. It is the practitioners of this last variety of *jap*, *tap* and *haṭh* who are remembered in the *ardās*.

JAPĪ

The sole purpose of *jap* in Sikhism is to please the Lord.[2] A Sikh is commanded ever to repeat *Satnām* or *Wāheguru*.[3] The

[1] The Riddhīs and Siddhīs are alien taste.—*Jap(u)*, p. 6

[2] *Jap* is that which pleases the Lord.—*Mājh* m 5, p. 100

[3] Repeat O my mind, Satnām, ever Satñam.—*Sūhī* m 1, p. 728

Repeat the one Name alone. All other rituals are superfluous.—*Dhanāsrī* m 5, p. 670

commoners' connotation of *jap* is to repeat the Name of the Lord with one's lips. However, the real *jap* is experiential. It is the practice of the presence of God and thereby of His coming to stay in one's mind.[4] When through the grace of the Guru, one awakens to the experience of the Divine Presence, the tongue automatically goes on saying repetitively, 'O Thou!' Such *jap* is only possible with undivided attention. One who practises this kind of *jap* escapes the throes of birth and death.[5]

In the Sikh thought, the relationship between the Guru and the Sikh is that of an 'attentive mind' with the 'Word'.[6] Guru Nānak himself first received the gift of *jap* from the Lord God Himself. During his mystical encounter with Him, Nānak was commanded, 'Go ye and make others repeat My *Nām*, the *Nām* that I have given you. Go and busy yourself with the task I have assigned you.' Then the Lord asked Guru Nānak, 'Do you discern me?' Guru Nānak then composed what we now call the *mūlmantra*.[7] The Lord approved of it and gave Nānak the following command:

> Only repeat One *Nām*,
> All else is futile.
> —*Sūhī* m 1, p. 728

Then Guru Nānak came back. He travelled far and wide to distribute the *jap* of the Lord's *Nām* to whomever he met in the world.

He told everyone that the faithful who practise the *Nām* transcend the fear of death and attain eternity. Where such *japīs*

[4]Everyone utters the Name of God,
But by mere uttering one doesn't Him attain.
If through the Grace of the Guru the Lord comes to stay in one's mind,
Then alone one gets the fruit.—*Gūjrī* m 3, p. 491

[5]With one-mind if one remembers the Lord,
He never falls into the throes of death—*DG: Akāl Ustat* 10.3

[6]The Word is the Guru and the one-pointed mind is the disciple.—*Sidh Gosht Rāmkalī* m 1, p. 943

[7]The *Mool Mantra is:*
ੴ ਸਤਿਨਾਮੁ ਕਰਤਾ ਪੁਰਖੁ ਨਿਰਭਉ ਨਿਰਵੈਰੁ ਅਕਾਲ ਮੂਰਤਿ ਅਜੂਨੀ ਸੈਭੰ ਗੁਰਪ੍ਰਸਾਦਿ ।
Ik Oaṅkār Sat Nām Kartā Purakh Nirbhau Nirvair Akāl Mūrat Ajūnī Saibhaṅ Gurprasād.

perform the *jap*, the earth at that place begins to resound with their *jap*; so do the sky, the sun and the moon and the entire Cosmos. It is such *japīs* who are remembered in the *ardās*.

TAPĪ

Tapīs are practitioners of *tap*. The two types of *tap* that *gurmat* approves of are 'cheerfully accepting the Divine Will and rendering service with faith to others'.

For those who cheerfully accept the Will of God, even suffering becomes endurable with pleasure. They consider even privations as the Lord's gift,[8] derive satiety from hunger and pleasure from pain.[9]

An outstanding and unique example of this kind of *tap* is illustrated by Guru Arjan Dev, the most supreme *tapī* of this genre, who while seated on a red hot iron plate, kept uttering, 'Thy Will, O Lord is sweet'.

The other *tap* in *gurmat* is that of *sevā* or rendering service with faith to others. Srī Amar Dās, practising the *tap* of *sevā*, was elevated to the rank of 'home for the homeless, Guru Amar Dās'. Bhāī Manjh became 'the Guru's ferry' and Bhāī Kanhaīyā became the founder of *Sevāpanthī* tradition.

In Sikh religion, *sevā* is considered the highest *tap* of all.[10] Living with contentment, being engaged in honest labour to earn one's living, leading a disciplined life, living frugally[11] and practising the presence of God are all elements of *tap* according to Sikh tenets.

HAṬHĪ

Haṭhī is one who has a firm determination. There are several variations of determination. There are those who realize the futility of their resolve but still do not give it up. Rāvaṇa is known to have

[8] Many have to endure distress, deprivation and continual abuse.
Even these are Your gifts O Lord.—*Jap(u)*, p. 5

[9] If You give me hunger, O Lord, I shall feel satisfied with it,
Give me suffering and I will derive pleasure from it.—*Sūhī* m 4, p. 757

[10] Service of the Guru is the highest penance.—*Āsā* m 3, p. 423

[11] Eat little and sleep frugally.—*DG: Hazāre Pātshāhī 10*, Rāmkalī

been such a one. Even after his gallant heroes, his siblings, his relatives and even his sons had all been killed, he was still not willing to hand Sītā back to Rāma. Such foolhardiness is called *man-haṭh* (self-willed determination), and is taboo in *gurmat.*

Alternatively, there is the determination to perform strenuous physical feats. This is practised particularly by *haṭh yogīs.* This *haṭh karma* is also taboo for the Sikhs.

Contrasted with these is the *dharma haṭh*—determination for righteous action. In it, the *haṭhī* does not shrink from his ideals even if he has to lay down his life. Such *haṭh* is termed *siraṛ* (resoluteness) in Sikh parlance. This is the all-steel *haṭh*—the *haṭh* of *Wāheguru jī kī Fateh.* Such *haṭh* is free of bigotry, pride and egotistic wilfulness. It springs from spiritual strength. In the *ardās,* it is the practitioners of this kind of *haṭh* who are remembered with reverence.

CHAPTER 20

Those Who Chanted the *Nām*

The term *Nām* is derived from the Sanskrit root *mnā* which means 'practice'. Hence, *Nām* is that which is practised. In *gurmat, Nām* is the Name of the Lord that one is commanded to practise.

In *gurbāṇī, Nām* also alludes to the state of the Lord that is between transcendence and immanence.

Himself He created Himself, and His *Nām.*
In the second place He created the Universe
In which He pervades and looks at it with affectionate pleasure.
—*Vār Āsā* m 1, p. 463

From His intent-less *samādhi,* the Formless One transmuted Himself into an 'intentioned state'. His intentionality was a *kvāo*[1]—the *Nām* from which emanated the entire cosmos. In other words, *Nām* itself became the universe and everything perceptible and non-perceptible is simply *Nām.*[2] *Nām* is the mainstay of everything:

The *Nām* is the Support of all creatures.
The *Nām* is the Support of the earth and the universe.
The *Nām* is the Support of the Simritis, the Vedas and the Purāṇas.
The *Nām* is the Support of listening, wisdom and meditation.
The *Nām* is the Support of the sky and the Nether Regions.
The *Nām* is the Support of all the bodies.
The *Nām* is the Support of the worlds and realms.
Being with the *Nām* and listening to it, one is saved.
—*Sukhmanī Gauṛī* m 5, p. 284

Through *Nām,* the Creator reveals Himself to His Creation.

[1] With one *kvāo* He made the whole expanse.
Therefrom a thousand streams began to flow.—*Jap(u)*, p. 3

[2] The entire Creation is simply *Nām,*
Bereft of it there is no place.—*Jap(u)*, p. 4

Those who contemplate *Nām*[3] receive the divine call. Beside the compositions of the Sikh Gurus in *Srī Guru Granth Sāhib*, only the works of those holy men who recognize the spiritual veracity of *Nām* and who laud it from their heart have been included. The works of Pīlū, Kāhnā and Shāh Husain each of whom did not subscribe to *Nām* were not accepted for inclusion in that holy book. The works of those who worshipped *Nām* throughout their life and went up the stages of spiritual progress to become aware of its multifarious mysteries have been enshrined in *Guru Granth Sāhib*. One such rare soul, Gurmukh Bābā Harī Siṅgh, has been an outstanding one. He has discussed these mysteries in his great book *Rāhnumā-e-Dīdār-e-Haq*[4] meaning 'Guide to the Vision of God'. The following account has been extracted from it:

There are many devices for the *jāp* of the exalted *Nām*, that have enormous significance in monotheistic worship. They include the following:

1. *Lom jāp* i.e. repeating the *Nām* with one's tongue.[5] When such repetition influences the heart, then one begins to discriminate between good and evil.
2. *Malom jāp* i.e. repeating not with one's tongue, but with one's heart. As a result of this, the practitioner transcends thirst and hunger[6] and becomes established in *Nām*.
3. *Kālpnik jāp* i.e. keeping some image constantly before one's mind. This is the favourite device of *Naqshbandī* Sūfis. It is also called *Ahaṅgreha Upāsanā* i.e. considering one's deity as inseparable from oneself and worshipping it from within.
4. *Praṅāyām* recitation. It is the same as *Habs-i-dam* of the Sūfis. With this, before long, a variety of spiritual lights appears within one's bosom and the mind is lit.
5. *Praṇ Saṅglī* or *Pās-e-nafs*, in which the *jāp* continues with every breath with its inspiratory and expiratory phases. The *Nām* to be repeated must have two syllables each of which can be repeated synchronously with the respective respiratory phase. That is why Guru Nānak prefixed

[3]Those who contemplate Your *Nām*, they alone get the Call.—*Mārū* m 1, p. 989

[4]Diwan Printing Press, Lahore, 1935.

[5]The tongue utters the *Nām*.—*Jaitsarī Vār* m 5, p. 709

[6]My mainstay, the Tue *Nām* has erased all my hungers—*Rāmkalī* m 3, p. 917

the numeral ੧ (1) to ੳ (Oaṅkār). For the same purpose, the Sūfis suffix *hū* after *Allah*. Such a practice enables one to attain the ultimate Truth.

In addition to these practices, there are additional prescriptions and proscriptions. These pertain to food, clothing, conduct and character. The practitioner must abstain from intoxicants, such as tobacco and alcohol. He must consume only consecrated food. He must pay attention to his conduct and character. He who indulges in evil simultaneously destroys his spiritual merit. A clean, isolated and quiet place is required for the spiritual practice.

By practising *Nām* with every breath, the devotee attains the *Sūkhamālambanā Samādhi* in which he hears mysterious celestial sounds in his ears. These sounds are extremely pleasant and bewitching. They present a mixture of 10 different notes in five pairs of nearly identical notes and are called *Pañc Shabad* or five notes.

During the emanation of these sounds, one first hears the chirping of sparrows. Along with it, a faint white light like that of early dawn appears. This condition has been described in *Gurbāṇī* as follows:

> The sparrows are chirping, and dawn has come;
> Waves and waves have been stirred up.
> This wondrous form, says Nānak, the Saints have fashioned through the Love of the *Nām*.
>
> —*Vār Gauṛī* m 5, p. 319

Another sound like the cry of a rain-bird (*bambīhā*) is also heard:

> The rainbird chirped in the ambrosial hours before dawn;
> Its prayers were heard in the Lord's Court.
> Order was issued to the clouds, to let the rains of mercy shower down.
>
> —*Vār Malār* m 3, p. 1285

Pañc Shabad is also called *anāhat nād* or *anhad shabad.* The spiritual state in which it appears is called *samīp mukti*, 'Closeness to the Lord signifying salvation'.

The consciousness of the devotee eventually transcends even this state and reaches the state of *turīā*, its fourth state.[7]

In brief, the stages through which the devotee ascends to the summit are as follows:

1. *Jap* or *jāp* (recitation) or *pāṭh.*
2. *Simrin* (remembering).
3. *Dhyān* (concentration)
4. *Sahaj Vismād* (spontaneous wonderment)
5. *Sunn Samādhi* (Ecstasy in Emptiness)

The *jap* of the mantra *Wāheguru* has been popular since the time of Guru Hargobind. The efforts of those who have performed *jap* of this *Nām, Wāheguru,* have yielded good fruit. Their faces are resplendent when they appear in the Court of the Lord. They have emancipated themselves and are busy emancipating others. Such souls that dwelt upon the *Nām* of the Lord in this way are remembered in the *ardās.*

[7]The other three states of consciousness are *jāgrit,* the wakeful state, *swapna,* the dream state, *sushupti,* the state of deep sleep. *Turīā,* the fourth state is the one of transcendent consciousness.

CHAPTER 21

Those Who Shared Their Bread with Others

Guru Nānak prescribed a three-item *dharma* for mankind:

1. *Nām japnā*, remembering God,
2. *Kirt Karnī*, earning one's living with honest labour, and
3. *Vaṅd Chakṇā*, sharing one's bread with others.

Nām is Divine Essence, an existential concept. Living to remember it is tantamount to fulfilling a spiritual obligation. Honest livelihood and sharing are both ethical concepts that stand close together. In the Gurus' works, social welfare (an ethical concept) is considered a variety of Truth (an existential concept):

> One knows the Truth only when on true counsel
> One shows mercy to others, and contributes to charities.
> —*Vār Āsā* m 1, p. 468

Charity, mercy and benevolence are ethical virtues, the practice of which tantamounts to 'truthful living'. 'Truthful living', the Guru says, is higher than Truth:

> Truth is higher than everything; but higher still is truthful living.
> —*Srīrāg* m 1, p. 62

Sharing, as its essential basis, must have honest earning. Kabīr said:

> Meditate on the Nām, as well as on the grain.
> —*Goṅḍ* Kabīr, p. 873

Here, grain stands for honestly earned bread. One who does not live by righteous earning has to fall back upon begging or stealing. Such acts are dishonest and have been proscribed by the Guru. A Sikh has been commanded to earn his living with uncorrupt labour with his own hands.[1] Manual work is hallowed and blessed.

When Guru Nānak was commissioned by the Lord Almighty, he was commanded, *inter alia,*

Nānak! You shall initiate the Way. . . . Unto your followers, prescribe three practices with due emphasis, *Nām,* charity, and cleanliness. Remain unattached while living as a householder. Live a disciplined life, earn your living with honest work, dole out a part of the earning to others for my sake. . . . Go and stress such work to your followers. Ask them to reckon none other than my *Nām.*

It may be noted that Guru Nānak was commissioned to propagate both the Divine *Nām* and the principle of honest hard work while giving away part of the returns in charity. That is living the divine way:

One who labours hard for what he eats, and
renders to others some of what he has,
O Nānak, he knows the real Path.
—*Vār Sāraṅg* m 1, p. 1245

An event of history illustrates the spirit of sharing:

Under the orders of Farrukh Saīyar, four Sikhs were imprisoned. They were of different ages—a child, a youth, a middle-aged one and a man well advanced in age. For four continuous days and nights, they were starved. Then, a small piece of bread on a plate was placed before them. For some time it remained lying there, and no one touched it or even looked at it. The old man picked up the plate and offered it to the child saying, 'My dear child, please take it.' But the child respectfully declined the offer and pushed the plate towards the youth, saying, 'I am too young to fight, but you can. Please you take this little piece of bread so that your fighting vigour can be revitalized.' The youth also declined and offered the bread to the middle-aged companion, saying, 'You please accept it. I can still easily endure starvation for a few more days'. The latter on his part said, 'Let us respectfuly offer it to the eldest among

[1]He should take to farming trade or works of skill,
Or service of a sort that pleases his fancy.
Save what he can out of his prescribed vocations,
Never indulges in thievery and robbery.
—*Rahitnāmā,* Bhāī Caupā Siṅgh

us'. Doing so, he addressed the old man with great reverence, and said, 'We can all easily live for a few more days without food. You have gone famished already. We all desire that you may agree to take it.' The old man slid the plate again before the child requesting him, 'Please take this and keep the hope of our future alive.' The child still did not accept the offer. Eventually, each took a little piece of the bread and gratefully thanked God for it. This event reflects the high morale and lofty moral character of the Sikhs of yore, their unity, unselfishness, and spirit of sharing.

To share is to accept the Fatherhood of God and brotherhood of man. This is also the way to earn the Guru's pleasure:

> One who prepares a meal and gives another Sikh to partake of it,
> The Guru will be so pleased that he would offer him his own life.
> —*Rahitnāmā,* Bhāī Prehlād Siṅgh

One should not share what one has only with one's own brethren-in-faith; rather, even one's enemy should be invited to share the food, for food is the gift of God and your adversary is also the son of your Father:

> . . . When the meal is ready, reckon it as the Guru's.
> At that time, even if an enemy comes,
> Let him partake of it the same way as you would offer your friend.
> Show him the same generosity as you would give a friend.
> You may then take what is left over.
> Even if nothing is left, remain content. —*Paṅth Prakāsh*

An event from the life of Bābā Sāhib Siṅgh Bedī[2] readily comes to mind as closely relevant to the theme.

Farrukh Siyar and his successors had avowed tyrannical enmity towards the Sikhs. The Bābā, being a revered leader of the Sikhs, was the special target. He had been declared a proclaimed rebel, and a prize had been announced for his head. At that time, the

[2]Bābā Sāhib Siṅgh Bedī has been a greatly revered leader of the Sikhs. He was the one who was chosen to perform anointing to Māhārājā Raṅjīt Siṅgh at the occasion of his coronation. He was a pious man who inspired people to practise remembering the *Nām* of God. In Batālā region, at one time, a ballad (*vār*) used to be sung, called *The Vār of Bābā Sāhib Siṅgh Bedī.* Its authors were Mohammad and Noora. The narration given here has been extracted from that *Vār.*

Bābā lived in a small hutment in Kahnūvān forest. Dīn Mohammad, an army officer had learned of it and started searching the forest for him. After many days, he identified him sitting on the bank of a shallow brook. Dīn Mohammad drew out his sword and approached the Bābā from behind. He found that the Bābā was trying to rescue a scorpion out of the stream. However, as the Bābā would lift it out, it would sting the Bābā's hand, making the Bābā's hand quiver, and the scorpion would fall back into the stream. This happened again and again. While watching what was happening, Dīn Mohammad forgot to kill the Bābā and was impelled to tell him, 'Why don't you let this tormentor go?' The Bābā looked back and retorted, 'If this scorpion will not give up its evil habit of stinging, why must I give up my good habit of helpfulness?' Dīn Mohammad was so impressed with the Bābā's character that he said, 'I had come with the intention of killing you, but now I won't, because you are a God-fearing man. But I can't altogether spare you either. You should quietly accompany me; I have to produce you before the governor. You are a proclaimed rebel and I have been detailed to capture you and produce you alive or, if you resist, I should kill you and take your severed head as proof. Come with me willingly so that I can produce you before my government.' The Bābā said, 'Who knows who has to produce whom before which government?' and then with a smile accompanied him. While they were travelling along, the sun began to set. Dīn Mohammad said, 'The evening is getting deeper. Let us stop somewhere and take rest for the night'. At that, the Bābā suggested, 'My hut is not far from here. Why not spend our night there. There we shall get something to eat as well.' Dīn Mohammad agreed. When they reached the hut a teen-aged deaf-and-dumb girl received them. Reckoning her of ill omen, her parents had abandoned her in the forest when she was a little child. The Bābā happened to find her abandoned, rescued her and raised her with tender care. After they entered the hut, the girl helped them wash their hands and made them sit down for dinner. The girl had cooked four *chapātīs*, two for the Bābā and two for herself, to be eaten with mango pickle. The Bābā placed two of those in Dīn Mohammad's plate and one each in the girl's and his own. Then he asked the girl to put the lamp out to prevent moths gathering and defiling their food. Dīn Mohammad was very hungry and quickly finished both the *chapātīs*. The Bābā did not eat his, but kept his jaw moving, pretending that he was eating. Before Dīn Mohammad had finished his *chapātīs*, the Bābā put his own *chapātī* into Dīn Mohammad's plate and the girl followed him. Dīn Mohammad was satiated and soon went to sleep, still wondering why the Bābā had turned off the light before eating. As he slept, he had a dream in which he saw that he was sitting for the meal like the previous night. He also saw the lamp being turned off. Then he saw that both the Bābā and that girl, in the darkness, put their *chapātīs* into his plate while pretending that they were eating. When Dīn Mohammad got up in the morning, he sought the Bābā's permission to bid him good bye, saying, 'O wonderful Sikh of your Guru, nobody can ever kill a worthy man like you.' While departing, he had tears in his eyes.

Those who share their bread with others are practitioners of selfless love. If we don't love God's creation, how can we love God? Sharing testifies our love for God.

Guru Nānak himself set this tradition when in Sultānpur, he worked as a storekeeper. 'Whatever rations Nānak would get, he let others eat for God's sake and at night sang the Lord's praises. People began to flock to his kitchen to eat and, from his benevolence, began to benefit. As the Bābā's kitchen got ready, crowds would gather there.'[3]

Guru's *laṅgar* and the institution of *dasvaṅdh* (tithing) arose from this tradition. The money collected through *dasvaṅdh* was always employed for common community projects.[4] 'Sharing one's bread', thus, is the motto of Sikh social life.

Social progress has two aspects:

(i) Collective upliftment, and
(ii) Common welfare.

Such phrases in the *ardās* as 'Wheresoever the Kh̲ālsā is, there

[3] *40B Janam-sākhī*.

[4] Bhāī Naṅd Lāl testifies this:
What one earns with one's ten fingers,
And brings the earnings home,
Let him render a tithe out of it
And earn merit and glory in the world.
—*Prashanottar*, quoted by Piārā Singh Padam

may O Lord, Your favour and protection be available', 'victory to the *Panth*' and 'welfare of all' are indicators of collective caring. The concept of sharing is indicative of common welfare and its foundation is universal love. Communism propagates class struggle as the means for inducting socialism; Sikhism advocates universal love as its basis. The Sikh socialism aims at the upliftment of the poor and the helpless, but does not demean or destroy the rich and the affluent. Sikhism reckons none as enemy—everyone is a member of the same divine commonwealth. It does not subscribe to a 'Bloody Revolution'. It rather vouches for a 'Revolution through Love'.

Homage is paid in the *ardās* to all those who strove to realize the 'Revolution of Love'. They sought to unite with God through love of humankind and sharing the sufferings of those in distress. That is how one remembers those who lovingly 'shared their bread' with others.

Rare Nineteenth Century painting of the Sikh Gurus with Bala and Mardana as depicted by the artist. Courtesy: Takhat Sri Hazur Sahib, Nanded.

Parkash of *Guru Granth Sahib* in the sanctum sanctorum of the Golden Temple, Amritsar.
Photograph by Malkiat Singh, N.I.P.S. Collection.

Jatha of Akali volunteers marching towards Guru-ka-Bagh for liberation of historic Sikh shrines.
Courtesy: Sir James Dunnett, London.

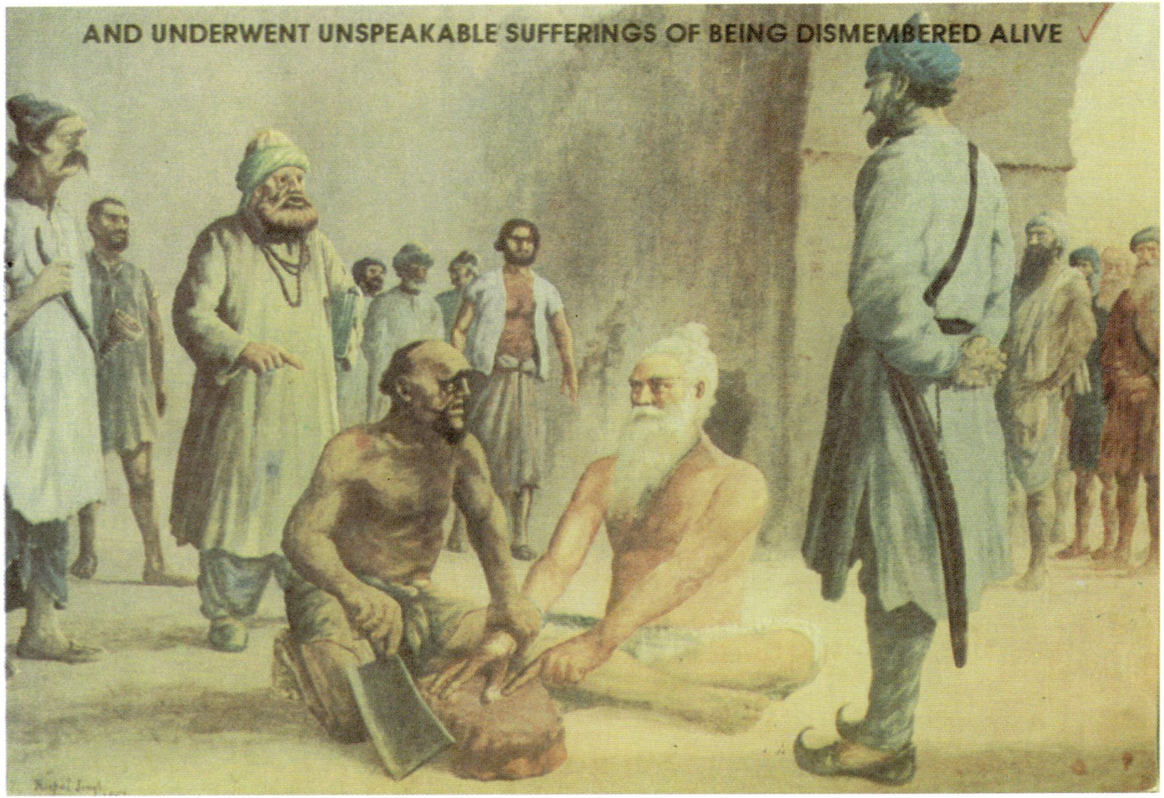

A painting depicting the one who was severed joint by joint. Courtesy: SGPC, Amritsar.

CHAPTER 22

Those Who Kept the Cauldron Warm

Deg means a cauldron, a wide-mouthed, large vessel in which food articles for the *laṅgar* are cooked. Its wide mouth and large size symbolize the great benevolence with which the Divine Grace sustains all.[1]

Deg also symbolizes one of the most basic needs of our life: the food that provides strength to our body and sustains our health. Without it, one becomes bereft of *shakti* (strength) and as Kabīr says, one cannot practise even *bhakti* (devotional worship).

> On empty stomach, I can't perform your worship.
> Here, Lord, take back your rosary.
> —*Soraṭh*, Kabīr, p. 656

He does not merely complain, he requests God for the grant of *deg:*

> I ask for two kilos of flour
> And half a pound of ghī, and some salt;
> I ask for a pound of beans as well.
> That should suffice (for my meals) twice a day,
> And to keep me alive and well.
> —*Soraṭh*, Kabīr, p. 656

The Gurus gave us the gift of *deg* (or *laṅgar*) so that none shall complain to God for want of food and that no one's worship is interfered with due to hunger.

In the Sikh parlance, the term *deg* is also employed to signify *kaṛāh prasād*.[2] *Prasād* means a blessing, a gift. One who receives

[1]The Great Giver keeps on giving, 'tis those who receive, get weary receiving.—*Jap(u)*, p. 2

[2]Just as the symbolic term for *Amrit* is *Bata* (steel bowl), so the symbolic term for *Kaṛāh Prasād* as well as *laṅgar* is *deg*.

kaṛāh prasād in his hands or partakes of the Guru's *laṅgar* sitting in a *paṅgat* (a row) receives divine blessings. Thus *deg* bears testimony to the limitless benevolence of God.

By remembering those who kept the cauldron warm, we affirm our faith in the Great Giver and thank Him for providing us our daily bread.[3] Puran Singh calls the *laṅgar* 'The Temple of Bread'. In this temple, formal interchange takes place between Divine Grace and human need.

The grace of *deg* was introduced by Guru Nānak himself. While going from Sultānpur to Eminābād, during his first odyssey, he stopped a little distance from Sultānpur at a picturesque spot. There, one Bhāī Tārā came to see him. The Guru asked him to bring him three commodities—flour, ghee and sugar. He gave instructions how to prepare the *deg* of *kaṛāh prasād.* When the *deg* was readied, he said grace to thank God and distributed it among those present. When Mardānā partook of it, he spontaneously remarked, 'Such sacred food one would like to take every day.' Thereupon Guru Nānak remarked, 'Mardānā! from this spot, this ambrosial food will indeed be distributed everyday. From here will run the combined stream of *bhog* and *mokh* (physical satiation and spiritual salvation).'[4] Years later, at that same location, the Golden Temple of Amritsar was established where *kaṛāh prasād* continues to be distributed everyday without a pause.

During Guru Nānak's days, *laṅgar* was established in Kartārpur. Every visitor to that place was provided food and services uninterruptedly.

During the time of Guru Aṅgad, in K͟hadūr, a lavish *laṅgar* was established under the supervision of Mātā Khīvī, the Guru's consort. This fact is testified by Bhatt Balvaṅḍ:

> Says Balvaṅḍ, K͟hīvī, the noble lady,
> Extends her soothing leafy shade over all.
> She distributes the bounty of the Guru's *laṅgar*
> In which is served the ambrosial butter-soaked rice-pudding.
> —*Vār Rāmkalī*, p. 967

[3]Hail Him from whom we receive our daily fare.—*Vār Āsā* m 1, p. 474.

[4]Based on Attar Siṇgh Bhadauṛ, *Sākhī Pothī*, Amritsar: K͟hālsā Samāchār, 1968.

During the time of Guru Amar Dās, it was mandatory for every visitor to partake of the *laṅgar* before the visitor could see the Guru in the congregation.[5] It is recorded in Sikh chronicles that when Emperor Akbar came to meet the Guru in Goiṅdwāl, he complied with this requirement. He was so impressed with the institution of the *laṅgar* that he offered to gift a fief for it. However, the Guru gracefully declined the offer, saying, 'The Guru's *laṅgar* is run by the meagre offerings of the devotee Sikhs. That is why it is so blessed. It is the symbol of honest earning of each individual devotee. It would not be appropriate to run it via a royal gift.'

Guru Arjan Dev's elder brother Prithī Caṅd, not having been selected to succeed his father as Guru, was jealous of his younger sibling. He created a rival camp and made arrangements to wean pilgrims away from going to Guru Arjan Dev. He was successful in blocking all offerings for the Guru's *laṅgar*. As a result, a time came when the tradition of *laṅgar* was temporarily interrupted. However, Bhāī Gurdās came down from Āgrā to revitalize it.

By the time of Guru Har Rāe, the kitchen of every Sikh household began to be considered as the Guru's *laṅgar*. It had been commanded by the Guru that before a Sikh sat down to have his meal, he must step outdoors and announce loudly, 'The Guru's *laṅgar* is ready. Everyone and anyone is invited. No one need stay hungry!'

During the time of Guru Gobiṅd Siṅgh, the Guru's *laṅgar* was sited at five different places in Ānaṅdpur. There, no individual kitchen functioned in any of the homes. The residents of the town, as well as all the visitors, could dine at any one of the five places. The *laṅgar* had really become the symbol of Paṅthic unity.

Today, the *laṅgar* continues to be an uninterrupted institution of the Sikhs. When the tyranny of the rulers had compelled the Sikhs to take refuge in jungles during the reign of Zakariā Khān and his successors, keeping the *deg* functioning was considered as important as wielding the *teg* (the sword). Even during times of intense privation, wherever the *laṅgar* was ready, the Sikhs used to make a loud announcement:

[5] *Pehle paṅgat, pāche saṅgat.* First visit the row of the *laṅgar* and after that join the congregation.

Is there anyone who is hungry ?
Come, the *deg* of the Guru is ready.

In the Guru's *laṅgar,* no discrimination of caste, class, creed, race or even between friend and foe has ever been observed.

Even today in the *gurdwārās, laṅgar* is organized wherein hundreds of thousands are fed without any charge everyday. This institution has been kept alive by those who prize the Fatherhood of God and brotherhood of man.

By remembering those in the *ardās* who kept the *deg* running, one identifies oneself with the ideals of service and of brotherhood.

CHAPTER 23

Those Who Wielded the Sword

In the Sikh parlance, *teg* (the sword) is not just a weapon of steel; it symbolizes Divine Glory. It enters the conflict between truth and untruth, good and evil and prepares truth to fight against untruth, standing by truth in every fierce contest.

In the entire world, God is not visible anywhere but is always active. In all places and at all times, He is busy protecting His men and chastising the evil. His sword shines everywhere. *His sword* means His nature, which is not only invincible, but can also dissever like a sword. Whatever is not within His nature is also not within His sword. He Himself is benevolent, and likewise His sword is benevolent too. It is the power of His Righteous Justice that protects the holy, decimates the egoist and raises the banner of Divine Victory (*Wāheguru jī kī Fateh*).

This invincible sword puts the human soul onto the spiritual whetstone to give it the sharpness of courage to wield it. This it is that converted *Tiāg Mal* into *Tegh Bahādur*.[1] It creates *shakti* (power) out of *bhakti* (devotion). The Gurus themselves donned the sword representing both *bhakti* and *shakti*. 'The sword that Guru Gobind Singh gave the Sikhs was wrought from the steel that Guru Nanak had prepared.'[2] The soul was first steeled before the sword was put into the sword-belt of the Sikhs.

Two Sikhs, Pigārū and Jaitā, appeared before Guru Arjan Dev and prayed, 'O our True King, at one time Nūrdīn, at another, Bīrbal, and at yet another, Sulhī came to raid us. If you permit us, we would like to don weapons to protect ourselves.' The Guru

[1]The Ninth Master, Guru Tegh Bahādur was formerly known as Bābā Tiāg Mal. During the battles with assaulting Mughal troops, he wielded his sword so skilfully that he was given the title of Tegh Bahādur by his father, Guru Hargobind. Later, this title began to be used in lieu of his name.

[2]Gokul Chand Narang, *The Transformation of Sikhism*, New Delhi: Kalyan Publishers, 1989.

said, 'Do not be hasty, we shall be plying weapons when Hargobiṅd assumes leadership'.[3] When, before his martyrdom, Guru Arjan Dev was leaving for Lahore, he summoned Srī Hargobiṅd and told him, 'Real hard times are about to follow. You shall wield weapons and keep the struggle going till this tyrannous rule is finished.' Then, he went over to embrace martyrdom in order to steel the souls of his followers. Thus during Guru Hargobiṅd's time, the all-steel spirit was actually butressed with the sword of steel.

Guru Hargobiṅd had a meeting with the Marāṭhā leader, Sāmarth Rāmdās (1609-81) in Srīnagar (Gaṛhwāl).[4] Noticing the royal elegance of the Guru, he observed, 'I have heard that Guru Nānak was an ascetic; but you are a householder. You also carry weapons. What kind of fakīr are you?' The Guru replied, 'Guru Nānak had discarded *māyā*, not the world. We have royalty outside, but mendicancy at heart. Our weapons are for the protection of the poor and for the destruction of the tyrant.' Rāmdās remarked, 'I can well appreciate that.'

When Emperor Bahādur Shāh presented a robe of honour to Guru Gobiṅd Siṅgh, he said, 'O Guru, show us some miracle.' The Guru pulled out his sword and said, 'This sword is my miracle. With its help, I got you the throne. If I wish, I can also decapitate you with it. But there is a difference between my *kirpān* (sword) and your *talvār* (sword). Behind your *talvār* lurks anger, behind my *kirpān*, only compassion. Yours only doles out death, mine rejuvenates life. Yours deprives people of their dignity, while mine saves their honour.'

A sword of such quality is symbolic of Divine Power. The *kirpān* is an emblem of power and a symbol of *mīrī* (temporal authority). However, in Sikhism it also symbolizes *pīrī* (spiritual authority). In fact, the Gurus have reckoned even God as a sword-bearer.

> O the sword-bannered God of the world!
> —*DG: Caritra* no. 405

[3]Bhāī Manī Siṅgh, *Sikhāṅ dī Bhagatmāl*, New Delhi: Bhāī Vīr Siṅgh Sāhitya Sadan, 2007.

[4]*Punjāb Sākhiāṅ.*

Guru Gobiṅd Siṅgh employs the *khaṅḍā* (the double-edged sword) as a symbol of divine creativity.[5]

The swords of *mīrī* and *pīrī* have distinct functions. During the battle of Hargobiṅdpur, the sword of Guru Hargobiṅd got broken. Bābā Buḍḍhā suggested, 'Please Master, take out your other sword'. The Master shook his head and said, 'While the sword of *mīrī* slays the demons, the sword of *pīrī* even then stays in its sheath. Even the sword of *mīrī* gets unsheathed for the purpose of redemption. It slays only to redeem. But the sword of *pīrī* is that of moral discipline. It symbolically slays the foes that lurk in the mind of man such as pride.[6] The *kirpān* of the Khālsā has a composite *mīrī* and *pīrī* function with precedence of *pīrī* over *mīrī*. Laying down one's life requires great courage and valour; but if living becomes more threatening than dying, then to steel one's soul to continue to live is more valorous than laying down one's life. When the naked sword of tyranny runs around on a despoiling spree, the sword of righteousness gets unsheathed only to compel the tyrannous sword to return to its sheath. He alone is capable of wielding the sword of righteousness,

> Who has the Name of God on his tongue
> While he ponders war in his heart.
> —*DG: Krishnāvtār* 2492.1

The heroes who plied their *teg* either for the protection of the meek and redress of injustice or for helping the helpless and oppressed are remembered in the *ardās*. Through it, we recharge our faith via the memory of such heroes and ourselves receive the inspiration for undaunted, but benevolent, courage.

[5] Having first fashioned the *Khaṅḍā*, He created the whole world.
—*DG: Vār Srī Bhagautī jī kī* 2.1

[6] O Nanak, he alone is a valiant hero who has slain the internal demon, pride.—*Vār Srirāg* m 4, slok m 3, p. 86

CHAPTER 24

Who Noticed, Yet Could Overlook

There is an instructive folk-tale that takes us straight to the heart of the saying 'those who observed, yet overlooked'.

There was a king whose queen was an inconstant lady. She had a dubious relationship with the king's minister. One day, the king was out on a hunting expedition. The queen and the minister got together in the palace and began to enjoy each other's company. Since the king was expected to be away for the night, the two also took the liberty of sleeping in the king's special personal bed. However, the king returned earlier than scheduled. As he entered his bedroom, he found the two asleep on his bed. The queen's loosened garments were telling a tale. The king overlooked what he saw, just took off his own wrap and covered both of them with it so gently that he would not wake the queen and her paramour. Then, very quietly, he left.

The next morning, when the lovers woke, they were startled to see the king's wrap over them. However, the king never mentioned anything to his queen, nor even to his minister. Many years passed uneventfully thereafter.

One day the king was taken seriously ill. The doctors lost hope of his recovery. The king then summoned all his courtiers and his queen. He addressed everyone in his feeble but audible voice and declared, 'After I pass away, my queen shall be my successor'. Hearing that, the queen burst into tears. The king took her into his arms and consoled her saying, 'My dear, you must not cry. My entire kingdom shall be yours. Your writ will run unchallenged. You will have obedient and devoted subordinates. Your children are nice and affectionate. They will take full care of you. You will have no want. Why must you cry?' The queen began to cry even more bitterly and said, 'I am aware that I will have everything, but there will be none whose wrap would cover my deeds.'

The generous disposition to cover up the faults of others is true overlooking.[1] It is indicative of a high moral acumen, a rare acquisition of the human soul. One who can overlook has a heart as wide as the universe; but there is no room in it for ill-will towards anyone, even for evil doers.

To perceive and yet to overlook is a divine disposition. It is the very covenant of our God, who

> Overlooks our faults, yet folds us into His arms.
> —*Mārū* m 5, p. 1101

He covers our sinfulness[2] and reckons not our transgressions. If we desire that He should not take our faults into account, then we must also practice overlooking the faults of others. Only He can spread His Wrap over our sins.

Pilgrims on the spiritual path look for other people's merits. Faults, they perceive only their own. The Sikh faith commands us to share merits with others.[3] Only a slanderer revels in the faults of others.[4] However, practising slander is a moral taboo.

> It is not good to slander anyone,
> In it, the foolish and the egoist indulge.
> The faces of the slanderers are blackened,
> And they are dumped in hell.
> —*Suhī* m 3, p. 755

In *gurmat* only forgiveness is prescribed:

> Practise forgiveness and
> Find the sanctuary of the true Guru.
> —*Mārū* m 1, p. 1030

Forgiveness is the highest expression of love. On a certain occasion, Guru Tegh Bahādur is reported to have said to his Sikhs:

[1] In the sense of allowing (offence) to go unpunished—*The Concise Oxford Dictionary*.

[2] By whose grace are my defects covered,
O my mind! take His Refuge.—*Sukhmanī* Gauṛī m 5, p. 270

[3] Share merits with others, leave alone faults.—*Suhī* m 1, p. 766

[4] The slanderer is pleased to notice faults in others,
Seeing merit, he is depressed.—*Bilāval* m 5, p. 823

Forgiveness is great penance. It is a great charity.
Forgiveness consecrates like a bath in a holy place,
In it rests human benediction.
No other merit equals forgiveness.
Have it always in your heart.

—*Gur Pratāp Sūraj*, Rās ii, A.17

Wherever forgiveness is, God Himself is.

Says Kabīr, where there is spiritual wisdom, there is righteousness,
Where there is falsehood, sin prevails.
Where there is greed, there is mortality,
Where there is forgiveness, God Himself is there.

—*Slok*, Kabīr, p. 1372

Doubt is often expressed that forgiveness contravenes justice. Forgiveness is not unjust; it is an acknowledgement of the jurisdiction of divine justice. To forgive is to leave the entire situation to the justice of the Lord. Justice at the lowest rung feels satisfied by punishing the transgressor. At the higher rung of compassionate justice, kindness is shown while giving punishment. Above this rung is that of forgiveness and further above it, forgiving and forgetting—like that of a mother who forgives her children and doesn't let their faults linger on in her memory.[5] Higher still is the stage of 'perceiving and still overlooking'. All the lower rungs are this worldly. Only *overlooking* is other worldly.

'Perceiving but overlooking' is an ideal, whose practice the Gurus demonstrated in their own lives. Guru Arjan Dev's brother Prithī Caṅd always troubled him. At the time of *dastār-baṅdī*, he slapped the Guru in the congregation and removed his turban, which is considered a great insult. He even tried to get Guru Arjan Dev's son Srī Hargobiṅd killed. Yet, when Prithī Caṅd fell ill, Guru Arjan Dev offered public prayers for his recovery in the midst of the holy congregation. He even composed a hymn of thanksgiving upon his recovery.[6]

[5] Though many faults the son may commit, the mother remembers them not.—*Āsā*, Kabīr, p. 478

[6] God, the great enlightener, showered His Mercy
and spared my brother.
I take His refuge, who always comes to our rescue.

—*Bilāval* m 5, p. 819

Guru Gobiṅd Siṅgh's entire family became prey to Auraṅgzeb's tyrannies. Yet, after perusing the Guru's epistle, *Zafar Nāmāh* (The Epistle of Victory), Auraṅgzeb became penitent and expressed a desire to meet the Guru. The latter, overlooking all the faults of Auraṅgzeb, travelled southward to meet him.[7]

We live under the abiding compassion of God. Though we transgress His commands, He lets His forgiveness prevail upon our disobedience in advance. We break away from Him time and again, but He overlooks our transgressions and sustains us with His Love without regard to any of our faults. It is incumbent upon every Sikh to make an effort to practise this divine virtue. Those lofty love-drenched, faith-soaked souls, who ever lived at this sublime plane and practised such 'overlooking' deserve the homage paid to them in the *ardās.*

[7]However, the emperor expired before they could meet.

CHAPTER 25

Those Who Gave Their Lives for Righteousness

Laying down one's life for *dharma* (righteousness) is termed *shahādat* or *shahīdī*. *Shahādat* literally means 'testimony'. Martyrdom (*shahīdī*) is testimony in more ways than one. The death of a martyr bears testimony to the faith for which he wilfully gives up his life and entrusts it to the custody of Divine Grace. Furthermore it bears testimony to the greatness of the deity for whose sake the martyr sacrificed his life, and who accepted the sacrifice and bestowed on it an honourable and holy status. That is how a martyr bears testimony to God.

Martyrdom also testifies to the determination that overcomes every terror, threat, seduction and allurement, and does not yield even at the pain of death. In laying down his life, the martyr renders a good account of his life and also gains a meritorious death.

The martyr neither fears death nor lets his faith turn into sick bigotry. On the contrary, he testifies to the healthfulness of his faith for which he gladly embraces death. A martyr bears testimony to the Truth for the sake of which he gives his life.

If a religious community produces an uninterrupted series of martyrs, it shows that the followers of that religion do not flinch from bearing testimony to righteousness.

Martyrdom is the highest miracle of a *dharma*. It is not a theatrical feat; it is a true miracle. Theatrical feats can be performed even by magicians, performers and pseudo-*yogīs*, but to give up one's life is the job of one whose soul is ablaze with intense love. To be able to lay down one's life is the one miracle that can take place only through God's Grace.[1] This kind of miracle has the ability to sustain *dharma*.

[1] Says Nānak, that alone is a miracle which one receives from gracious God.—*Vār Āsā* m 1, sl. m 2, p. 475

Auraṅgzeb offered Guru Tegh Bahādur a choice between the following three alternatives:

1. Conversion to Islam,
2. Displaying some miracle, and
3. Accepting death.

The Guru accepted death and embraced martyrdom. According to one tradition, the Guru said, 'Ask the executioner to strike his sword. The miracle that you shall see will be my survival.' The sword was struck, and his head was severed, but

> Who can say that the revered Guru died ?
> —*Sawayīyā* 5, Harbaṅs, p. 1409

Guru Tegh Bahādur is still alive and is with us. Today, if people can keep their own faiths, it is all due to his martyrdom. He laid down his life for the freedom of faith—not for his personal faith but that of those who wore the sacred thread that Guru Nānak had declined to wear. The ungrateful might forget his favour, but sincere men of faith following in his footsteps have been laying down their lives at the altar of righteousness ever since.

In the first stanza of the *ardās,* we remember Gurus Arjan Dev and Tegh Bahādur as being the foremost among martyrs. In the next stanza, homage is paid to the memory of other martyrs: the five loved ones, the four young sons of Guru Gobiṅd Siṅgh, the 40 *mukte* (the salvaged ones) and the others who were cut joint by joint, broken on the wheel, descalped, sawn through, who endured unendurable agonies and never winced nor flinched from their faith. They accepted the Lord's Will cheerfully. Especially remembered with reverence are the mothers whose infants were snatched away from their breasts, torn into pieces and hurled back at their faces. Also refreshed are the memories of the martyrs who gave up their lives to re-establish the sanctity of the *gurdwārās* and the memories of those who gave up their lives during more recent pogroms on the Sikhs but did not yield their faith.

Their mention in the *ardās* does not merely preserve an oral historic memory. Rather, it inspires fresh sacrifice and martyrdom if the situation demands it.

In his work *Muṅtakhib Lubāb,* Khāfi Khān narrates an event which illustrates the spirit of martyrdom that continued to permeate through the Sikh people. When Baṅdā Bahādur and his companions were captured and sentenced to death, one among them was a 10-year old child. His mother learned of it and approached the authorities. She pleaded, 'My son is not a Sikh. The Sikhs have forcibly taken him along with them. His life, pray, be spared!' The order was given to spare the child and to set him free. When the child was told about it, he asked, 'Why are you freeing me?' He was told, 'Your mother says you are not a Sikh.' The boy wrinkled his brow with scorn and said, 'My mother is simply telling a lie. I am from my heart and soul a devoted Sikh of my Guru.'[2]

In 1922, *jathās* of Sikhs embraced martyrdom during the Gurdwārā Reform Movement. In the Guru kā Bāgh, they were subjected to a cruel *lāṭhī* charge which they endured peacefully with no retaliation whatsoever. An eyewitness to that event was C.F. Andrews, a British Christian priest. He was struck with what he considered to be the perfect example of non-violence, and he recorded his impressions in a series of letters to the press. In one of them, he wrote that 'what I saw reminded me of the shadow of the Cross: the same passive suffering and the same holiness of atmosphere'.[3]

The Sikh history offers an almost uninterrupted series of martyrs. Whoso brings before his mind's eye the agonies that they had to undergo before their life departed, one is impelled to bow to them. They did not flinch from their faith in spite of such tyrannies, and that inspires fortitude among the Sikhs even now. A miserable heart may find peace by remembering the suffering of these martyrs. By remembering them, hearts simply melt and faith is replenished.

If this particular section of the *ardās* that recalls martyrs is read with feeling, and if the memories of the martyrs are revived before one's eyes, the softened soul will essentially be charged with reburnished faith.

Death comes to everyone, but only heroes die the death of martyrs:

> Death is the right of heroes if they die an approved death.
> —*Vaḍhaṅs* m 1, p. 580

[2]Khāfī Khān: *Muṅtakhib Lubāb.*

[3]Quoted by Teja Singh in *Sikhism and Non-violence,* Amritsar: Chief Khālsā Dīvān, 1960.

CHAPTER 26

He Who Was Severed Joint by Joint

Innumerable martyrs have been referred to in the *ardās* but without mentioning their names. The reason is that martyrdom has been considered the collective achievement of the Sikh character. That is why it became an item of national pride for the Sikhs and hence its inclusion in the *ardās* has become imperative. Most of the martyrdoms have been remembered in the *ardās* by naming the tyrannies to which the martyrs were subjected. They all fulfilled the vow:

> We shan't forsake righteousness,
> Even if we may fall dead to the ground.
> —Bhaṭṭ Cāṅd

The sole martyr who was severed joint by joint was Bhāī Manī Siṅgh, one of those who played a select role in Sikh history. His grandfather was in the fighting force of the sixth Guru. He had 12 sons, one of whom was Srī Manī Das, the father of Bhāī Manī Siṅgh. Bhāī Manī Siṅgh had 11 brothers and 10 sons. It is nothing short of a miracle that of this holy family, all the 11 brothers and 10 sons of Bhāī Manī Siṅgh embraced martyrdom for the sake of righteousness.

Bhāī Manī Siṅgh was 13 years old when he accompanied his father to visit Guru Har Rāe at Kīratpur. At that time, his name was Manī Rām and his parents lovingly called him Manīā. The Guru was so very impressed with this promising child that he said, 'This Manīā will shine as a Gunīā (a man of great merit) in the entire world'. After Guru Har Rāe, he was with Gurus Harkishan and Tegh Bahādur. At the time when Guru Tegh Bahādur left for his last journey to Delhi, Bhāī Manī Rām was left in Ānaṅdpur to look after Srī Gobiṅd Rāe.

The service he rendered in the Guru's Court from the time of

Guru Har Rāe to that of Guru Gobiṅd Siṅgh included preparing manuscript copies of the holy book, instructing others in the religious lore, narrating to the Sikhs tales of the Gurus' lives and training the Sikhs in the use of weapons.

He was also a poet, and among the 52 poets of Guru Gobiṅd Siṅgh's Court, he had a special position.[1] He demonstrated many feats of valorous courage in the battles of Bhaṅgāṇī and Nadauṇ.[2] After the Order of the K͟hālsā was ordained, he and all his brothers received the *pāhul* (baptism). Impressed by the strength of his faith and selfless survice, Guru Gobiṅd Siṅgh appointed him the *dīvān* (manager) of his Court. In Ānaṅdpur he routinely unfolded unto the congregations exposition of *Guru Graṅth Sāhib.* The manner of his expositions has continued uninterrupted to date through generations of scholars and is known as the tradition of *giānīs*.[3]

After the demise of Sodhī Harī ji, Bhāī Manī Siṅgh was detailed to Amritsar to reinstate the sacred traditions of the Harmaṅdar—the holiest of the holies. There, he revitalized the practice of *caukīs*,[4] exposition of the text of the holy book, baptizing those who were desirous of receiving *amrit* and abolishing the mal-practices that had been indulged in by the *mīnās*.[5]

When *Baṅdaī K͟hālsā* fell out with the *Tat K͟hālsā* after the martyrdom of Baṅdā Siṅgh Bahādur, the wise Bhāī Manī Siṅgh wrought mutual reconciliation between them.

Around the Dīvālī festival of AD 1733, Bhāī Manī Siṅgh obtained the Mughal ruler Zakarīā K͟hān's permission to organize an assembly of the Sikhs in Amritsar. This was granted on the promise of paying a huge amount as tax, which the Bhāī agreed to pay after the assembly. He then sent letters to the Sikhs to

[1] Giani Gian Singh, *Panṭh Prakāsh.*

[2] Garjā Singh, ed., *Shahīd Bilās,* Ludhiānā: Punjabi Sahit Akademi, 1961, p. 25.

[3] Bhāī Saṅtokh Siṅgh, *Gur Pratāp Sūraj,* R.3 A.20.

[4] *Caukīs* were parties of traditional singers of holy hymns from *Guru Graṅth Sāhib* who went round *the pool of nectar* performing *kīrtan* in traditional tunes.

[5] *Mīnās* were the ostracized relatives of the Gurus who had been creating problems for the Sikh community especially by creating apocrypha of the Gurus' hymns.

attend the assembly. In the meantime, however, the intention of the rulers turned sour, and a conspiracy was hatched to attack the assembled Sikhs and destroy them. Learning of it, the Bhāī sent letters to all the Sikhs warning them about the threatening danger. Very few Sikhs gathered on that occasion, so the offerings were too meagre to make payment of the tax possible. The Governor sought Bhāī Manī Siṅgh's explanation. He explained the situation and asked for the payment to be deferred till after the Baisākhī fair. However, the same story repeated itself even at Baisākhī—in fact, the situation was somewhat worse because forces had already been dispatched from Lahore to Amritsar to surround the Harmaṅdar, and no fair could be held. Bhāī Manī Siṅgh and some other well-known Sikhs were arrested and taken to Lahore. The rulers ordered that the sacred tank at Amritsar be filled up with trash and the seventy-year old Bhāī be slain by severing him joint by joint. He was executed in that way in Nakhās Chowk of Lāhore[6] along with other Sikhs. The Bhāī started reciting *Sukhmanī Sāhib* and continued with it as long as his life lasted.

The memory of Bhāī Manī Siṅgh's martyrdom has been enshrined in the *ardās,* and everyday, wherever the Sikhs assemble, congregations pay their homage to the brave and noble leader who was mercilessly martyred.

[6]There, at that spot, Gurdwārā Shahīd Gaṅj was later established.

CHAPTER 27

The One Who Was Descalped

The troubling tale of a man being descalped pertains to Bhāī Tārū Siṅgh, a resident of the village Pūlā in district Lahore. He worked hard, farming his little piece of land and lived contentedly. He shared with others the grain that he harvested from his field. He was very compassionate, especially with his brethren-in-faith. Everyone in his village, whether Hindu, Muslim or Sikh, respected him for his sincere humanism and exemplary moral character.

That was the time of Zakarīā Khān, the tyrant governor of Lahore, and the Sikhs were a particular target of his atrocities. Hence they sought refuge deep in forests. If anyone gave the Sikhs help of any kind, he also became the target of the ruler's brutality. An entry in *Prāchīn Paṅth Prakāsh* testifies to the cruelty to which Sikhs were subjected.

> Whoso came forth to save the Sikhs
> His life was invariably taken.
> One who withheld the information of the presence of a Sikh around,
> also met his life's end.
> Whoso gave supplies to the Sikhs,
> The tyrant rulers would see him dead.

Nonetheless, Bhāī Tārū Siṅgh secretly helped the homeless Sikhs by providing them with necessary supplies.

In that region, there lived a *Nirañjanī*[1] *mahaṅt*, Har Bhagat by name. He felt jealous of Bhaī Tārū Siṅgh's high reputation, and reported to the Governor of Lahore that Tārū Siṅgh gave refuge to Sikhs and secretly supplied them rations and other necessities.

[1]Haṅdāl (AD 1630-1705), a disciple of Guru Amar Dās was known as *Nirañjanī* because he used to utter *Nirañjan* (unaffected by Māyā) as the name of God. His son, Bidhī Caṅd turned out to be a devil. He made improper changes in the *Janam Sākhīs*. Har Bhagat was a *mahaṅt* of the same *Nirañjanī* tribe.

Without making any enquiry, Zakariā ordered that Tārū Siṅgh be arrested.

When he appeared before the rulers, they demanded that he give away the knot of hair over his head and accept Islam. Tārū Siṅgh said, 'I can give up my head, but not the knot of hair over my head which is the gift of my Guru'. He was offered many temptations to win him over to Islam, but nothing was of avail. With an undaunted voice he said, 'Even if you were to make me ruler of the entire world, and offer me beauties of heaven, I will never agree to part with my sacred hair'. Thereupon, a verdict was given, 'If you cannot give your hair, we shall remove your scalp'.

On 26 June 1747, Bhāī Tārū Siṅgh's scalp was removed with a shoemaker's knife. While he was being descalped, Tārū Siṅgh kept reciting the holy text of *Jap(u)jī*. As his scalp was removed inch by inch, his face flushed with pride. Eventually, the removed scalp was thrown onto his face, and he was pushed into a trench, left for dogs and jackals to eat. However, even in that miserable state, Bhāī Tārū Siṅgh continued reciting *gurbāṇī*.

The same day that Bhāī Tārū Siṅgh was descalped, Zakariā developed retention of his urine. Some of his courtiers who had been impressed by Bhāī Tārū Siṅgh's personality told him, 'You have made a great mistake in performing such an atrocity on Tārū Siṅgh.' Zakariā became penitent, went to where Tārū Siṅgh was lying and sought his pardon for the cruel affront caused to him. Bhāī Tārū Siṅgh told him, 'All this happened under God's will. I have no grievance against you. As far as I am concerned, you stand pardoned. You may render the account of your deeds at the Court of God almighty, where you may reach before I do.' Zakariā did not survive his illness, but for the next twenty-two days, Bhāī Tārū Siṅgh remained alive; throughout that time, he kept reciting *gurbāṇī*.

When his last hour arrived, he addressed the Sikhs who had been attending on him, 'I am now about to sever my relationship with this world. Pray for me.' The Sikhs stood up and said the *ardās* with folded hands. As the *ardās* ended, Bhāī Tārū Siṅgh breathed his last.

> The servant's love triumphed at last.
> —*Mārū* m 5, p. 1000

This dreadful event cemented the relationship of the Sikhs with the sacred hair even more firmly. The hair became the symbol of their faith, determination, honour and dignity.

The memory of this man of faith who accepted descalping rather than part with his sacred hair has been preserved by the *Paṅth* in their congregational *ardās*.

CHAPTER 28

Those Who Were Broken on the Wheel

The two martyrs who were broken on the toothed wheel were a father and his son, Subeg Siṅgh and Shāhbāz Siṅgh. Subeg Siṅgh was a 'cooperative' Sikh. In the Sikh parlance, a 'cooperator' was one who cooperated with the rulers. Being a government contractor, he had influence and easy access to Zakarīā Khān's court. However, because he helped the Sikhs, he was also on good terms with them despite being a 'cooperator'.

Zakarīā received instructions from Delhi to effect a change in governmental attitude towards the Sikhs. The Delhi government had apparently realized that the Sikhs cannot be exterminated by atrocities and tyrannies nor could they be terrorized into subjugation. They decided to try softer methods to win the Sikhs over. Instructions were accordingly issued to Zakarīā to offer the Sikh people, Nawābdom of three *pragnās* and a *jāgīr* with it that yielded Rs. 1 lakh per year.

In order to negotiate this offer, Zakarīā chose Subeg Siṅgh and dispatched him with a robe of honour and the deed for the grant of the *jāgīr*. Taking those offerings, Subeg Siṅgh arrived at the *Akāl Ta<u>kh</u>t*. At that time, prominent Sikhs who were present on the spot declared Subeg Siṅgh a *tan<u>kh</u>āhīā*[1] for being a 'cooperator'. After he had completed the prescribed punishment, he was permitted to present his credentials before the congregation. When he presented the robe of honour, the congregation declined to accept it, saying,

> To us the Guru promised kingdom,
> Which we perceive is already close by.

[1] *Tan<u>kh</u>āhīā* means one liable to punishment.

How can we leave that and accept Nawābdom?
That would make us subordinates and that is not good.
—*Prāchīn Panth Prakāsh*

After persistent pleading by Subeg Singh, it was decided to accept the offer, but the person who served the *Panth* most must be made the Nawāb. At that time, Kapūr Singh was fanning the congregation. The congregation requested that he accept the Nawābdom on their behalf. He initially declined but relented after being persuaded by prominent Sikhs. He took the robe of honour, touched it to the feet of five prominent Sikhs and accepted it on their behalf.

Zakariā Khān was succeeded by Yāhyā Khān who did not have the same regard for Subeg Singh as his father had.

Subeg Singh's son was a pupil with a Qāzī in the Islamic school. The Qāzī was very fond of him. He thought that if this promising lad could be converted to Islam, he would marry his daughter to him. He began to influence Shāhbāz Singh for the purpose and openly conveyed his intentions to him. Shāhbaz Singh told his father what the Qāzī had hinted. His father said, 'Dear son, you have before you the example of the sons of Guru Gobind Singh who preferred to be walled alive than accept conversion to Islam. You also are a son of the same Guru. Do not get taken in by any inducements. You too should prefer to give up your life than give up your faith.' After these words of advice from his father, Shāhbāz Singh declined the Qāzī's offer.

The Qāzī, terribly upset by this, falsely accused Shāhbāz Singh of using irreverential words in respect of Bībī Fātimāh, the daughter of Prophet Mohammed. For his 'offence', both he and his father were arrested and dispatched to Lahore. There, they were given the option between conversion to Islam and death. They declined the first option and were sentenced to be broken on the toothed wheel to death.

The Sikhs of Lahore collected a large sum of money to induce the rulers with it to spare at least the child. When they discussed it with Subeg Singh, he said,

For our sake, the Guru sacrificed his family.
Would it be proper to think of saving my family?
—*Prāchīn Panth Prakāsh*

Subeg Siṅgh was tied onto the wheel first. He shouted the slogan 'Akāl!' and got onto the wheel. When he was half dead, they put his son also on to the wheel to shake Subeg Siṅgh's firmness. The son also shouted a similar slogan and got on to the wheel. Until they breathed their last, the tyrants kept breaking their bodies on the wheels while flakes of flesh flew out of them.

Thus, even the 'cooperative' Sikhs did not let down the glory of the Sikh tradition. The *Paṅth* decided to commemorate that martyrdom by preserving its memory in the *ardās.*

CHAPTER 29

He Who Was Sawn Through

Of the long list of barbarous atrocities perpetrated by the Mughals on the Sikhs, one was sawing a man through into two pieces. The man was first tied between two wooden rafters in the manner of a sandwich and then sawn through from top to toe.

Under the orders of Emperor Auraṅgzeb, Guru Tegh Bahādur and three Sikhs were arrested and taken prisoner in Malikpur Ranghṛāṅ[1] by Nūr Mohammed. The three Sikhs were Bhāīs Matī Dās, Satī Dās and Dayālā.[2] All of them remained imprisoned along with the Guru in Bassī Paṭhānāṅ prison-house for a week short of four months. The Emperor then issued orders from Hassan Abdāl that all four prisoners be put into steel cages and transferred to Delhi. There all the three Sikhs were put to atrocious death in front of the Guru. Bhāī Matī Dās was the first of them to be martyred.

When he was produced before the Qāzī, he was asked, 'Will you accept conversion to Islam or would you rather be put to death?' He replied, 'What better luck can I have than being able to embrace martyrdom in the presence of my Guru?' He was told, 'If you do not accept Islam, you shall be sawn through'.

He replied, 'I would love to be sawn through. Hurry up and do the needful. I will let my life go, but I will not let my faith falter.'

He was then asked, 'Do you have any last requests?' He said, 'My only wish is that when you kill me, my face should be towards

[1]According to Bhāī Saṅtokh Siṅgh and Giānī Giān Siṅgh, Guru Tegh Bahādur offered himself in Agra. But according to *Bansāvalī Nāmā* of Kesar Siṅgh as well as Bhaṭṭ *Vahīs*, he was arrested from Malikpur Ranghṛāṅ near Ropaṛ and interned for nearly four months at Sirhind before being despatched to Delhi.

[2]Of these, Bhāī Mati Dās was sawn through, Bhāī Satī Dās wrapped in cotton wool and set ablaze and Bhāī Dayālā was boiled alive in a cauldron.

the Guru so that I can behold his holy visage until I die.' Sandwiched between two wooden rafters, he was then sawn into two.

As the process of sawing started from his top, he started reciting *Jap(u)jī*. As he completed the text of that *bāṇī*, he took his last breath.

He accepted death, but did not let his faith falter, and in the presence of his Guru, embraced martyrdom. Thus he demonstrated through his death the truth of Kabīr's words:

Even if you cut me apart,
I shall not withdraw myself.
Even if my body falls,
I shall not let my love falter.
—*Āsā* Kabīr, p. 484

The memory of this martyrdom has been preserved in the *ardās* for all times to come.

CHAPTER 30

Who Cheerfully Accepted the Lord's Will

If martyrdom is a divine gift, the strength and courage to accept the Lord's will is a benediction. Only those hearts that have been purified in the fire of faith deserve it. At higher spiritual levels, the relationship of a devotee with *Wāheguru* becomes so close that he knows the will of the Lord spontaneously and stays under its umbrella with the utmost pleasure:

Whatever has my Lord designed,
That alone shall come to happen.
—*Gūjrī* m 5, p. 496

Even if a man is unable to know the divine will, accepting it is unexceptionable for him. None can deny it. There is no room for raising an objection. He who recognizes His will becomes really and truly human.[1] In the Sikh faith, accepting His will requires doing so cheerfully and reverently. It involves giving up one's own self-willed nature and submitting unflinchingly to the Lord's command.[2] Who does not know that one comes into the world through the Lord's will, and spends his whole life within its gamut:

Sent by Him, we come, says Nānak,
Beckoned by Him we return to Him.
—*Vār Sāraṅg*, sl. 2, p. 1239

[1]The word for 'human' used in *gurbāṇī* is *baṅdā* which also means a bondsman. The relevant lines are:
He who cognizes His Will and Him to be the One,
He alone can be called a *baṅdā*.
—*Prabhātī*, Kabīr, p. 1350

[2]He turns not his face away from the Lord's command.
Who has filled his house with peaceful bliss,
Should He beckon him, he would leave thither at once.
—*Mārū* m 5, p. 1000

A person endures pleasure and pain for as long as one lives in the world. Even if hardships occur, they are believed to be God's gift.[3]

The test of whether one accepts the Lord's will comes particularly during times of distress. God-oriented men pray not for the removal of distress but for enough strength to endure the hardship. That certainly is a higher level of *ardās*. The great souls who remain at peace and in cheer even during distress, reckoning it as His gift, and thank Him for it, perform an even higher *ardās*. Such souls are ever in *sadā vigās* (perennial bloom).

Those who realize that man can do nothing by his own will,[4] live in a state of self-surrender. They neither sink in sorrow nor jump up in merriment. Such men accept sorrow and happiness with equanimity. They never desert their faith and make no complaint[5] under any circumstance. On the contrary, they hail His will.

> Hail! You the wonderful Lord. Hail! Your wondrous Will.
> —*Prabhātī* m 1, p. 1329

They assemble all their desires and hopes and submit them to the Lord. Indeed, it was the Lord who even generated these[6] desires and hopes Himself. Then having made that submission, they rise above hopes, desires, fears and apprehensions of all kinds and dwell in the state of *nirvāṇa*.[7] Even while they dwell in the world, they do not become of this world. Though they discharge all the responsibilities of a householder, they do so in a disattached manner. Whatever happens around them, they reckon

[3] Many a man suffers from hardships and privations,
Even those, O Lord, are your gift.—*Jap(u)*, p. 5

[4] Nothing that I propose ever happens.
That alone happens which the Lord does.—*Bhairoṅ* Nāmdev, p. 1165

[5] Never have I ever complained.
Sweet have I always reckoned Your Will.—*Naṭ Nārāyaṇ* m 5, p. 978

[6] Submit unto Him the hopes He gave you,
And stay in the state of Nirvāṇa.—*Prabhātī* m 1, p. 1329

[7] *Nirvāṇa* literally means blown out (like light or fire, etc.). The mind out of which the hopes and desires have been blown out, is considered to have attained the state of *nirvāṇa*.

it as the play of their dearest Friend, and they revel watching His feats.[8]

Those wonderful men of faith who cheerfully accept His will, and even under an executioner's sword, shout *Sat Srī Akāl* (True is the Lord). They recite *gurbāṇī* while being sawn alive; they shout 'Akāl! Akāl!' while being broken on the wheel; they mind the Lord even while being boiled in a cauldron and recite *Sukhmanī* while being descalped.

The families of these martyrs are also a source of inspiration for the Sikhs, because they never sank in sorrow. Instead, they took pride in the martyrdom of their dear ones and thanked the Lord for it.

There is no option but to accept what He wills, and yet most of us do so unwillingly, often even protestingly. However, men of faith cheerfully accept the most trying demands of His Will, and these lofty souls are remembered reverentially in the *ardās.*

[8]I have accepted what my Friend is doing.
His feats I enjoy with pleasure.—*Gauṛī* m 5, p. 187

CHAPTER 31

Who Upheld the Dignity of the Sikh Faith and the Bestowed Form Until the Last Breath

Faith is the breath of spiritual life. The Lord pervades as Love everywhere.[1] Faith is the response to His all-pervasive Love. A number of terms occur in *gurbāṇī* that are synonymous with 'faith'.[2] It is a covenant with God—a covenant of truthfulness, sincerity, faithfulness, love and sacrifice.

Faith is the posture of a self-aware mind. It is the declaration of good intentions and joyful readiness for good deeds. It saves us from becoming self-centred. It rests on the surety of the Lord's own presence with us and ensures the certainty of Divine Victory. It is the declaration of spiritual optimism and ascending morale (*caṛhdī kalā*). Inspired with ideals, it has the courage to fight for them even when all alone.

Faith has the power of challenging the impossible. It transcends possible victory or defeat and keeps the struggle for righteousness going. It lends transparency to aspirations and strength to valour. It steels determination and buttresses determined effort.

Faith fortifies character, sublimates deeds and disciplines thinking. It prepares us to harness benign opportunities. It inspires thankfulness and makes us sing the praises of Him who always nurtures us. Faith and Truth are twins and reflect the resplendence of God's presence.

In the Sikh religion the practice of faith has four important loci: God, the Guru, the Word and the Panth. God is the fulfiller of the

[1] Here, there, and everywhere, the Lord spread Himself as Love.

—*DG: Jāp* 80

[2] These include *sidak, bisvās, visāh, bharosā, bharvāsā, niscā, yakīn,* and *partīt.*

hope of salvation. The Guru rekindles this hope in the devotee, unites him to God and thus saves him.[3] God alone nurtures our faith, shapes it, embellishes it and makes it blossom. He inspires it through his holy Word which is our mainstay throughout life.[4]

There is a saying that was prevalent in old Sikh circles:

Āsrā Akāl kā, parchā shabad kā, dīdār Khālse kā.

It means: we crave for refuge with the Lord, identification with the Word and appearance of the Khālsā.

Identification with the Guru is that with his Word, because the Word is the real Guru. The *Panth* is also the embodiment of the Guru. The light of the Guru is in the Word and the form of the Guru is in the *Panth.* The *Panth* is a spiritual community whose spiritual constitution consists of nothing but faith. One who subscribes to this constitution naturally becomes an embodiment of faith.

The Sikh faith has a special relationship with *siraṛ,* i.e. spiritual determination. A Sikh can lay down his life, but cannot weaken his spiritual determination.[5] Even when the heads of the Sikhs were being hunted, and they had resorted to living in forests, they would move about in small groups singing:

If my head is chopped off, I'll let it go;
But shall not let the determination of my faith falter.

During those trying times, the sacred hair (*kes*) became the recognizable symbol of the Sikh faith. That is why their hair was such an eyesore to the Mughals. If any Sikh was caught, his hair was sought to be shaved off before he was slain. Thus, their cruel sword was plied not only on the faith of the Sikhs but also on their head. The sacred hair became the symbol of the spiritual determination of their faith and was considered the stamp of the Guru's grace on the physical appearance of a Sikh.

[3] Rekindling faith in me, and blending me with the Lord,
My Guru, thus, does save me.—*Naṭ Nārāyaṇ* m 4, p. 983

[4] Study, O dear ones, the holy Word that is our support in life and death.
—*Rāmkalī* m 5, p. 916

[5] He gave his head but not his spiritual vow.—*DG: Bacitra Nāṭak* ch. 5: 14.2

Their hair also symbolized their love for independence and their self-respect. That is how hair came to assume prime importance in the Sikh way of life.

If an object comes to symbolize a nation's dignity, liberty and faith, then naturally it becomes dearer than life itself for the members of that nation. That is why the Sikhs could part with their life but not with their sacred hair. To be shorn of their hair meant for them to have become faithless slaves bereft of dignity, honour and self-respect. Such high regard for their hair symbolizes the respect for the heroes who upheld the dignity of their faith until their last breath.

CHAPTER 32

The Five High Seats of Authority

While the achievements of the Sikh nation are reminisced in the *ardās,* so also are their national institutions, that inspire them. 'Individuals may form communities, but it is institutions that can create a nation'.[1] Institutions not only set-up traditions, they ensure their future as well. The *takhts, gurdwārās, caukīs, jhaṇḍe* and *buṅge* are all important *Paṅthic* institutions which the *Paṅth* has always prized. That is, perhaps, why they find such a special mention in the *ardās.* Foremost among these institutions are the five *takhts.*

A *takht* literally means a royal throne. In the Sikh parlance, it stands for a seat of authority from where the Gurus conducted the mundane affairs of the Sikhs. There consultations and discussions on *Paṅthic* matters were held. Differences were sought to be resolved as per the justice of righteousness in preference to resorting to the judicial system of the rulers. The Sikhs visiting these *takhts* of authority would bring offerings *inter alia* of weapons and steeds. Decisions were made here for any expedition to be mounted for a righteous cause. Thus, these thrones established a self-government of the Sikhs. The *Khālsā,* then, would not accept any authority other than that of *Akāl Purakh* (the Perennial Lord). That is why they considered it obligatory to seek the permission of *Akāl Purakh* for any undertaking of theirs. The *takhts* were the centres from where such permission was obtained in the form of a *gurmattā*[2] which was considered equivalent to the Guru's order.

[1] Benjamin Disraeli: Speech, *Manchester Guardian,* 1866.

[2] *Gurmattā* means a decision taken according to *gurmat* (the Gurus' view). Ancient Sikhs used to arrange a consultative congregation on a *takht* prior to any undertaking, religious or mundane. Whatever was decided by consensus was called a *gurmattā* which was accepted by all without demur. Everyone in the congregation had the right to express his/her opinion. After all the various opinions had been heard, five impartial senior individuals (who were deemed as *Paṅj Piāre*) would take a joint decision. That was the *gurmattā* which everyone honoured. Anyone acting or behaving contrary to it was subject to censure.

There are five *takhts* currently accepted by the *Panth.* For a long time, only four *takhts* were considered as having been duly established. These were:

1. *Akāl Buṅgā* or *Akāl Takht* at Amritsar;
2. *Harmandar Sāhib* at Paṭnā;
3. *Kesgaṛh Sāhib* at Ānandpur; and
4. *Abchal Nagar* or *Hazūr Sāhib* at Nāndeṛ.

Recently, historical documents were discovered that established that another *takht* at Damdamā Sāhib at Talvaṇḍī Sābo, was constituted during the time of Guru Gobind Singh. According to Bhāī Giān Singh Giānī, the four copies of *Guru Granth Sāhib* that Guru Gobind Singh got prepared were sent to the following *takhts:* (i) Akāl Buṅgā,[3] (ii) Paṭnā Sāhib and (iii) Kesgaṛh Sāhib. The fourth one was kept at Damdamā Sāhib.

Hazūr Sāhib at Nāndeṛ was established by Guru Panth after the demise of Guru Gobind Singh.

Of the five *takhts*, *Akāl Takht*, previously called *Akāl Buṅgā*, is considered of prime importance. It was established by the order of Guru Hargobind, the sixth Guru, in AD 1665 in Amritsar right in front of Harmandar Sāhib. It functioned as a throne of royalty for the Guru where he sat and held his court twice a day. This is mentioned in the story of the coronation of Guru Hargobind that was recorded by two minstrels, Nathā and Abdullāh.[4]

This *takht* became the supreme centre for organizing the *Panth.* Here, the congregation of *Sarbat Khālsā* (representatives of the entire Sikh community) took place, and decisions were made for joint Panthic undertakings. Guru Hargobind, the Master of *mīrī* and *pīrī*, had authority over this *takht*, but *Akāl Takht* itself was the centre of *mīrī* alone and not of *pīrī*.[5] The latter remained vested in the Harmandar Sāhib as before.

[3]There are two more *buṅgās* of the same name, viz., *Akāl Buṅgā*—one in Ānandpur Sāhib, and the other in Paṭnā Sāhib; but neither of them is called *Akāl Takht.*

[4]They were the court minstrels of Guru Hargobind. They used to sing the ballads of heroes in order to instill martial spirit among the Sikhs.

[5]Although *mīrī* and *pīrī* both have coexisted in Sikh thought, their fields of authority have been quite distinct. Even Guru Gobind Singh vested the Guruship of *pīrī* in *Srī Guru Granth Sāhib* and that of *mīrī* in Gurū *Panth.*

During the Sikh rāj, a military regiment was established at *Akāl Takht* under the leadership of Akālī Phūlā Siṅgh. It was called *Akāl Regiment.* It did not draw its salary from the royal treasury. It was paid by the Sikh people since it was considered established to defend the ideals of Sikhism. Only the *Jathedār* of *Akāl Takht* had authority over it, an agreement that Mahārājā Raṅjīt Siṅgh had accepted.

Harmaṅdar Sāhib of Paṭnā is the second throne of the *Khālsā* and is the place where Guru Gobiṅd Siṅgh was born. The building of the *takht* was initiated by Mahārājā Raṅjīt Siṅgh.

Kesgaṛh Sāhib (Ānaṅdpur) is the third *takht* where Guru Gobiṅd Siṅgh initiated the Order of the *Khālsā* on Baisākhī Day in the year AD 1699.

Damdamā Sāhib (Sābo kī Talwaṅḍī) is the fourth *takht.* It was designated as the seat of Sikh learning by Guru Gobiṅd Siṅgh, and under his order, a seminary of Sikh learning was established there. Indeed, Guru Gobiṅd Siṅgh had a new reclension (*biṛ)* of *Guru Graṅth Sāhib* prepared there. The service at the *takht* was entrusted to Bābā Dīp Siṅgh Shahīd.

Abchal Nagar Hazūr Sāhib (Nāndeṛ) is the fifth *takht* and is situated on the bank of river Godāvarī. Here Guru Gobiṅd Siṅgh left his earthly abode in 1708. The construction of this *takht* was initiated by Mahārājā Raṅjīt Siṅgh.

The weapons of the Gurus and Sikh heroes have been preserved within the precincts of the *takhts.*

The authority of the *Jathedārs* of these *takhts* does not pertain merely to religious affairs, but is also extended to the polity of the Sikhs including their social and self-governmental roles. Even at these *takhts,* a *bīṛ* of *Guru Graṅth Sāhib* is installed. It indicates that both religious and socio-political matters are under the suzerainty of the Guru. It is a reminder that the *Jathedārs* of the *takhts* also serve *Guru Graṅth Sāhib.*

Recalling these *takhts* in the *ardās* brings to mind the religious and socio-political centres of authority of the Sikh people.

CHAPTER 33

All The *Gurdwārās*

Among Sikhs a place of public worship is called a *gurdwārā*. During the period of the first five Gurus, it was called a *dharamsāl*. From the sixth Guru onward, its designation changed to *gurdwārā* and has stayed that way. Now every place that is devoted to the practice and propagation of the Sikh faith and where *Guru Granth Sāhib* has been installed is called a *gurdwārā*.

Guru Nānak Dev, wherever he went, established a *saṅgat*, that is, a congregation of the faithful. *Dharamsāl* was the place for the assembly of such holy congregations. If there was no specific *dharamsāl*, congregations would assemble in the private house of a devotee. This used to be designated as *Choṭī Saṅgat* (small congregation). When a *dharamsāl* was established in its own premises, its designation changed to *Baṛī Saṅgat* (the big congregation). When a *saṅgat* became established firmly with a *dharamsāl* and arrangements for its services and ancillary affairs had got formalized, it was designated as a *Pakkī Saṅgat* (a permanent congregation).

In the Sikh faith, great value and merit is attached to participation in the congregation. Such participation affirms a feeling of brotherhood and deeper mutual affection among the devotees. It encourages exchange of views and experiences and enhances cooperative undertakings. It also provides opportunities for serving others, that enhance the firmness of faith.

In a *saṅgat*, there is an opportunity for the practice of *Nām* collectively. It helps in building concentration in meditation. It also provides a forum to resolve conflicts. In a *saṅgat*, wisdom prevails; the mind is cleared and the soul becomes transparent. The Guru affirms:

> In the holy congregation, the Lord God Himself abides.
>
> —*Mājh* m 4, p. 94

A *saṅgat* is both the root and a branch of a *gurdwārā*. No *gurdwārā* can be established without a *saṅgat*. Once established, the *gurdwārā* becomes a locus point for the functions of the *saṅgat*.

The prime function of the *saṅgat* is chanting and propagating the holy *Nām* and attending to the spiritual quest of the devotees through singing praises of the Lord and insightful discourses on *gurbāṇī*.

Another important function of the *gurdwārā* is the Guru's *laṅgar* (free kitchen) where everyone, regardless of caste, class, creed or colour sits in one *paṅgat* (row) and partakes of the holy food. Besides providing the basic need of food, *laṅgar* serves as a training school of Sikh character. By engaging in *sevā* (labour of love), one inculcates the virtue of humility, observes the dignity of labour, rises above all divisive distinctions and becomes an instrument of philanthropy. Enjoying the food cooked with humble devotion, we are impelled to thank God for His gift.

In a *gurdwārā*, charitable board and lodging for visiting guests would ideally be available. Guru Har Rāe instructed that every guest be served devotedly and his needs attended to, even if the guest arrived at an odd hour.

Another annexed function of a *gurdwārā* is to organize a *Gurmat Pāṭhshālā* (a School of Sikh Learning) where one may learn the *Gurmukhī* script, proper chanting of *gurbāṇī*, instruction in the diction, hermeneutics and grammar of *gurbāṇī* and classic as well as folk styles of *kīrtan* (holy choir).

Many *gurdwārās* also establish a dispensary or a hospital for taking care of the sick. Guru Arjan Dev had set-up a hospital for lepers in Taran Tāran where he personally looked after patients.

Thousands of *gurdwārās* exist the world over. Besides being places of worship and instruments of Sikh learning, they function as institutions of the corporate power of the Sikh *saṅgats*. A *gurdwārā* is not the property of any one individual. It belongs to the whole *Paṅth*.

In a *gurdwārā*, congregations of devotees engage themselves in *Nām simran*, recognizing the Presence of God, singing the praises of the Lord, supplicating through the congregational *ardās*, receiving *hukamnāmā,* the divine message, and partaking of the sacrament (*parsād*).

Every Sikh is expected to attend the services of a *gurdwārā* daily and to make an effort to preserve its cleanliness and sanctity, as also of its precincts. The Guru sternly warns us against desecration of a holy place:

> If the places of worship are polluted,
> The whole world sinks.
> —*Dhanāsrī* m 1, p. 662

The managers of a *gurdwārā* have no personal authority over the offerings made by pilgrims. The collection is the Guru's trust with them. Additionally, the *granthī,* the caretaker of the *Granth Sāhib,* must be treated with great respect. He is the Guru's viceroy. The management of the *gurdwārā* cannot treat him as merely an employee. He is a religious minister and his dignity ought to be be upheld.

CHAPTER 34

Let us First Pray on Behalf of the Entire *Khālsā*

In the congregational *ardās*, the foremost supplication is on behalf of the *Sarbat Khālsā* (the entire commonwealth of the *Khālsā*). Whoever offers the *ardās* does so as a representative of the entire *Khālsā* fraternity.[1]

There is no exclusive priestly class for the Sikhs. Everyone and anyone is entitled to offer *ardās* in a congregation. Even a child has the prerogative of offering *ardās* on behalf of the *Sarbat Khālsā*.

The *Khālsā* is always *sarbat* (complete), and every member of the brotherhood is an inhabitant of Ānandpur. Everyone's father is Guru Gobind Singh and mother is Mātā Sāhib Devān. The nation of the *Khālsā* was born out of the unique union of these two sacred spirits. For the first time, this nation gave India the idea of nationhood.[2] Within years, this nation established a valuable legacy of rich religious traditions, the essence of which has been preserved in the *ardās*. It embodies a vivid aspiration for corporate life. Every individual after the *amrit sanskār* (the baptismal ceremony) loses his previous loyalties—be they tribal, occupational or religious. His loyalty is now towards God, the Guru and the *Khālsā* brotherhood. The birth of the *Khālsā* took place after the undaunted devout offering their head. This amounts to taking a standing vow to lay down one's life whenever there is a call. That makes every baptized Sikh a *dvijā*[3] (twice born). His second birth is in the Guru's house

[1]That is why, it is important for every Sikh to commit the *ardās* to his/her heart.

[2]'. . . the work of Guru Gobind Singh can be divided into two parts: the creation of a nation and his armed campaigns. When I say the creation of a nation, I mean the words to be taken quite literally, for when Guru Gobind Singh began his work, there was no such thing as a Hindu nation. . . .'—Gokul Chand Narang, *Transformation of Sikhism*, Lahore: New Book Society, 2nd edn., p. 135.

[3]In Hindūism, only the Brāhmins and Kshatriyas are considered twice-

by virtue of which he transcends the cycle of transmigration.

It behoves every Sikh, therefore, to pray on behalf of the entire *Khālsā* fraternity before making any other supplication. It appears that behind every undertaking of the *Khālsā*, collaborative objectives, collective sentiments and corporate faith happened to be at work. Every member of this family prays for the gift of the holy *Nām* for every member of the brotherhood with the firm belief that reminiscing over the Name of God ensures comprehensive happiness and peace of mind for everyone.

Such corporate aspirations ensure national unity. The heart of every Sikh beats for the entire nation. The prayer for 'protection and favour for the *Khālsā* wherever they be' springs naturally and spontaneously from the tongue of every Sikh in the *ardās*. Every morning and evening, when thousands of devoted hearts supplicate for protection and special favour for the *Khālsā*, the *Khālsā* get spiritually revitalized wherever they are—in their homes or in deserts, jungles, hills or jails.

This section of the *ardās* indicates the unity of the *Paṅth* as a nation. The basis of this unity is our faith in one universal God, one source of the Divine Word and the same spirit working in the *Khālsā* that worked in the Gurus. We are not only one in spirit, we are also one in form—characterized by a flowing beard and turbaned head.

The faith of the Sikhs serves to preserve their unity. It not only ensures the affirmation of a singular loyalty, but also negates any sectional allegiance. The affirmation of their national unity distinguishes them from other people without making them stand in opposition to them. Indeed, it even binds them to all.

We must pray for the entire *Khālsā* with this sentiment of unity. Every devotee participating in the *ardās* should feel enveloped in a collective spiritual embrace. Affirming the unity of the *Paṅth* is a collective obligation, and the preservation of such unity should be an unrelenting effort. The inspiration for this effort is the natural outcome of the prayer for the safety and protection of the entire *Khālsā* commonwealth.

---

born. None of the lower castes have this privilege. In Sikhism, there is no consideration of caste. Anyone and everyone can get baptized and earn the status of twice-born.

CHAPTER 35

May the *K͟hālsā* Enshrine *Wāheguru* in Their Heart

There is an intimate relationship between the *ardās* (prayer) and *simran* (meditating over the *Nām* of God). The *ardās* is primarily a prayer for the maturation of *simran.* That is why, of all the gifts supplicated for in the *ardās,* the foremost is 'May the entire *K͟hālsā* enshrine the holy Name *Wāheguru* in their heart'. Later in the *ardās,* there is another supplication for 'the greatest of all gifts, the *Nām*'. Those who continually chanted the *Nām,* therefore come to a prayerful mind first of all. Towards the end of the *ardās,* prayer is made for the company of those 'meeting whom, O Lord, we remember your *Nām*'. In the penultimate line of the *ardās,* *caṛhdī kalā* (enhanced spiritual power) is sought and that is based on *Nām.* Thus, the gift of *Nām* is repeatedly besought in the *ardās.*

In the supplicatory line, 'May the *Sarbat K͟hālsā* remember *Wāheguru! Wāheguru!! Wāheguru!!!*' the gift of *Nām* has been supplicated for by repeating it three times, thus affirming *simran.* It suggests that the holy congregation must repeat the holy Name *Wāheguru* all the time. Thus, besides praying for the gift of *Nām,* praying for its practice has also been included in the *ardās* in a suggestive way.

Furthermore, the uttering of *Wāheguru* is repeated every time the *ardāsīā* enthusiastically invites the congregation to utter this holy syllable after him, and the congregation responds to his call. Since everyone present in the congregation makes an audible response that all can hear, the spiritual fruit of *simran* becomes manifold. Therefore, it should be considered obligatory for everyone in the congregation to be attentive to the *ardāsīā's* call and respond to it in an audible way. One who hesitates in uttering *Wāheguru* can hardly have conversation with Him. Isn't *ardās* primarily meant to be conversation with *Wāheguru*?

The syllable *Wāheguru* is our *gurmantra.* By remembering and reminding oneself of it, one can cross the *Ocean of Being.*

A story in the *Janam-sakhīs* has relevance here. Once during their travels, Guru Nānak and Mardānā came upon a river that they had to cross. Guru Nānak told Mardānā, 'Keep repeating *Wāheguru* and you will be able to cross the river'. Symbolically, the river stands for the Ocean of Being, and the instructions given to Mardānā are not for him alone, but for the entire mankind.

This *gurmantra* was apparently kept a secret during the time of the first five Gurus and was whispered only in the ears of a baptized Sikh.[1] During the sixth Guru's time, the observance of secrecy was relaxed, and when the tenth Guru initiated the Order of the Khālsā, with *khaṇḍe dā pāhul* (the baptism of the sword), he asked the initiates to utter *Wāheguru-jī kā Khālsā, Wāheguru jī kī Fateh* several times—thus making public what used to be a secret *gurmantra.*

The syllable *Wāheguru* enshrines in it the spirit of *Vismād* (spiritual wonderment) and its repetition wafts the practitioner into that transcendent emotive state. It also unites the devotee with the Guru and through him to God.

If one remembers *Wāheguru* and enshrines Him in his heart, his life becomes replete with eternal joy. Human life is the opportunity for attaining the Lord, and this opportunity can be availed of through *simran.*

> Meditate the Lord and forget Him never,
> This is the benefit of human incarnation.
> —*Bhairon* Kabīr, p. 1159

One who does not practice *simran* forfeits the great opportunity of meeting the Lord. One who misses this opportunity is cautioned:

> He alone is alive who keeps the Lord in mind.
> Says Nānak, none else is truly alive.
> —*Vār Mājh,* sl. m 2, p. 142

[1]The baptismal ceremony at that time used to be *Caranpāhul.* The Guru used to touch a bowl of water with his big toe and the disciple would drink from that bowl.

That is why *simran* of the *mantra Wāheguru* has been prescribed as a compulsory practice for the Sikhs. That seems to be why the inspired souls who composed the *ardās* incorporated its practice even in the *ardās*.

CHAPTER 36

Wheresoever the *Khālsā Jī* Abide

Khālsā jī Sāhib is a reverential phrase that expresses the extent of the love and respect the Sikhs have had for each member of the *Khālsā* brotherhood. The entire *Panth* as well as every individual Sikh can be addressed as *Khālsā jī Sāhib* because the Gurū is believed to abide in the *Khālsā jī*. It also indicates the sanctity of the relationship that any member of the *Khālsā* fraternity has with the others, considering them, like himself, as the spiritual offspring of Guru Gobiṅd Siṅgh.

The term 'wheresoever' indicates that the jurisdiction of this phrase extends to the entire world and spiritually covers every individual Sikh who may be living in any place in the world. Everyone of them is considered a member of one's own spiritual family, and divine protection is sought for him/her the same way as a mother might pray for the safety of her children who may have settled in different places at home and abroad.

This particular phrase of the *ardās* was composed during a great holocaust. For forty years, bearded and turbaned Sikhs were hunted like animals and killed on sight. The few that survived went into hiding in forests, hills or deserts.

The climax of this brutality reached during the rule of Mīr Mannū. He spared no one—neither women, nor children, nor even infants. He arrested even women and forced them into harsh labour while giving them only a thin slice of bread to eat. The infants were snatched from mothers and cut into pieces that were strung together and hung around the necks of the mothers. The tyrants would then exhort, 'This is the penalty given you for having produced a Sikh child'. Under such atrocious conditions, every Sikh heart throbbed for every other Sikh living anywhere. The phrase seeking protection and favour for the Sikhs wherever they may be was added to the *ardās* then.

In this phrase, faith surges high. Belief in the presence of God wells up. Safe and secure protection by the Gurus appears to be assured. It seems that every time there was distress, the *Paṅth* received special favour and protection. Whether it was a struggle for freedom to wear *kirpān* as in the UK or a struggle to wear a turban in Canada, sincere good wishes and help always came to the affected Sikhs from all over the world showing even trance-oceanic solidarity. When, in AD 1984, armed onslaughts were made on the *Akāl Takht* in Amritsar, the heart of every Sikh living anywhere cried out in agony. The surge of such feelings reflects the mystic power inherent in this phrase.

This phrase also contains the secret of the separate national identity of the Sikhs. The *Khālsā Paṅth* is not a state-nation, but a non-state universal commonwealth. That is why its ideals are higher and vaster than patriotism.

Sometimes the Sikhs received favour and protection in very mysterious ways. Khushvaqt Rae has recorded a strange incident in his *Tarikh-i-Sikhāṅ*. The entire Sikh population of the village Niāz Beg including women and children had been wiped out by Mughal tyrants. Only a very old woman survived. Even her survival was noticed by the attackers and a few cavalrymen came back to find her and eliminate her. As she saw the horsemen returning, she went indoors and tearfully prayed, 'O Master of the *Paṅth*, have you really deserted us? I have heard that whenever someone sought your help from the depth of the heart, you invariably came to help. Why don't you come now? My husband and my sons have been slaughtered. My whole village has been devastated. Tell me, who but you can come to my rescue? If you also have decided to desert us in this calamity, then why did you make us your Sikhs?' Then suddenly, as if from nowhere, a knight-at-arms dressed in blue and riding a blue steed appeared and asked that woman, 'What is your desire?' She replied, 'I only desire Guru Gobiṅd Siṅgh. He alone can save me from the evil tyrants.' Then the man in the blue drew out his sword and attacked the cavalrymen. In minutes he killed them all and then just disappeared. The woman firmly believed that it was none other than Guru Gobiṅd Siṅgh himself who came to her rescue.

In *Dasam Graṅth*, the Book of the Tenth Master, there is a sacred text called *Akāl Ustat* (Laudation of the Timeless). The first four lines of it that were inscribed in the original manuscript in the hand of Guru Gobiṅd Siṅgh himself, read thus (in translation):

We have protection of the Timeless Lord.
We have protection of the All-steel.
We have protection of the All-Time.
We ever have protection of the All-steel.

The *Khālsā*, who consider themselves as God's very own, have always wanted to continue to deserve such omnipotent and omnipresent protection. That is why in their *ardās* they daily pray: 'Wherever the *Khālsā jī* are, your favour and protection, O Lord, may prevail over them.'

CHAPTER 37

May Our Rations and Weapons Ensure Victory

In *ardās,* the Sikhs not only remember those who kept their *deg* (cauldron) warm and their *teg* (sword) plying, they also pray that their *deg* (signifying rations) and *teg* (standing for weapons of war) should always ensure their victory. In a war, victory rests on availability of rations as much as on that of weapons.

Deg is symbolic of the great Divine Benevolence, whose cauldron the whole globe is.

Once for all has the great cauldron of the globe
been bequeathed unto you.
Your destiny, however, is your disbusor.
—*Basant* m 1, p. 1190

This alludes to the fact that their nutriment was created in anticipation of the creatures.[1] So, before there were any creatures, there was their food. *Deg* thus represents all the many gifts that the Lord has created for us. In a manner of speech, the grain is to be worshipped as also the Giver of the grain:

Meditate on the Nām and meditate on the grain.
—*Gond* Kabīr, p. 873

Food and drink are sacred.[2] Appeasing the stomach is also part of devotion, for sustenance is required even before devotion. Thus *deg* is the preamble to devotion.

Hunger of the stomach is trifle compared with that of the spirit. For the latter, appropriate nourishment is also required.[3] Thus,

[1] First you created their nutriment, and thereafter the living beings.
—*Mājh* m 5, p. 130

[2] Food and drink are sacred nourishment, You've given us all.
—*Vār Āsā* m 1, p. 472

[3] Your True Name is my nourishment, which all my hungers appeased.
—*Anand, Ramkalī* m 3, p. 917

deg also symbolizes spiritual satiation. The Guru's Word is the *deg* that feeds hungry souls to satiety:

> The Ambrosial Nectar of the True Nām has become my food.
> Through the Guru's instruction whoever ate to his fill, comfort found. —*Vār Mājh* m 5, p. 150

Deg also represents the cooking quarters; these in turn represent the life of a householder. There is a basic difference between the fire in the householder's hearth and the smouldering fire of Nāth *yogīs.* While the former represents hospitality, the latter is associated with beggary. In the Sikh religion, begging is taboo. The Sikhs are not a community of beggars but one of philanthropists. It is the householder who is able to practise philanthropy, and from him alone all other denominations can benefit.

> Of all other denominations, the householder's is better,
> For from him all others benefit.
> —*Vār Vadhaṅs* m 4 sl. m 3, p. 587

This *deg* is not any individual's personal possession; rather, it is the Guru's *deg.* 'Grain and water, they belong to the Guru, only to serve these is our good fortune.' The only hospitality we can give is to pass on the Lord's gifts into more deserving hands.

Deg also stands for *kirt,* or earning through honest labour. If there was no *kirt,* no *deg* could run. *Deg* is run by honest labour done with one's hands and taking pleasure in giving away from those very hands.

The term *deg* is also used to signify *laṅgar,* the 'Temple of Bread', where *sevā* of sorts is continually practised: the floors are washed, provisions are obtained and stored, the fuel is stacked, lentils are picked, vegetables are sliced, dough is kneaded, bread is made, dishes are cooked, pilgrims are seated, food is distributed, and their plates are collected and washed clean.

A European pilgrim at Harmaṅdar Sāhib, Amritsar, saw the service being rendered in the *laṅgar* and remarked:

> Here one witnesses a living faith—providing a clear acceptance of the Fatherhood of God and the brotherhood of man. The gift of God is distributed here, and brothers-in-faith receive it, put it together, distribute it, partake of it and thank the Giver for it. This is truly a heavenly affair. —An entry in the Visitors Book

In the *laṅgar*, spiritual discipline prevails. Before the food is distributed, grace is said through *ardās*, and the Guru's permission sought to distribute his gift to the *paṅgat* (every row of pilgrims). No one starts eating until everyone has received their food. Then a *jaikārā* is called out to signify that all have received their fare. The pilgrims then start eating together. Until then, they continue chanting *Satnām, Wāheguru*. Everyone takes only as much as he can consume. Leaving uneaten food in one's plate is taboo.

Victory of *deg* signifies Divine sustenance for one and all. *Deg* also signifies worship through bread, dignity of labour, equality of mankind and the great merit of the householder's way of living.

2

Like *deg*, *teg* is also a multipotent symbol and not just a thing of utility. It is not only a weapon for self-defence, or for repulsing violent aggression but also a symbol of spiritual courage. It is always the last resort for the Sikhs.[4]

Real *ahimsā* lies in not using force despite having the requisite strength. If one lacks the requisite strength and pretends to be non-violent, he is practising cowardice, not *ahimsā*.

The *K͟hālsā* was initiated when, one by one, five Sikhs rose to offer their head to the Guru's sword. Defying death was a demonstration of undaunted courage. After the Order of the *K͟hālsā* was initiated, the *kirpān* (the sword) became a part of their *rahit* (discipline of life).

Teg is primarily a symbol for God Almighty. Guru Gobiṅd Siṅgh named God as *Srī Aspān* (having a sword in His hand)[5] and *Khaṛagket* (having a sword on His flag).[6] The Lord God was also named as *Srī Bhagautī* (the Revered Sword),[7] and in *ardās* homage is paid to it even before it is paid to the Gurus.

[4]When all peaceful methods have been tried and they failed,
Then alone would it be legitimate to employ the sword.
—*DG: Zafar Namah* 22

[5]*DG: Rāmavtār*, 863-4.

[6]*DG: Benaṭi Chaupāī*, 25.

[7]*DG: Vār Srī Bhagautī jī kī*, 2.

The Sword has been used as a symbol of God's Power even in Christianity:

> And take . . . the Sword of the Spirit, which is the Word of God.[8]

The Sword, thus, also symbolizes the Divine Power of God.

The Sword has also been designated as *Giān Kharag* (the Sword of Wisdom):

> I've received from the Guru, the powerful Sword of Wisdom.
> —*Vār Mārū* m 3, p. 1087

It is with this Sword that war can be waged against one's own mind.[9] With it, the five enemies—lust, anger, avarice, attachment and ego—can be defeated.

Teg is also a symbol of power. When one becomes bereft of power, one can fall into bondage.[10] *Teg* alone can free us from bondage. Hence it is also a symbol of freedom.

Even in the Christian Bible, two symbolic swords are mentioned:

> And they said, Lord, there are two swords.
> And he sayeth unto them, it is enough.[11]

3

Deg and *teg* are the gift of *Wāheguru* to the *Khālsā*. If the *Khālsā* have both *deg* and *teg*, they will keep a vigil on their duties. That is why, they yearn:

> Our *deg* and *teg* should both keep active in the world.
> —*DG: Krishnāvtār,* 436.3

The juxtaposition of *deg* and *teg* also spells a vow for the *Khālsā* that they, while partaking of *deg*, shall remain vigilant of the duties for which they were bedecked with the *teg*.

[8] Ephesians 6: 17.

[9] With the Sword of wisdom can one fight against one's own mind.
—*Mārū* m 1, p. 1022

[10] When our power abdicated us, we found ourselves slaves.
—*Slok* m 9, p. 1429

[11] Luke, xxii.38.

Deg is the *prasād* (sacrament) of the Lord. By touching it with *teg*, it not only symbolizes approval of *Srī Asket* but is also a reminder of the pledge that having taken the food consecrated with the sword, the dignity of the Sword shall be held high. To consecrate the *kaṛāh parsād* with a *kirpān* (sword) is to symbolically re-emphasize the ideal of *Deg-Teg-Fateh*.

In *ardās*, *Nām* and *Fateh* are yearned for a number of times. Both are related with *Caṛhdī Kalā* (the ascendant spirit). Three levels of *Fateh* are sought for in the *ardās:* (a) of *deg-teg*, (b) of the *Paṅth*, and (c) of *Wāheguru*. Victory of *deg-teg* is subsumed under that of the *Paṅth*, and that of the *Paṅth* subsumed under that of *Wāheguru*.

CHAPTER 38

May Our Reputation be Preserved

Bird ki paij is a phrase that has multiple meanings:

1. The term *bird*, derived from the Sanskrit root *vird*, has 'reputation' as one of its meanings. Traditionally, when a king or emperor approached the gate of his court, the doorkeeper would enthusiastically chant laudation of the ruler and his reputation in elaborate and hyperbolic epithets. This citation was called *bird*.[1]

   The root meaning of *paij* is a pledge, a vow. Its secondary meaning is 'honour', 'pride' or 'glory' (of a vow having been fulfilled). In Sikh parlance, it is used in this secondary sense.[2]

   The meaning of *bird kī paij*, in this context then is that 'the glory of the reputation should ever remain intact'.

   This prayer for the maintenance of the glory and reputation is on behalf of *Sarbat Khālsā jī*.
2. A second meaning of *bird* is 'obligation'. The complete phrase *bird ki paij* would mean that 'the obligation be fulfilled'. One who is capable of fulfilling one's obligation becomes eligible to rise to the status of even a Guru. Others, even though they may be the Gurus' offspring, were overlooked by the Gurus when selecting their successor. Rāe Balvaṅḍ, a minstrel in the court of Guru Arjan Dev testifies to this:

   When the sons did not obey his word,
   The Guru turned his back upon them.
   —*Vār Rāmkalī*, Rāe Balvaṅḍ, p. 967

[1]Bhāī Kāhn Siṅgh Nābhā, in his *Mahān Kosh*, gives a *bird* in respect of Guru Gobiṅd Siṅgh.

[2]As in *Jan ki paij rakhī Kartare*, i.e. the honour of His own man, the Lord has saved.—*Gauṛī* m 5, p. 201

Here, it may be added that *bird* can also refer to *Akāl Purakh's* covenant with His Creation; that His promise of being a benevolent protector shall ever stand fulfilled irrespective of whether we deserve it or not.

He does not consider my merits and demerits,
Such benevolence is inherent in His Nature.
—*Srīrāg*, m 3, p. 72

3. A third meaning of *bird* is 'a religious symbol'.[3]
   The holy hair are considered the *Khālsā's bird.*
4. If *bird* is understood to be synonymous with the Persian term *vird* (the regular daily remembrance of God) then *bird kī paij* means that the daily observance of performing the *Nit Nem* should be fulfilled.

Each of the above meanings of *bird kī paij* appears to be in accord with the ideals of *gurmat.* Hence, all of them may be considered applicable to the supplication *bird kī paij* in the *ardās.*

[3]As in *Bird sees par se utravo*, i.e. Remove this religious symbol (i.e. hair) from your head.—Bhāī Saṅtokh Siṅgh, *Gur Pratāp Sūraj.*

CHAPTER 39

May the *Paṅth* be Victorious

M.A. Macauliffe once asked an elderly Sikh, 'What is *Paṅth*?' The old man replied, 'I cannot explain to you the real meaning of the *Paṅth*. It is our spiritual path, it is our nationhood, it is our Guru, it is our deity, it is our life.'

The literal meaning of *Paṅth* is 'the way'. The applied meaning is 'the Way for the attainment of God'.

In Sikh parlance, 'the organized Sikh *dharma*' is also called the *Paṅth*. In this context, *Paṅth kī jīt* would be a prayer supplicating for victory both for *dharma* and for the Sikhs. It is, thus, both a desire and a belief.

'Certainty of victory is a precondition for victory.'[1] Confidence that the *Paṅth* shall be victorious has been optimized in this phrase. Every Sikh believes at heart that the *K͟hālsā* is the 'pampered army of the Timeless Lord'.[2] Victory is certain because that is victory for the Lord Himself. So, this phrase of the *ardās* reflects both confidence in the self and confidence in the Lord. However, as already observed, personal victory is subsumed under the victory of the *Paṅth* and both these under victory of the Lord. Yet, all signify the three aspects of the devotee's confidence.

'It is men's to fight, but heaven's to grant success.'[3] Hence, petition for victory can only be made to the Lord. However, only moral victory can be asked of God. 'In victory, the hero seeks glory, not prey.'[4] Glory is possible only if the victory is moral, the

[1] With certainty I should achieve victory.—*DG: Ukt Bilās* 231

[2] The *K͟hālsā* is the pampered army of the Timeless Lord.
The *K͟hālsā* became manifest at the express pleasure of the Lord.
—*Sarab Loh Graṅth.*

[3] Homer: *Iliad*(ninth century BC), tr. Alexander Pope.

[4] Sir Philip Sydney (1554-86) quoted in *The New Dictionary of Thoughts*, comp. Edwards Tyron, Standard Book Co., 1966.

struggle is justly motivated, fearlessly fought without any pressure and for any favour. One should have God on one's side and with the desire even to sacrifice one's life should it come to that.

A sacrifice never suffers defeat. Indeed, it is the highest victory. Those who live for ideals do not find it hard to lay down their life for them. For them, it signifies the fulfilment of the purpose of life. Sacrifice is particularly victorious when it is made to root out tyranny. The awareness of belonging to the *Panth* has continually been heightened through the process of serial martyrdoms. *Panthic* consciousness flowers as much under the shadow of death as it does through non-violent tolerance.[5]

Panth kī jīt is victory of the Way adopted by the *Khālsā*. It is the way of monotheism, of *Ik Oankār.* It is the way of egalitarian humanism that condemns all distinctions of caste, creed, class and colour. It is the way of valourous manliness. Only live manliness is able to attain victory. 'Dead men can have no victory.'[6]

Victory is a mental state. The heart that doesn't accept defeat is never vanquished. Victory of the mind is victory of the world.[7] He who considers himself the 'wrestler of the Lord' receives the Guru's pat on his back.[8] Such fighters alone become the means of *Panthic* victory.

A couple of Sikhs once asked Guru Gobind Singh, 'How can the victory of the *Panth*, the progress of the *Panth* and the ascendant spirit of the *Panth* be assured?' The Guru replied,

> The *Panth* belongs to the Guru. Its progress rests with him. However, beware of the pretender Sikhs—nominal Sikhs who are looking for personal profit, not looking for the welfare of the *Khālsā*. For insignificant personal benefits they allow themselves to be used as a cat's paw against the *Panthic* interest. They may look like Sikhs but within themselves, they have disowned the Guru. Every Sikh should look within himself and check lest a pretender Sikh might be sitting there in masquerade. He should check lest he may have inwardly turned away from the Guru. If

[5]That individual in this world is great who has God's name on his lips
And desire for war at heart.—*DG: Krishnāvtār,* 2492.1

[6]Euripides, *The Phoenecian Women (c.411-409 BC)*, tr. Elizabeth Wycloff.

[7]*Jap(u)*, p. 6.

[8]*Srīrāg* m 5, p. 74.

that be so, then one should reunite oneself with the Guru even at the cost of one's life.

The prayer for victory of the *Paṅth* is, in a way, prayer for the unity of the *Paṅth.* The vow for *Paṅthic* unity ensures *Paṅth kī jīt.*

CHAPTER 40

May the Holy Sword Help Us

Srī Sāhib is a characteristic expression in the Sikh vocabulary which has two meanings. On the one hand, it represents *Srī* (*Lakshmī*)'s *Sāhib* (Master) or God Almighty. On the other hand, it stands for the Sword.[1] Thus, it represents both *pīrī* (spiritual authority) and *mīrī* (temporal authority). In other words, it is simultaneously the All-Steel sword as well as the Sword of enlightenment. It may be thought of as *Sarab-Loh* (All-Steel) of *Sarab-Kāl* (All-Time). That is how Guru Gobiṅd Siṅgh invokes it.[2]

The Order of the *K͟hālsā* is an order of spiritual valour. It was initiated with the blessing of the sacred Sword. That is why every member of this Order has been advised to sever his own head and put it on his palm as an offering and only then think of treading on the path of love.[3] To put one's severed head on one's palm symbolically means getting ready to sacrifice one's life. A Sikh has to have the Name of the Lord on his lips and the longing for war in his heart. The sacred Sword becomes deified for the *K͟hālsā* because the *K͟hālsā* was initiated with *kirpān*. When they begin their *ardās*, they first invoke *Srī Bhagautī jī* (the supreme Sword) and yearn for its assistance. Whenever a Sikh invokes the sacred Sword, he verbalizes sentiments of worship. He goes further and deifies his weapons.

[1] According to Bhāī Kāhan Siṅgh, this name Guru Gobiṅd Siṅgh gave to the Sword holding the *Kharag* to be the Master of *Lakshmī*.

[2] May we have protection of the Timeless One. May we have protection of All-Steel.
The protection of All-Time is with us. The protection of All-Steel is with us.
—*DG: Akāl Ustat*

[3] If you desire to play the game of love with Me,
Then step forward with your (severed) head on your palm.
—*Slok* m 1, p. 1412

The meaning behind this phrase is longing for being potent and adequate. The sword of the *Khālsā* severs all bondages and grants freedom. It establishes righteous justice and abolishes injustice of all kinds.

Real valour is that which remains ready for dying while still alive. It considers death as a right. However, if conditions of life appear worse than death, then it has the fortitude for accepting the Will of God.

Assistance by the sacred Sword has been considered basic to *Panthic* victories along with the yearning that 'the *Khālsā* shall rule'. Once, Adinā Beg dispatched a letter to Sardār Jassā Singh in which he offered peace with the *Khālsā* and said, 'The Sikhs should give up fighting which only harms them. You should adopt peaceful ways.' To this, Sardār Jassā Singh replied,

> The *Khālsā* is not prepared to accept the subservience of Delhi at any cost. They will establish their rule over India with the help of their sword the same way the Mughals did. Heroes always meet in the battlefield. Without martyrdom and blood flowing in streams, none cedes royalty, and none gets freedom. So far, you have only seen the shine of our sword. When it comes into play, the royalty shall fall at our feet. The *Khālsā* will not rule through anyone's favour, but with the help of the sacred Sword and the grace of the Lord.

Weapons cannot be held by the hands of cowards. Only heroes can wield them. That is why the first five Gurus initially concentrated on developing spiritual valour and moral strength in their Sikhs so that they shall not misuse weapons. Moral courage was induced first, and the sword was handed over afterwards for fighting against injustice. A Sikh is basically peace-loving, but he will not brook injustice. Overlooking injustice and putting up with it is culpable non-violence. Yet, the Sikhs have been advised to unsheath their sword when *all other* peaceful methods have failed.

That is why after the martyrdom of Guru Arjan Dev, the sixth Guru wore two swords—of *mīrī* along with that of *pīrī*. After the martyrdom of Guru Tegh Bahādur, Gurū Gobind Singh made wearing the *kirpān* on one's person obligatory for the *Khālsā*. Thus, the sacred Sword became a part of their body-image itself.

Whenever and wherever this sword rises to protect the

tyrannized, uproot the tyrant and re-establish *dharma*, the Lord Almighty comes to provide His help.

The *Khālsā* have always defended their right to wear a *kirpān* on their person. They have never accepted a ban on the sacred Sword—a sword that they worship as their deity. From time to time, various governments have attempted to enact a ban on the wearing of *kirpān* because they considered this as a challenge to their authority. The Mughals first imposed this ban not merely on the Sikhs but on non-Muslims of all denominations. Only the Sikhs defied that ban to authenticate their freedom. The British imposed a restriction on the size of *kirpān*. For forty years, the Sikhs opposed this restriction till it was rescinded. Even in 'free India', the Congress government in UP imposed a ban on the *kirpān*. However, even they were obliged to withdraw it. It should be apparent how the *Khālsā* has on all such occasions defended their right to wear the sacred sword on their person.

CHAPTER 41

May the Word of the *Khālsā* Ever Prevail

The phrase *Khālsā jī ke bol bāle* in *ardās* has multi-layered meaning. *Bol* means 'word' and *Bāle* (from Persian 'Bālā') means:

1. loud, of high tone,
2. authentic and credible,
3. sublime, and
4. authoritative.

All these connotations fully apply to the word of the *Khālsā*.

1. That the *Khālsā* have the roar of a lion is testified to by their *jaikārā* (the war-slogan).[1] Their thundering exclamations testify the confidence with which the *jaikārā* has always been uttered.
2. Authentic words have established credibility. They are words based on truth. Neither does truth wear out nor does the glory of the word. Neither does truth alter, nor does the reliability of truthful word. Their luster endures perpetually.

   Speakers die, their words remain alive. The only authentic words are the ones uttered by those who would give away their life to vindicate them.

   Whoever relies on God does not feel subservient to any temporal power. Freedom authenticates their words. Every word they speak is fearless. Each intent of theirs has moral courage.

   Slavery lowers the value of one's words. The words of slave India had ceased to be her own. It was when Guru Nānak

[1]The *jaikārā* is: *Sat Srī Akāl.* It means 'The revered Eternal Lord is Truth'.

spoke out the truth that the conscience of enslaved India got stirred. He spoke when there was real need to speak up. He challenged the people, saying:

In every home, you address each other as *mīāṅ*,
Folks! Your very tongue has become alien.
—*Basaṅt* m 1, p. 1191

Even Kshatriyas, who were supposed to defend the country, had discarded their language. The Guru alluded to them and said:

The Kshatriyas too have forsaken their *dharma*,
They too speak the tongue of *malechhas*.
—*Dhanāsrī* m 1, p. 663

Not just the Kshatriyas, even Brāhmins had begun consuming meat of the animal slaughtered 'under foreign idiom'.[2] In an agonized voice he tried to awaken the hope that:

Hindustān[3] will take care of its word.
—*Tilaṅg* m 1, p. 723

3. He alone is a spiritual hero whose words are sublime, and lofty. Self-sacrifice makes real testimony to the validity of any words. Even under atrocities of the worst kind, the Sikhs did not utter any unbecoming word. Under the most trying circumstances, they kept their faith aloft without any complaint.
4. *Bol Bāle* also means words of authority. Reportedly, Guru Gobiṅd Siṅgh wanted to see the word of the *Khālsā* ascendant even in this sense. He wanted them to be upright, powerful, scholarly and authentic *Sardārs*. He said:

Out of them shall I see scholars arise.
They shall give authentic exposition of the scriptures.
I shall make them such chiefs as would rule wisely.

[2] *Vār Āsā* m 1, p. 472. Here the allusion is to Arabic *kalimā* which is recited by Muslims when they slaughter an animal.

[3] Guru Nānak was the first to employ the term *Hindustān* in literature.

> I shall make them kings, so that they remember me as their Guru.
> —*Panth Prakash*

Thus, when we yearn for our *bol-bāle* in the *ardās,* we in fact, make a pledge that our words should meet our Guru's expectations.

CHAPTER 42

Beseeching the Right Gift

Man constantly suffers from one want or another. He may even have many privations together. That is what spells his dependence on others. He needs others for his living, security, learning and progress in all other spheres of life. He needs others to inspire him, instruct him, goad him, nag him and encourage him. Thus viewed, man is a perpetual beggar. When he goes out to beg, he finds that all others are also beggars only. He then thinks, 'Why beg from beggars?'

Whenever such feeling arises, it turns one toward God, and seeks to beg only of Him. God is the only one who gives, and having given, never regrets.[1] The Sikhs have been instructed to beg from none other than God. 'Begging from others only makes one feel ashamed.'[2]

What is it that we should beg of Him? He is the supreme Giver, so what is the right gift to ask of Him? He can give anything.[3] He is never miserly. It is we alone who swerve and stumble while asking some gift of Him.

A king, it is said, was pleased with a man and told him to ask for anything, and that his request would be granted. That man had not had anything to eat for many days and was very hungry. He could not think of anything else except rice pudding and so he asked for that only. Was he not insulting the king by requesting

[1] How Eternal is the greatness of my Lord,
He gives and never regrets having given.
—*Vār Soraṭh* m 4, sl. m 3, p. 653

[2] Beg from the One Lord, and obtain your heart's desire,
If you beg from someone else you shall suffer deadly shame.
—*Āsā* m 5, p. 401

[3] My benevolent Father has issued these instructions,
Should my child open his mouth and request a gift, that he must be granted.—*Malār* m 5, p. 1266

him for that paltry gift? How much more absurd it must be if we request the Emperor of Emperors, our God, for equally measly favours?

Let us look at what we generally ask of Him. Don't we pray, for example, for affluence, comfort, offspring, success, power, status or popularity? Are they not measly things? Seldom if ever, we ask Him for a gift, after which nothing else would be required. Why not ask Him to unite us with Himself? Either we think, we don't deserve that or He won't grant us that. Instead we ask Him for a house, a job, success in examination, a nice bride or a dutiful son. Are they not trifles? Even worse, we may ask him to save us from the police though we have committed a culpable crime? Don't we insult Him? But this is what we easily do. Who prays for His grace, for His *Nām* or for enthusiasm to laud Him? Are these not the best things to request?[4] Should we not approach Him to grant us His *Nām*? The composers of the *ardās* have incorporated it for us in the prayer as 'the best gift of all gifts'.[5] Not just this, they make us petition for other valuable gifts as well—the Sikh faith, the sacred hair, disciplined life, discriminating wisdom, faith, and trust. Such lofty gifts take the seeker up the ladder to the Lord:

> In this way, we climb up the ladder step by step
> And come to merge with Him.
>
> —*Jap(u)*, p. 7

[4]The best thing to beg of Him is His Praise.—*Marū* m 5, p. 1018
[5]*Dānāṅ sir dān.*

CHAPTER 43

The Gift of the Sikh Faith

Guru Nānak was commissioned by God Almighty to propagate what is now known as *Sikhī*, the Sikh Faith. *Sikhī* is disciplined spiritual life bequeathed us by enlightened Masters.[1]

According to Guru Amar Dās the school of the Gurus leaves behind all the six schools of Indian philosophy because it enables one to achieve salvation as well as to attain God.[2]

The way of *Sikhī* is not prescribed for any particular sect or caste. It is for the entire mankind. Whoever follows the Guru's instructions becomes our brother-in-faith.

The *Bhagat Ratnāvālī* mentions that Guru Nānak imparted the following instructions to Bhāīs Phiruā and Jodhā:

> The Sikh faith prizes humility. Render unto Sikh brothers whatever service you can. Get up during the last quarter of the night and concentrate on the Lord's Word. Reckon God as your Lord and yourself as His serf. Participate in the holy congregation, listen to the Guru's Word with devotion and faithfully carry out his instructions.

Sikhī involves the virtues of humility, zeal for effort (*uddam*), service (*sevā*) and *simran*. It matures through congregational worship, observing the brotherhood of all.[3] Similar qualities of *Sikhī* were described by Guru Hargobiṅd to Bhāī Cūhaṛ:

> One who stays humble, engages in honest work and service, keeps the company of godly men, makes effort to receive *giān* (enlightenment) by

[1] *Sikhī* is practised when the Sikh carries out what the Guru instructs.
—*Bhāī Gurdās Vār* 28.10

[2] The six systems of philosophy are pervasive,
but the Guru's system is profound and unequalled.
The Guru's system is the way to liberation.
The True Lord Himself comes to dwell in the mind.
—*Āsā* m 3, p. 360

[3] *Bhagat Ratnāvalī*, Tīkā Pauṛī 14.

which one recognizes the world as illusory and the Light of the Lord as True, is an accomplished Sikh. All of you, Sikhs, should reckon only one God.

The *Rahitnāmā* of Bhāī Caupā Siṅgh provides a more detailed picture of *Sikhī*:

Sikhī preserves the sanctity of the holy hair unto the last breath, discourses on the holy word, profits from the holy congregation, sows the seeds of noble acts, contemplates over the Guru's instructions, earns one's livelihood through honest labour, wields self-control, speaks the truth, and harvests the fruit of such actions. A devout Sikh would elevate the glory of the Guru's *laṅgar,* worship the Timeless Lord, revere the sacred weapons, preserve his merit and credibility. He would spread the fragrance of *Sikhī* through dignified service, sweetness of speech, modesty in the eyes, and by honouring women. Women, as good wives and mothers should mind house-holding. All should recognize the Presence of God, uphold healthy traditions, obey the Guru's commands, serve the Lord like a Sikh, receive instructions from the *Granth,* recognize the Guru in the *Khālsā,* wake up early, take a bath including hair-wash and sit for prayer. Avoid evil, interact with others with due deference and make controlled utterance, accept the prescribed discipline sincerely and practise the wisdom of discrimination between good and evil. Serve and love the Sikhs as siblings. Serve your parents and study with interest. Sing (the Lord's praises) throatfully. Conquer your own mind. Find eminence through service, love from the heart, share with others what you have, remain mindful of virtue, slay sin, live frugally—habituated to nothing but food. (Be ever prepared to) engage in war (with evil). Your word should be powerful (i.e. reliable), your manner should reflect and promote spirituality. Relate (with the Lord) through *Sikhī,* be desirous of meeting the Lord.

Bhāī Saṅtokh Siṅgh recognizes five levels of *Sikhī:*

1. *Merely professed:* indifferent to the Gurus' instructions and selfish in outlook.
2. *Imitative:* merely copying others and doing what they do without knowing the significance thereof.
3. *Covetous:* interested in profiting materially, devoid of any knowledge of the real self, bereft of *gurmat.*
4. *Faithful:* reposing trust in the Gurus, staying firm and steadfast even in trying times, willing to do anything to uphold the ideals.

5. *Ardent:* staying in constant love (of the Lord), lauding the Lord as well as the Guru and having sentiments of fraternity for brethren-in-faith.

The prayer for the gift of *Sikhī* in the *ardās* is a prayer for those who are faithful and ardent. This gift is not asked for oneself only but for all members of the fraternity.

Living as a true Sikh is not an easy job. Indeed, it has been likened to walking on the edge of a sword.

Sharper than the edge of a sword
And narrower than the breadth of a hair
Is the path you have to tread.
—*Rāmkalī* m 3, p. 918

In real *Sikhī*, one shuns the counsel of one's egoistic mind and submits oneself wholeheartedly to the Gurus' guidance:

Tread this path following the Guru's advice
And do what he ordains.
Eschew your own mind's counsel and abstain from duality.
—*Sūhī* m 5, p. 763

Once, Guru Arjan Dev was asked, 'Dear Master, how many true Sikhs have you known?' He replied, 'Only four and a half'. Further, he named his four predecessors as true Sikhs in every sense of the word and counted himself as a half-baked Sikh trying to become a true one.[4]

Sikhī is mysterious. Here, if one becomes a true Sikh, he can reach the status of a Guru. However, at times, even after touching the summit of *Sikhī*, one might prefer remaining a Sikh to becoming a Guru. Bhāī Pāro Julkā pleased Guru Arjan Dev so much by his missionary work that the Guru told him, 'I feel like installing you as my successor'. But, Bhāī Pāro said, 'My true King, I would love to remain a Sikh. Only a Guru can glorify that office.'

One cannot attain real *Sikhī* through one's own efforts. The Guru's grace is required as well for its attainment. That is why a special prayer is made in the *ardās* for the grant of *Sikhī*.

[4]This reminds one of George Bernard Shaw who was asked, 'How many true Christians do you know of?' He replied, 'It is hard to be a true Christian. There has been only one, and you know what happened to him.'

CHAPTER 44

Gift of the Holy Hair

Hair holds a special significance in the history of religion. Thomas Decker observed, 'Hair is the robe which curious nature weaves to hang upon the head and to adorn our bodies. When we are born, God doth bestow that garment. When we die, then like soft and silken canopy, it is still over us.'[1]

Hair is a gift of God, designed by divine wisdom and received by us through divine grace. Since obedience to God is our singular duty, preserving our hair intact is our bounden obligation. Wilfully disregarding this obligation is tantamount to insubordination to God's Will and believing that our puny intellect is superior to Divine Wisdom.

The etymological origin of *kes* (Sans. *kesh*), according to Pāṇinī is *kash* which means 'light'. Hair is believed to attract celestial light and to be an instrument in enlightenment.

According to *Atharvaveda*, 'The hair cannot be sown. To trim them or to pluck them is not proper. Instead, it would be advisable to preserve them in order to enhance dignity and vigour.'[2]

Hair is a symbol of the spiritual culture of India. All the *rishīs* and *avatārs* kept unshorn hair. Lord Buddha, who had shorn his hair when he gave up palatial comforts in search for truth, grew it back when he got enlightened.

Preservation of the hair has been sanctified in the Indian as well as the Semitic tradition. 'In enumerating the wonders of creation, God pointed out to Job the wisdom shown in making human hair. A penalty of one hundred salain is imposed by the Rabbi for pulling out an antagonist's hair.'[3] Even Jesus kept his

[1] Quoted in Tyron Edwards, comp., *The New Dictionary of English Thought*, Standard Book Co., 1966.

[2] *Atharvaveda:* 19.32.2.

[3] *Jewish Encyclopedia*, New York, 1925.

hair unshorn. One of the epithets employed for Prophet Mohammad is *gesū darāz*, which means 'one with long hair'.

Even today, men with spiritual endowment preserve their hair. Examples include those of Aurobindo Ghosh, Rabindranath Tagore, Bhagwan Das, Digamber Vishnu and Vinobā Bhāve.

Even God has been described as *Keshava* (one with hair).[4]

Hair has been held sacred from the beginning and has been believed to be symbolic of advanced spiritual life.

Hair symbolizes not only *bhakti* (devotion for the deity), but also *shakti* (physical vigour). According to *Atharvaveda*, 'Preserving the hair is conducive to increasing one's vigour and pride.' Well-kept hair symbolizes vigour, beauty, lustre and health.

... ...

A faith that aims at producing saint-soldiers naturally would relate to the archetypal significance of the hair. In the Sikh faith, considering hair as sanctified began with its founder Guru Nānak. When he took Mardānā as his lifelong companion, he asked him to take three vows: that he will never shear his hair, that he will not miss his morning prayers and that he will affectionately welcome and lovingly serve visiting guests.

With the baptism of the sword introduced by Guru Gobiṅd Siṅgh, maintaining unshorn hair became obligatory in the Order of the *K͟hālsā*.

Where people accepted Guru Nanāk's faith but lost contact with subsequent Gurus, even they continue to preserve their hair.[5]

[4]Your eyes are pretty, teeth luscious, beauteous nose and long hair.
—*Vadhaṅs* m 1, p. 567

[5]Major Jagat Siṅgh in his little booklet *Kes Mahattā* (published by Guru Nānak Dev Mission, Patiala), writes that he met some Tibetans who were keeping full-length unshorn hair. He asked them, 'Are you Lamas?' They replied, 'No, we are Sikhs of the Rimpoche Guru.' The Major asked, 'Who is Rimpoche?' They replied, 'The same as your Guru.' 'My Guru is Guru Nānak Dev,' said the Major. 'So is he ours,' they remarked, 'we only do not pronounce his name out of reverence'. The Major asked them, 'How is it that you all wear unshorn hair?' They said, 'When on the Sumer Mountain the Guru had a dialogue with the *siddhas*, our ancestors who were until then

In *gurbāṇī*, the beard is a symbol for purity of conduct.

True are those beards, that brush the feet of the Guru.
They serve their Guru and live in bliss, night and day.
Their faces appear beautiful in the Court of the True Lord.
—*Slok* m 3, p. 1419

Attacks by tyrannous rulers on the Sikhs' sacred hair started during the Gurus' time itself. If the Mughal rulers arrested any Sikh, they ordered that he be shorn before he was slain. The Sikhs accepted martyrdom but did not accept disgrace to their sacred hair. Bhāī Tārū Siṅgh was descalped but he refused to cede his sacred hair.

Guru Gobiṅd Siṅgh ordered the unshorn hair to be a mandatory part of the exterior of the baptized Sikhs. All the *Rahitnāmās* are unanimous on this issue.[6] Any disgrace to or indignity of the hair has been unacceptable to the Sikhs. Such an act is looked upon with contempt.[7]

Those who accepted baptism and observed the inner discipline as well as the outer form (inclusive of unshorn hair) prescribed by the Gurus were *amritdhārī* Sikhs in contrast to the *sahijdhārī* ones.[8] If an *amritdhārī* Sikh committed violation of any taboo, one

---

disciples of the *siddhas* found them no match to the Guru and so they became Sikhs of the Guru. Since then, generation after generation, we have been his Sikhs'.

The same author quotes some armymen who said, 'In Baghdad, there is a monument set up in the memory of Guru Nānak's visit there. The Muslim keeper of that place was wearing long hair and a flowing beard. On enquiring, he averred that his ancestors had kept these on the order of Guru Nānak. Since then, it has become a family tradition.'

[6]For example, the *Rahitnāmā* of Bhāī Chaupā Siṅgh says, 'The Guru's Sikh should consider the hair as the seal and keepsake of the Guru'.

Likewise, Bhāī Desā Siṅgh, in his *Rahitnāmā* says, 'Keep the hair, fragrant, clean and free of pollution. Know that they are the Guru's charming stamp'.

[7]One who walks about with uncovered hair and allows dust to gather in them, deserves to be punished. . . . He who touches his hair with dirty hands needs to be censured. . . . So too the one who removes the turban of another Sikh.

[8]Those who had not yet kept their hair unshorn but had adopted the Sikh faith were called *sahijdhārīs* (the gradual adopters). Those *keshadhārīs* (who

of which is desecrating the sacred hair, he is dubbed as *patit* (a fallen one). Those who grow their hair but do not intend to take *amrit* (baptism) are considered *bhekhī* (impersonators).[9]

However, unshorn hair seems to have become the *nishān* (identity) of the Sikhs in general and so reckoned as the declaration of one's faith in *Sikhī*. A Sikh must not conceal his identity; so has the obligation of taking care of his/her sacred hair. The unshorn hair became the flag of high moral character.

The sacred hair, in a way, seem to declare who one's Guru is. One who ignores the responsibility of keeping the hair unshorn appears to be disavowing his Gurus. So, *gurbāṇī* declares:

> One who publically disavows his Guru,
> Is not a good person.
> —*Vār Gaurī* m 5, p. 304

During the Mughal rule, barring a *hājī*,[10] nobody was allowed to maintain an unshorn beard. By commanding his disciples to keep unshorn hair and beard, the Guru, expected his Sikhs to affirm their freedom. Hence, the sacred hair became the symbol of freedom for the Sikhs.

Hardly any ruler would tolerate an upsurge of the sentiment of freedom among his subjects. To them, it smelt of rebellion. That is why unshorn hair began to irk successive governments.

First of all, it irked the Mughals. Not only did they forbid having long hair and flowing beard, they even ordered hunting out and slaying those who wore them. Rewards were offered for Sikh heads. Under these circumstances the Sikhs supplicated that they should live with their sacred hair intact until their last breath.

Ahmad Shah Abdālī captured Sardār Ālā Siṅgh and ordered that his hair be shorn. His wife consented to Abdālī's demand

---

keep unshorn hair), who had not yet received baptism, but were working towards it, were also *sahijdhārīs*. However, if one has grown long hair, but has no intention of receiving baptism, he is simply impersonating.

[9]About such *bhekhī* Sikhs Guru Gobiṅd Siṅgh said:

> By keeping long hair (alone) one cannot meet God.
> —*DG: Akāl Ustat* 5.252

[10]*Hājī* is one who has performed *haj* (pilgrimage) of the Muslim holy place in Mecca.

for a huge sum of money in order to spare the Sardār's hair. It is clear that the hair had become the symbol of Sikh dignity. Those wearing the sacred hair were addressed as 'Sirdār Sāhib'.

After the British defeated the Sikhs in the Anglo-Sikh wars, they wanted to exterminate the Sikh religion completely. They began by converting Sikh chiefs to Christianity. They even converted the minor Mahārājā, Duleep Siṅgh, sheared his hair and put him under an official Trust. Later, they realized the valour of the Sikhs and noted that it was linked with the honour and dignity of their hair. Then they issued an order forbidding any Sikh official causing indignity to his hair.

Even in free India, those who wore the *kes* were made the target of a pogrom in 1984. Once again, the Sikhs realized that the sacred hair was the symbol of their corporate dignity. Although many with wavering faith sheared their hair for the sake of their life, there were many others who stuck to the ideals of their faith and preferred martyrdom.

Thus, the history of the Sikh people has been an uninterrupted account of struggle for freedom. During the entire span of this struggle, the sacred hair has remained a symbol of freedom for them.

It is natural, then, that in their *ardās* the Sikhs supplicate for the gift of the sacred hair.

CHAPTER 45

The Gift of Disciplined Life

In Sikh parlance, *rahit* means 'discipline of life' that aims to bring worldly desires under control, inspires one for higher ideals, aids the advent of spiritual enlightenment and, thus, makes life really meaningful.

THE INTERNAL DISCIPLINE

The internal discipline has been designated in *gurbāṇī* as *ātam kī rahit*[1] (spiritual discipline). It spells the fundamental approach to spiritual life. It has been said, 'Real discipline is spontaneous discipline, and real spontaneity is disciplined spontaneity'.[2] *Gurbāṇī* emphasizes:

> True living is when the True One abides within.
> Through the *rahit* (lifestyle) of Truth,
> the True Lord comes to dwell in us.
> The self-willed *manmukh* talks about it,
> but puts it not into practice.
>
> —*Bilāval* m 1, p. 831

The inner *rahit* in Sikhism is both individual and corporate. In individual *rahit*, is *Nām*, *dān* and *ishnān*. *Nām* stands for spiritual, *dān* for fiscal, and *ishnān* for physical cleanliness.[3] *Nām simran* is remembering the Lord and practising His presence. *Dān* means earning one's livelihood with honesty and donating generously a portion thereof to charity.[4] *Ishnān*, literally 'a bath', stands for physical cleanliness in a wider sense.

[1] *Sukhmanī*, *Gauṛī* m 5, p. 269

[2] Harold Kelman: *Eastern Wisdom and Psychoanalysis*, Personal communication.

[3] *Srīrāg* m 5, p. 74.

[4] Bhāī Gurdās *Vār* 6.12.

Inner discipline includes remaining busy in benevolent endeavours,[5] being humble in thought and speech,[6] accepting happiness and sorrow with equanimity,[7] remaining undaunted during struggles against tyranny[8] and being ready to lay down one's life for upholding righteousness.

There are specific commands for obseving daily liturgies. Early morning, one must recite *Jap(u)*, *Jāp Sāhib*, *Anańd Sāhib* and *Tav Prasād Savaīye*; at sunset, one must recite *Raherās* and at bedtime recite *Kīrat Sohilā*.

There are some proscriptions also. Lust, greed, worldly attachment and egoism have to be shunned.[9] There are admonitions against coveting others' wealth and women and indulging in slander and calumny.[10] Lying[11] and vain argumentation[12] have also been forbidden.

The following sacred verse epitomizes the inner *rahit:*

One who calls himself a Sikh of the True Guru,
shall rise early morning and meditate on the Lord's *Nām.*
Early in the morning, he should bathe,
and cleanse himself in the pool of nectar.
If he follows the Instructions of the Guru and chants the *Nām* of the Lord, all his sins and misdeeds shall be erased.
At sunrise, he should sing *gurbāṇī;*
Whether sitting down or standing up,
he is to meditate on the Lord's *Nām.*
One who meditates on the Lord
with every breath and every morsel of food—
that Gursikh pleases the Guru.
If my Lord has compassion upon any Gursikh,
unto him are the Guru's Teachings bestowed.
Servant Nānak begs for the dust of the feet of that Gursikh,
who himself chants the *Nām,* and inspires others to chant it.

—*Vār Gauṛī* m 4, p. 305

[5] *Gauṛī Mājh* m 5, p. 218.
[6] *Srīrāg* m 3, p. 31.
[7] *Bilāval* m 5, p. 801.
[8] *DG: Ukt Bilās* 231.2.
[9] *DG: Ukt Bilās* 1-7.
[10] *Āsā* m 5, p. 379.
[11] *Āsā* Farīd, p. 488.
[12] *Bhairoṅ* Nāmdev, p. 1164

COLLECTIVE INNER DISCIPLINE

Collective inner discipline incorporates *sādhsaṅgat* (participating in the holy congregation), *kīrtan* (devotional singing), *kathā* (exposition of the holy word), *sevā* (devotional service) and *ardās* (prayer).

Sādhsaṅgat or *Satsaṅgat* (the true congregation) is the basic unit of the collective organization of the Sikhs. Whatever the organizational level of the *saṅgat,* its functions have primarily been devotional. The Gurus affirmed that:

> In the *saṅgat* abides the Lord Himself.
>
> —*Mājh* m 4, p. 94

Hence, its decisions were considered to be Divine commands.

Its function had two aspects: *jot* (spiritual radiance) and *jugat* (practical strtegies). The former was wrapped in the holy Word. Hence, every *saṅgat* is now supposed to be presided over by the holy book, *Srī Guru Granth Sāhib.* The *saṅgat* is also concerned with practical operations and decisions relating to emerging problems. These decisions were expected to be unanimous or at least based on consensus, so that they could represent the spirit of the congregation. The *saṅgat* eventually evolved into the *K̲hālsā.*[13] The *K̲hālsā,* over a period of time, evolved into *Sarbat K̲hālsā.* Faithfulness remained the basic tenet of the congregational organization.

Kīrtan is one of the major activities of the holy congregation:

> Singing the praises of the Lord in the *sādhsaṅgat*
> is the loftiest of all spiritual actions.
>
> —*Soraṭh* m 5, p. 642

It has been considered the supreme medium of salvation in the Dark Age of *Kaliyuga.*[14] Guru Nānak himself performed *kīrtan* accompanied by minstrel Mardānā on his rebec. During Guru Aṅgad Dev's time, Bhāī Bādū and Sādū performed *kīrtan* for the congregation. Guru Amar Dās was a great enjoyer of *kīrtan* and

[13] Bhāī Gurdās II *Vār* 41.1; Saināpatī *Gur Sobha* 7.27.

[14] *Kīrtan* is the most sublime spiritual activity during the *Kaliyuga.*
—*Mārū* m 5, p. 1075

invented a musical instrument called *sāraṅdā.* Sattā and Balvaṅd were the twin minstrels who performed *kīrtan* for the congregation during the time of Guru Rām Dās and Guru Arjan Dev. Once, they became annoyed and did not show up to perform *kīrtan.* The Gurū himself went to their home and requested them to join the *saṅgat* and perform *kīrtan,* but they declined to come. The Guru returned and asked the *saṅgat* to perform *kīrtan* on their own, joining them with a *sāraṅdā* in his own hands. Since then, *kīrtan* has been a major congregational function.

Kathā is exposition of the holy word. Several hermeneutical traditions have evolved over time. The Bhāī tradition is reputed to have been started by Guru Gobiṅd Siṅgh who provided the exposition of *Srī Guru Graṅth Sāhib* to Bhāī Manī Siṅgh and Bābā Dīp Siṅgh. After several generations, it came down to Bhāī Vīr Siṅgh who is known for his *Saṅthyā Pothīs.* The tradition of Nirmalās started with those Sikhs that were sent by Guru Gobiṅd Siṅgh to Banāras to receive education in Sanskrit. Their exposition is scholarly, though, naturally, influenced by Vedāṅtic thought. Yet another tradition is that of modern scholars. Of these, Bhāī Sāhib Siṅgh is known for his contribution as a grammarian. Principal Tejā Siṅgh and Professor Bāwā Harkishan Siṅgh are best known for their *Shabdārth.* Giānī Mohiṅder Siṅgh Rattan's explication of *gurbāṇī* promises to be a noticeable addition to the traditional lore in *gurbāṇī* hermeneutics.

Sevā is serving others with devotion. It is an outstanding activity of the holy community. Selfless devotion to it can make one rise to the level of a Guru. Srī Lehṇā jī became Guru Aṅgad Dev, and Srī Amar Dās became Guru Amar Dās by virtue of their *sevā.* It can earn one a place of honour in the Court of the Lord:

> In the midst of this world earn merit through *sevā,*
> And you shall be given a place of honour in the Lord's Court.
> —*Srīrāg* m 1, p. 20

Through *sevā* one practises *humility,* sanctifies labour and learns selflessness. However, that is possible through divine grace only. Guru Nānak said:

> How can I possibly serve, O Lord,
> When even my soul and my body are Yours?
> —*Sorațh* m 1, p. 635

The discipline of *sevā* has its own distinctive *samādhī* (ecstasy). When the *bāolī* (step well) was being sunk in Goiṅdvāl, a woman performed the service of labour day and night. However, occasionally, she would fling her hand forward in the air in the manner of pushing something. This surprised the onlookers. Some of them talked about it to Guru Amar Dās. The Guru told them, 'This devoted woman hails from Kabul. She is all the time in the *samādhi* of *sevā*. She leaves her child behind at home when she comes for *sevā*. Whenever that child cries, she becomes aware of it in her *samādhi* and pushes her child's cradle from here itself by pushing her hand.' The devotees who revel doing service are engrossed in it body and soul. Such servers find divine approval.

> Those humble servers who follow the Guru's teachings
> And serve the Lord receive approval at His Court.
> —*Tukhārī* m 4, p. 1115

Ardās (prayer) is a means of establishing direct relationship with one's deity. In the Sikh religion, congregational *Ardās* is a unique institution. Through it, a congregation links itself with the entire community, its national pride, its religious centres, and through universal consciousness with the Lord Himself.

THE EXTERNAL DISCIPLINE

The external discipline of the Sikh religion is that of *pāhul* or *amrit*, the baptismal ceremony, which was first performed by Guru Gobiṅd Singh. It is currently performed the same way as was done by the *Paṅj Piārās* for Guru Gobiṅd Siṅgh.

The all-steel bowl symbolizes divine protection.[15] The *bāṇī* (liturgical texts) is symbolic of *bhakti* (devotion). The double-edged sword and the heroic posture symbolize *shakti* (vigour). Water represents the intermingling of *bhakti* and *shakti*. Sugar candy symbolizes sweetness of thought, word and deed.

Initiation with this sublime potion into the Order of the Khālsā is designated as *amrit saṅskār* (ceremony of immortality). One initiated thus is expected to be ready to struggle for upholding

[15]We have protection of All-Steel.—*DG: Akāl Ustat*

righteousness and curbing evil while staying imbued with *caṛhdī kalā* (spiritual optimism) even in adverse circumstances. One who imbibes *amrit* becomes a member of the *Khālsā* fraternity, and the *Khālsā* is the Lord's personally pampered army.[16] The *Khālsā* follows no orders except from the Lord under whose Will they function to uphold virtue and punish evil:

> I honour the saints and punish the wicked—
> This is my duty as God's police official.
> —*Rāmkalī* Kabīr, p. 969

This army has a distinctive discipline. To wear on their person the five archetypal symbols is obligatory for all members. All these symbols begin with the phoneme 'k'. These are *kes* (unshorn hair), *kirpān* (the sword), *kachhehra* (pair of shorts), *kaṛā* (bangle) and *kaṅghā* (comb). The first three of these have been known as *traimudrā* (three signs). According to *Sarab Loh Graṅth* and *Gur Pratap Suraj* only these had been initially prescribed by the Guru. However, it has been claimed by a historian that there is a *hukamnāmā* issued by Guru Gobiṅd Siṅgh to the *saṅgat* of Kabul in which all the five symbols have been mentioned.[17]

The *kes* has long been recognized as symbolic of spiritual life. Accepting them and respecting them is our obligation. They have been considered the composite symbols of *bhakti* and *shakti*, pride and honour, valour and courage, freedom and dignity.

Kaṅghā is a requirement for the cleanliness of the *kes*. This symbol of cleanliness literally sits next to the symbol of Godliness, i.e. *kes*.

Kirpān is the symbol of upholding righteousness through courage and valour. As a weapon, it is never unsheathed in wrath. While wearing a *kirpān*, a saint turns into a knight-at-arms of God Almighty.

Kaṛā is the comrade of *kirpān*, just as *kaṅghā* is the comrade of *kes*. The fighters used to wear a set of all-steel bangles over the

[16] *Khālsā* is the army of the Immortal, Timeless Being.
Khālsā appeared through the fond Will of the Lord.
—Bābā Saṅt Siṅgh, *Sarab Loh Graṅth*, p. 527.

[17] However, the present writer has not been able to confirm the existence of such a *Hukamnāmā* from any knowledgeable source.

wrist of the *kirpān*-wielding arm as a protective device. It is also considered a symbol of self-control.

Kachehrā discretely symbolizes temperate application of the instinctive power of procreation.

The *rahit* of the 5 ks symbolizes not only the saint-soldierly role of the *K͟hālsā*, it also reminds the *amritdhārī* of his other obligations and commitments.

In case the internal *rahit* is not being observed, observing the external *rahit* alone becomes blasphemous wearing a deceptive façade. Such faking is hardly acceptable in Sikh ethics.

> Displaying guise to the world, one might overpower people,
> But at the end, one gets chopped as if with a scythe
> And thrown into hell. —*DG: Bachitra Nāṭak* 6.5

One who observes the internal as well as the external *rahit* is a well-disciplined Sikh. The inner *rahit* directs a Sikh's spiritual life and the external *rahit* vouchsafes his identity.

Rahit is the Guru's gift. It cannot be observed without the grace of the Guru. Most individuals profess it, but few can live up to it.[18] That is why the gift of *rahit* is so ardently yearned for in the *ardās*.

[18] *Rahitnāmā*, Bhāī Caupā Siṅgh.

CHAPTER 46

The Gift of Discriminating Wisdom

Bibek (Sanskrit *Vivek*) is a sublime wisdom by which one can discriminate between truth and untruth, good and evil, right and wrong. It is that wisdom which can lead us to enlightenment—to know that *Brahman* (the Creator) and *Prakriti* (the Creation) are not two separate entities but only one. Thus, *bibek* is that which transforms the conception of 'two' (*bib*) into that of 'one' (*ek*).

According to a mythological story, *man* (mind) had two wives: *Pravritti* (worldliness) and *Nivritti* (asceticism). With each of them, he had a son. *Pravritti* bore *moha* (worldly attachment) and *nivritti* bore *bibek* (discriminating wisdom). *Moha* tempted *man* with objects that give immediate sensual pleasure, thereby turning one away from *bibek*. In order to enjoy those sensual pleasures, *man* gets engrossed in sensual pleasures and believes 'I enjoy'. Thus, it has been caught in the duality of 'I' and 'enjoyment'. *Bibek* has nothing to present which yields immediate pleasure. It can enable *man* only to understand his own real self. If ever, *man* may be able to break the bond of worldly attachment and turn to *bibek*, it can get released from the duality of 'I' and 'enjoyment'. He comes to know that he himself is not only the enjoyer, but the joy and the process of enjoyment also inhere in himself.[1] Thus, *bibek* brings *man* out of duality and makes him experience unity.

Reading may yield scholarship, but it cannot yield *bibek*. Wisdom without literacy is better than literacy without wisdom. Indeed, one who treads the path of spirituality often finds scholarship superfluous baggage.

Bibek, according to one tradition, has four aspects:

1. Wisdom that does everything with discretion;
2. Truth that does not leave justice out;

[1] He Himself is the enjoyer, Himself the Essence and Himself the Ravisher thereof. —*Srīrāg* m 1, p. 23

3. Courage that is linked with fearlessness; and
4. Discipline that tames desires and enables life to transcend worldly attachments.

The path of *gurmat* is lit by *bibek*. Every Sikh is ordained to remember God, for He is the source of *bibek:*

Says Kabīr:

Say 'Rām' and nothing but 'Rām'
For in saying this lies *bibek*.
—*Slok* Kabīr, p. 1374

Bibekī (a discriminating person) is one who lives according to the Guru's instruction, for the Guru is perfect in *bibek*,[2] and he can also bestow *bibek* upon others.[3]

Bibek is flawless intellect, self-enlightened sublime consciousness. Opposed to it is *abibek* (lack of *bibek*) that lures one away from spiritual joy to sensual pleasure.

Our sensual passions are powerful
And discriminating intellect weak.
Hence we have no access to Supreme Values.
—*Soraṭh* Ravidās, p. 658

Abibek has also been identified with 'proud' and 'egotistic' intellect. It is that which generates the 'ego' and makes us the slave of the *duality* caused by the senses:

Though I performed many rituals,
I could not escape the passions caused by the five senses,
Then I fell at the door of my Master,
And of Him I begged Discriminating Wisdom.
—*Soraṭh* m 5, p. 641

It is only through *bibek* that we can free ourselves from the bondage of duality.

[2]The Guru is *bibek* incarnate. He looks upon all alike.
Meeting with Him doubt and skepticism depart.
—*Naṭ Nārāyaṇ* m 4, p. 981

[3]Discriminating intellect I got from the Guru,
He reveals the spiritual wisdom of God.
—*Toḍi* m 4, p. 711

Belief yields spiritual inspiration, trust provides spiritual support, and *bibek* leads to spiritual enlightenment. These are the three pillars of spiritual *rahit* and in the *ardās,* there is supplication for all the three.

CHAPTER 47

The Gift of Conviction

The next two gifts supplicated in the *ardās* are *visāh* (conviction) and *bharosā* (trust), which are inseparable constituents of faith. Conviction is firm and indubitable belief in the existence of God, and Trust is the assurance of protection by Him.

Visāh is called *īmān* in Sūfī parlance. It is not only an acknowledgement of God being our Creator, but also a belief that He is also our sustainer and protector and benevolent towards all His Creation.

The primary requirements for *visāh* are love for and devotion to the Lord. Anyone who is deeply in love, continually misses his beloved. Such loving remembrance of the Lord is called *simran.* A man of conviction lives a life of *simran* and does not give it up even in trying times. On the contrary, he considers even tribulations of life as the grace of God;[1] so, accepts them cheerfully. He never gives up his faith; might give up his life for it. That way, he proves his conviction by embracing martyrdom.

Conviction provides the foundation to spiritual life. Without it, there would be no chance of human consciousness grasping the experience of God. God Himself awakens conviction in ordinarily slumbering consciousness. Conviction is thus the call that God himself generates. It is the call of His grace and the tug of His love.

The basis of conviction is the movement of divine mystery in the human soul. It spells man's first step out of time, into eternity. It never errs because God guides it.

Conviction is not a half-baked belief nor a half-convincing certainty. It is a fully consummated belief which entertains no doubt. It is not linked with the world; it is linked with *Akāl Purakh,*

[1] So many endure distress and deprivation,
Even these are Your gifts O Giver Lord.—*Jap(u)*, p. 5

the 'Timeless Person'. It testifies our theism and the assurance of protection of God. When conviction sprouts, ego begins to vanish.[2]

Those devoid of conviction smoulder in the fire of evil.[3]

Those who have conviction of the Lord are designated as *gurmukh*; those devoid of it are termed *manmukh*. It is the Guru who awakens true conviction in us.[4]

The Guru's testimony kindles divine light in our hearts.[5]

Hence, the Sikh has conviction in the testimony of the Guru.[6]

This conviction does not relate to the person of the Guru but to his Word:

> Everyone in the world beholds the Guru,
> Liberation isn't attained by merely seeing him;
> It comes by contemplating his Word.
> —*Vār Vaḍhaṅs* m 4 sl m 3, p. 594

Confidence in the Guru is actually confidence in God. God has installed Himself in the Guru who out of his Divine experience, creates *gurbāṇī*, the holy Word.

In the *ardās*, the supplication for conviction stands on the one hand for our confidence in God, longing that it remains steadfast, and on the other, that our deeds are accepted as worthwhile.

[2]When conviction of Your Presence sprouted in my heart,
My egoistic intellect was simply driven out.
—*Mārū* m 5, p. 1072

[3]The heart devoid of conviction of God's Presence
O brother, shall simply burn.
—*Soraṭh* m 5, p. 640

[4]Says Nānak, the true conviction comes from the Gurū.
—*Gauṛī* m 5, p. 284

[5]Enlightenment occurs through the Guru's testimony.
—*Dhanāsrī* m 1, p. 13

[6]The perfect Guru has given me conviction.
—*Gauṛī* m 5, p. 18

CHAPTER 48

The Gift of Trust

The term *bharosā* is derived from Sanskrit *bhadra āshā* meaning 'good hope'. We trust one who can promise us good hope. *Bharosā*, thus, means Trust. If trust is injured, apprehensions emerge. One knows that every worldly trust is unreliable. Truly reliable Trust is one that relies on God Almighty. This is the only Trust that the Guru advises us to rely on.

I've seen that no relationship is truly worthy of trust,
So, Lord, I have grasped the hem of Your robe.
—*Vār Rāmkalī* m 5, p. 963

Bharosā has many synonyms in *gurbāṇī*[1] and each of these appears very many times. That alone testifies to its importance in the life of a Sikh.

'Trust' has a reciprocal relationship with 'patronage' known as *khasmānā* in *gurbāṇī*. It is the powerful patronage of our Lord that generates the feeling of immense trust in us; our trust, in return, invites for us the Lord's patronage. This reciprocity is the foundation of spiritual life.

How does our trust in God arise? When do we begin to rely entirely on Him? When our powers fail, our wisdom puts its hands up, our cleverness admits defeat, things go wrong, everything appears lost and the feelings of utter helplessness well up in us. It is then that we cry out:

I am an orphan—pray, put me up with You!
—*Gauṛī Pūrbī* m 5, p. 204

Him alone can we trust[2] who will stand by us under all circumstances. Apart from this nothing endures, when nothing endures, nothing is really trustworthy. One cannot trust one's

[1]These synonyms include *bharvāsā, āsrā, tek, ādhār, ot, panāh, takīa,* etc.
[2]One who stands by you at all times.—*Bhairoṅ* m 3, p. 1129

wealth, one's property, one's relations, even one's own body.[3] Then what in this world is trustworthy? It is God only. None else[4] but the Almighty Lord. It is His strong arms that generate such unfailing trust in us.[5]

Placing trust on one who is incompetent, is bound to disappoint us. Our trust breaks and we feel hurt. All kinds of apprehensions surge up. Yet, are we not accustomed to trusting the incompetent? It is no wonder that anxieties and regrets don't leave us. If we trust the Lord Almighty, our concerns and apprehensions will vanish. He has immence concern for us.[6] That is what generates our trust in Him.

One who reposes his trust in the Lord, does his work, takes all the necessary steps, but does not feel anxious about the outcome because he relies on the Lord. That is how he remains at peace.

> I took all measures, gathered all devices, and left all concerns
> Trusting in the Lord,
> It has begun to set my home and all my undertakings right.
> —*Malār* m 5, p. 1266

A Sūfī story has an interesting bearing on trust in God:

Bū Alī Qalandar gave up all his belongings except a bucket and a long piece of string and went away to the forest for meditation. He spent years there contemplating on the Lord. One day, he felt thirsty and was looking for water when he saw a deer drinking water at a pool a short distance away. He walked thither. As he approached, the deer galloped away, but the water of the pool sank as if it wasn't a pool but was actually a well. Seeing that happen, Bū Alī beat his brow and lamented, 'O God, all these years I have been contemplating on You, yet this deer was dearer to You. When the deer came, the water was up, when I came, it

[3]The body of which you are so proud does not belong to you.
Nor do power, property and wealth;
Your offspring, spouse and siblings are not yours,
Close friends and even parents are not yours.
Gold, silver and wealth are not yours,
Your Steeds and elephants are of no use.—*Gaurī* m 5, p. 187

[4]Only the One Lord is our comrade, no one else!—*Jaitsarī* m 5, p. 704

[5]Mighty Arms alone generate strong trust.—*DG: Bacitra Nāṭak* 1.92

[6]Says Nanak, have no concern; He has concern for us all.—*Vār Rāmkalī* m 3 sl. m 2, p. 955

sank into a well.' It is said that a voice then came from on high, 'Bū Alī! this deer had nothing else to rely upon; it placed its entire trust in me. You have the string and the bucket. Why not lower your bucket and draw out as much water as you require?'

This story has a lesson. God even looks after those of His creatures whom He has not endowed with much resource. However, He expects those whom He has provided with much resource to make use of it.[7]

Trust in God does not mean that we discard our resources. On the contrary, we must understand that even these have been provided us by God. According to *gurmat,* one must utilize one's resources fully but not rely on them entirely. Reliance must still be placed on God. Resources are useful, but they become useless without the grace of God.

To supplicate God for the gift of 'trust' means that we rely on Him. It also means that we must also be trustworthy, That can be possible only if we have known how trust is generated.

[7] However, Bū Alī did not draw this lesson. On the contrary, he threw away his bucket and the string and reposed his entire trust in God. However, in Islam (as in Sikhism) it is considered advisable to make use of resources also. It is said, once a Sahābī went to meet Prophet Mohammad. As he kissed the prophet's feet, Mohammad enquired of him, 'Where have you left your dromedary?' he replied, 'I have left her outside on God's trust.' The Prophet said, 'Go and tether your dromedary first and then leave it on God's trust.'—*Tarmāzī,* referred by Manhājulslāhīn, Bairut, p. 246

CHAPTER 49

Nām the Gift Above All Other Gifts

Bhāī Gurdās, narrating the story of Bābā Guru Nānak, says:

> The Bābā was decorated in *Sach Khanḍ*[1]
> with the nine treasures of *Nām* and humility.
> —Bhāī Gurdās, *Vār* 1.24

The Bābā then came back to the world to distribute the wealth of *Nām* to one and all. For twenty-seven years of his life he observed severe austerity. This was the austerity of *simran* (remembering the Lord). Even before these austerities, he first received the Lord's grace:

> At first the Bābā received Grace from the Lord's door,
> Thereafter did he engage in his spiritual efforts.
> —Bhāī Gurdās, *Vār* 1.24

The Divine Grace came first, and the effort of *Nām simran* followed later. *Nām*, therefore, is an undoubted Divine gift.

Having received this gift, the Guru went out, distributing it to everyone.[2]

Nām has been qualified in *gurbāṇī* as *nidhān*, that is a treasure. All worldly treasures are expendable, only the treasure of *Nām* is not.[3] All other treasures can be priced. *Nām* only is price-

[1] *Sach Khanḍ*, literally, 'the Realm of Truth', in Sikh theology, is the celestial abode of God.

[2] That teacher is *gurmukh* who imparts wisdom to his pupils:
'Contemplates the *Nām*, gathers it well, and earns profit in the world.
On the True tablet, writes with a pure heart and reads the true word.'
Says Nānak, he alone is a learned scholar who ministers the *Nām* of God. —*Rāmkalī* m 1, p. 938

[3] *Nām* is an unexpendable treasure received through good luck.
—*Srīrāg* m 3, p. 29

less.[4] No other gift equals it.[5] That is why it has been designated as 'the gift above all other gifts'. Guru Arjan Dev himself supplicates for it:

> Give me the gift of Your *Nām* through Your Grace
> So that I forget You not even for a moment.
> —*Sūhī* m 5, p. 784

It is *Nām* that provides comprehensive support to man. Through it, your tasks are accomplished, your mind gets regulated, sins are removed, fear and anxiety disappear, the cycle of birth and death ceases, and in the Court of the Lord your head shall be high with pride. Thus, it is *Nām* that protects you here as well as in the hereafter. Indeed, there is no greater gift than *Nām.*

In *gurbāṇī*, *Nām* is everything; and everything is from *Nām.* There is no difference between the Name (*Nām*) and the named.[6] Whoever receives His *Nām*, and dwells on it, attains God.[7] In this Dark Age, *Nām* is the medium for man's deliverance.

> In the *Kaliyug, Nām* is supreme;
> Through it the devotee attains deliverance.
> —*Mārū* m 4, p. 995

It is natural that it has been considered 'the gift above all gifts'.

What is *Nām*? It is hard to describe, but the following is an event from Guru Nānak's life:

A *fakīr* called Miāñ Miṭhā of Mithankoṭ once asked the Guru, 'What is *Nām*?' The Guru replied, 'Who has ever found its worth? It is not a thing that can be known through intellect, it can only be experienced.' The Miāñ then said, 'Pray Sir, introduce me to this mystery.' Then the Bābā said, 'Miāñ, do you hear any sound?' 'No!' replied the Miāñ. Then the Guru held his arm and asked, 'Do you now hear any sound?' 'O my Lord!' said Miāṅ, 'I experience

[4] *Nām* is a priceless entity. Only a *gurmukh* receives it.—*Āsā* m 2, p. 425
[5] There is no other gift as valuable as *Nām* . . . —*Vār Sūhī* m 3, p. 787
[6] See no difference between the Name and the Named.
For in the resplendence of His Name is the splendour of God.
—Khwājā Muīn-ud-Dīn Cishtī
[7] Whoever from his heart has accepted *Nām,*
He alone, says Nānak, knows the immaculate Lord.—*Gauṛī* m 5, p. 281

waves of *Nām* in every pore of my being.' Ineffable *Nām* is thus an awful experience.

Nām has been considered supreme in many creeds[8] and is the mainstay of everyone in all the three worlds.[9] The entire universe is the expanse of *Nām*. Devoid of *Nām*, there is nothing whatever.[10]

The nameless Almighty became *Nām* before he created the universe:

> He created Himself, He created His *Nām*,
> In the second place, He shaped Nature,
> Then he took His seat and saw His Creation with pleasure.
> —*Vār Āsā* m 1, p. 463

It appears that *Nām* is the creatively throbbing (*sphur*) state of *Brahm*—between His *nirguṇ* (unattributed) and *saguṇ* (attributed) states. The entire Creation was present as a creative intent in *Brahm*, but his *māyā* had not yet come into action. *Brahm* was still *Niraṅkār* (formless). That was *Nām*. From it emerged the entire Creation.[11]

Nām alone supports the entire universe: worlds, regions, skies and netherworlds:

> The *Nām* is the Support of all creatures.
> The *Nām* is the Support of the earth and the solar system.
> The *Nām* is the Support of the Simritis, the Vedas and the Purāṇas.
> The *Nām* is the Support by which we hear intuitively and meditate.
> The *Nām* supports the celestial ethers and the Nether regions.
> The *Nām* is the Support of all forms.
> The *Nām* supports all settlements and abodes.
> Associating with the *Nām*, and hearing it with ears, men attain deliverance. —*Sukhmanī* Gauṛī m 5, p. 284

[8]The essence of all creeds is only the *Nām*.—*Gauṛī* m 5, p. 281

[9]The True Name of the Creator is my festive dish of rice balls on a leafy plate.
Here and hereafter, in the past and the future, this is my support.
—*Āsā* m 1, p. 358.

[10]All that has been created is the manifestation of Your *Nām*.
Without Your *Nām*, there is no place whatever. —*Jap(u)*, p. 4

[11]From *Nām* everything came into being.—*Sūhī* m 3, p. 753.

We can only contemplate *Nām,* but even that is not possible without His Grace. An individual can only contemplate *Nām* if the Lord is pleased.[12] *Simran* of *Nām* is, indeed, great benediction. It is appropriate therefore, to pray for it:

> A supplicant supplicates only for Your *Nām.*
>
> —*Kaliāṇ* m 5, p. 1321

[12] They alone remember Him whom He Himself inspires.

—*Gauṛī* m 5, p. 263.

CHAPTER 50

A Dip in the Pool of Immortality

'Amritsar' literally means 'the Pool of Immortality'. Its location was established by Guru Rām Dās. Around it arose the town Rām Dās Pur, which after the name of the pool, later came to be known as Amritsar. It became the supreme religious centre of the Sikhs. There we have *Harmaṅdar*, the capital of *pīrī* (spiritual authority), and *Akāl Takht*, the capital of *mīrī* (temporal authority).

According to an oral tradition, the foundation of the Harmaṅdar Sāhib was laid by the Muslim Sūfī *fakīr* Mīān Mīr at the request of Guru Arjan Dev. This *maṅdar* (temple) houses the Holy Book, *Srī Guru Graṅth Sāhib* that preserves the spiritual heritage of five centuries (from the birth of Jai Dev in 1171 through to the demise of Guru Tegh Bahādur in 1675) and contains the works of the Sikh Gurus alongside that of many Hindu and Muslim holy men This pluralism is the first message of the Harmaṅdar.

God is not the exclusive reserve of any one religion. He belongs to entire mankind. That is the motto of this temple. It has four doors, one on each of its sides. This signifies that anyone from any quarter is welcome to the temple without any discrimination of caste, creed, class, colour, race or domicile.

Here, day and night, flow the currents of *kīrtan* (devotional singing), *simran* (chanting the Name of God), *ardās* (prayer) and *sevā* (devotional service) in the setting of the *saṅgat* (holy congregation). Live faith is at work at all hours here. At this temple, crowds flock and receive Divine benediction. Intention here is blessed and desires fulfilled.

Opposite Harmaṅdar Sāhib stands *Akāl Takht*, the centre of the temporal authority of the *Khālsā*. The *Sarbat Khālsā*, a representative body of the entire *Khālsā* have, from time to time, held their sessions here and passed *gurmattās* (resolutions) of import. From this seat of authority, *hukamnāmās* (epistles of command) have been issued to congregations located elsewhere.

The sacred 'pool of immortality', *Amritsar*, surrounds the Harmaṅdar. Here, earth, water and heaven comingle peacefully. Everyday, many pilgrims take a dip in the sacred pool and refresh their faith.

Surrounding the pool is the circumambulatory path (*parikarmā*) where, all the time, pilgrims can be seen moving along with faith in their hearts, the Lord's *Nām* on their lips and *prasād* (consecrated food) in their hands. During the appointed hours, *caukīs*[1] may be seen marching in the *parikarmā.*

Around the *parikarmā* are the *buṅgās* (hospices). These are centres of Sikh religious missions as well as official quarters of Sikh *misls* (principalities). From the *Jhaṅḍā Buṅgā,* two flags, one of *pīrī* and the other of *mīrī,* can be seen fluttering.

On one side behind the *buṅgās* is the Guru's free kitchen along with the attached dining hall. *Laṅgar* is prepared and served for all the 24 hours everyday and night. Here more than a hundred thousand visitors partake of food gratis everyday. In this way, the Guru's grace rains down unceasingly here.

The city of Amritsar is the religious centre for the Sikhs and many other major communities. In the city are many *gurdwārās*—outstanding among which are Bābā Aṭal, Guru ke Mehal, Qilla Lohgaṛh, Gurdwārā Maī Kaulāṅ, Gurdwārā Shahīd Gaṅj, Gurdwārā Khushāl Siṅgh Nihaṅg, and Burj Akāli Phūlā Siṅgh. Yet, in the old city alone there are sixty-nine *thākurdwārās* (Hindu temples). Even to this day, the city has nineteen *shivālās* (temples of Shiva). There are twelve *akhāṛās* (cloisters) of *udāsī mahātmās.* There are also six mosques, the first of which was ordered to be erected by Guru Arjan Dev.

Ten *taquiās* (hermitages) of Muslim *fakīrs* are extant even to this day. At one time, there were three hundred pools and ponds and around three hundred large and small wells in the city, many of which are still in use despite municipal water supply having replaced many of them. So many ponds, pools and wells give an idea of how many individuals must be taking their bath every morning. The *buṅgās* and *dharamshālās* indicate how many pilgrims must have been visiting and staying there. The *akhāṛās*

[1] For a description of *caukīs* see the next chapter.

of *Nirmalās*, the *ḍerās* of *Sevāpanthīs*, the *ṭikāṇās* of *Addaṇshāhīs, shivālās, ṭhākurdwārās*, mosques, *taquīās* and *gurdwārās* tell us what a large number of people worship and pray daily. All of these religious places functioned as schools and training centres of religious learning. These centres produced *giānīs* of *gurbāṇī*, teachers of the six schools of Indian philosophy, scholars of Vedic lore and expositors of the Holy Quran. Thus, the city has been a comprehensive religious centre.

Twice a year, a fair is held here. The fair of Baisākhī was introduced by Guru Arjan Dev and of Dīvālī by Bābā Buḍḍhā. A dip in the 'pool of immortality' and devotional attendance at Harmaṅdar Sāhib at least once annually is considered obligatory by all Sikhs.

The importance of Amritsar—particularly of Harmaṅdar Sāhib and *Akāl Ta<u>kh</u>t*—grew so great for the Sikhs that adversaries of the *Paṅth* several times in history tried to take possession of these or to raze them to the ground.

During the time of the Gurus, Prithī Caṅd and his descendants had wrested possession of the Harmaṅdar Sāhib; so much so that when, in 1669, Guru Te<u>gh</u> Bahādur came to pay a visit there, the doors of Harmaṅdar Sāhib were closed on him. He made his obeisance from outside and returned.

In AD 1740, the Sikhs of Bīkanīr received the heart-rending information that Massā Raṅghaṛ had at that time wrested the possession of Harmaṅdar Sāhib and was putting its premises to all kinds of immoral use. Incited, a Sikh Mehtāb Siṅgh, along with a companion journeyed to Amritsar, and brought back Massā's slain head and presented it to the congregation in Bīkānīr.

In AD 1762, Ahmad Shāh Abdālī, during his invasion of India, ordered genocide of the Sikhs before advancing further. Thousands of Sikhs were killed. The Sikhs remember it as their *ghalūghārā* (great holocaust). During his return, he ordered the twin buildings of Harmaṅdar Sāhib and *Akāl Ta<u>kh</u>t* to be destroyed. As soon as Abdālī left, the Sikhs began to reconstruct these pilgrim spots of theirs. On Dīvālī of the same year, a congregation of *Sarbat <u>Kh</u>ālsā* was convened over the debris of the *Akāl Ta<u>kh</u>t*. Abdālī, who was still in Lahore, sent an emissary to offer peace. The offer was summarily rejected by the Sikhs.

Abdālī returned but the Sikhs fought him so vigorously that he was forced to retreat. To avenge his defeat, he returned again in AD 1764. On that day, only thirty Sikhs were present in the precincts of Harmaṅdar Sāhib when he mounted his attack. They fought bravely and embraced martyrdom while inflicting great damage to the invading forces. The two holy centres were again ordered to be blown up. However, while the Harmaṅdar Sāhib was being demolished with gun-powder, a brick hurtled out and hit the Durrānī's nose. The wound that it caused never healed and eventually in 1769 caused his death.[2]

During the days of Farrukh Saīyar and Mīr Mannū, when a bounty had been assigned for bringing a slain Sikh head, the Sikhs would come out of their hiding places at night and, evading all vigil, take a quick dip in the holy pool and retreat into hiding. Many times, they lost their lives, yet they were not willing to give up their right to visit Harmaṅdar Sāhib and take a dip in the *sarovar*.

It appears, whenever an invader or a ruler decided to undermine the collective strength of the Sikhs, he first attacked Harmaṅdar Sāhib and *Akāl Takht*, then persecuted devoted Sikhs and finally sought to undermine Sikh doctrines and symbols. However, history stands as evidence that during every such holocaust, the *Paṅth* emerged stronger.

Many Sikhs believe that Massa Ranghar, Ahmad Shah Abdali and Indira Gandhi met a violent end because they had desecrated these holy places.

Many times, governments banned visits to these holy places, but it naturally only sharpened the Sikhs' desire to visit them, a desire that naturally came to be incorporated into their *ardās*.

[2]The Sikhs since then have believed that this would be the end of those who desecrate these holy places. In fact, Durrānī made one more attack on India in 1767, but did not touch these holy places.

CHAPTER 51

Long Live Choirs, Banners and Hospices

A line in the *ardās* yearns for eternal life for the traditional institutions and symbols of the Sikhs. That line is:

Caukīāṅ, jhaṅḍe, buṅge jugo jug aṭal.

CAUKĪĀṄ

The term *caukī* means 'vigilant watch'—actually, a group of four watchmen as is suggested by the following lines of *gurbāṇī*:

> The Word of the Guru's *Shabad* is my safety.
> It is a *caukī* (vigilant watch) on all four sides around me.
> —*Soraṭh* m 5, p. 626

In the Sikh faith, whether one is attacked from without or from within, it is considered essential to invoke vigil of the divine Word. Hence, our *caukīs* are *caukīs* of the holy Word.

In an implied sense, it means pilgrim-parties singing holy hymns to alert us to dangers from within and without. Such a *caukī* is a *bhajan maṅḍlī* (choir) circumambulating the *sarovar* (pool) singing hymns.[1]

Caukīs are of three types: (i) *caukīs* of *Nitnem*, (ii) historical *caukīs* and (iii) pilgrim *caukīs*.

There are five *caukīs* of *Nitnem:*

1. *Caukī* of *Āsā-dī-Vār*—sung early morning.
2. *Caukī* of *Bilāval*—at sunrise.
3. *Caukī* of *Caran Kaṅwal*—about four hours after sunrise.
4. *Caukī* of *Sodar*—just after sunset.
5. *Caukī* of *Kaliāṇ*—when the night has advanced an hour and a half.

[1]A group of four *rāgīs* is also called a *caukī*.

HISTORICAL *CAUKĪS*

Historical *caukīs* are linked with historical events: Once, Guru Hargobiṅd went to villlage Daraulī to meet some of his Sikhs but stayed longer than expected. The congregation at Amritsar began to miss him. They persuaded Bābā Buḍḍhā to petition the Guru to come back soon. In reply, the Guru wrote, 'I shall return as soon as my work here is done. Until then, you and the congregation may sing the Gurus hymns. That shall protect you here as well as hereafter.' The Bābā read out that command to the *saṅgat.* The same evening, the congregation re-assembled and walked behind the holy standard singing *kīrtan.* Since then, that *caukī* has been mounting everyday.

Likewise, when Guru Hargobiṅd was interned in the Gwalior Fort, groups of Sikhs under the leadership of Bābā Buḍḍhā flocked towards Gwalior in the form of *caukīs.* In front was always the Sikh flag symbolizing freedom. It was accompanied by two torches symbolically inviting the monarch to see light. These *caukīs* moved from village to village doing nothing but singing *kīrtan* and arousing feelings of indignation among the people. Arriving in Gwalior, the *caukīs* went around the wall of the fort and upon reaching the place behind which the Guru had been incarcerated, they would make tearful obeisance. This went on relentlessly everyday till the Emperor Jahāṅgīr felt impelled to order that the Guru be released. The Guru, however, would not agree to be freed until the fifty-two princes who were also incarcerated in the fort were also released. The Guru thus became their *baṅdī-choṛ* (the deliverer). The Guru returned to *Akāl Takht* and blessed the tradition of *caukī,* saying, 'Whenever, in order to protest against tyranny and injustice, my Sikhs revive this tradition of *caukī,* I shall spiritually be with them.'

PILGRIM *CAUKĪS*

On specified days, these *caukīs* set out for the pilgrimage of specific holy places. For example, on the day of every new moon, a *caukī* sets out from Amritsar to Taran Tāran, and on every 5th of a lunar month from Taran Tāran to Goiṅdvāl.

Supplicating for the perpetual continuation of *caukīs* in the *ardās* signifies asking for protection from external and internal dangers.

JHAṄḌE (THE FLAGS)

A belief prevails among many Sikhs that the Sikh flag as we know it today came into vogue during the time of Guru Hargobiṅd representing *mīrī*. However, there is indication that a flag of *pīrī* had been in use before that. Bhaṭṭ Kalashār records the following about Guru Amar Dās:

> Whose patience planted His white banner
> that fluttered since time immemorial on the bridge of heaven.
> —*Savaīye* m 3, p. 1392

There is an apparent indication in this verse that during the time of Guru Amar Dās, a white flag flew in Goiṅdvāl. Some scholars hold that on this white flag was inscribed ੧ੴ (One *Oaṅkār*). That seems to have been the flag of the spiritual kingdom that Guru Nānak had started.[2]

It appears that after the martyrdom of Guru Arjan Dev, the flag became saffron in colour and on its banner were inscribed two *kirpāns*—of *mīrī* and *pīrī.* This Akālī flag was first flown at the *Akāl Ta<u>kh</u>t* in 1609 during the time of Guru Hargobiṅd. After that, this flag became part of the Sikh tradition. During the time of Guru Tegh Bahādur, whenever a mission was established, the Guru furnished it with an ox, the book and the flag.

Guru Gobiṅd Siṅgh gave God the name 'Flag of Dharma'—thus he consecrated the flag and even deified it.[3]

The flag, also known as *Nishān Sāhib* was flown in front of the *Akāl Ta<u>kh</u>t* in 1609. It was flown in front of Harmaṅdar Sāhib during the time of Bhaṅgī Misl by Jathedār Jhaṅḍā Siṅgh.

In 1775, two *udāsī sādhus,* Bāvā Saṅtokh Dās and Bāvā Prītam Dās, set-up two flags at the site of *Jhaṅḍā Buṅgā*—one pertaining

[2]Nānak established the true fortress of his kingdom on the strongest foundations.—*Savaīye* 5, p. 966

[3]Guru Gobiṅd Siṅgh himself would circumambulate this flag. Orthodox Sikhs when they visit a *gurdwārā* first bow before *Gurū Graṅth Sāhib* as well as circumambulate it, and then do the same with the *Nishān Sāhib.*

to the Harmaṅdar Sāhib and the other to the *Akāl Ta<u>kh</u>t*. In 1881, the flags were uprooted due to a strong windstorm. Then Mahārājā Sher Siṅgh got one very high and firm *Nishān Sāhib* installed there and another one, by its side, was installed by Desā Siṅgh Majīṭhīā.

At the *Jhaṅḍā Buṅgā*, in front of the *Akāl Ta<u>kh</u>t*, both these flags still flutter. One of them is that of *pīrī* and the other of *mīrī*.[4] However, the two later got tethered together with the following symbol:

The *cakra* (circle) between the two *kirpāns* stands for *Brahm Cakra*, the Circle of the Absolute. It also symbolizes universal equanimity. The two *kirpāns* surrounding it represent *pīrī* and *mīrī*. The *khaṅḍā* (double-edged sword) in the middle symbolizes Divine Justice.[5]

Records indicate that during the second Battle of Ānaṅdpur, Bhāī Ālā Siṅgh was the standard-bearer. He was surrounded by the enemy who challenged him,

'Drop your flag or else . . .'.
'This flag is dearer to me than my life; I shall not let it go!'
'But how, if we cut-off your hands?'
'Should that happen perchance, I will hold it with my feet.'
'Then your feet will be slashed away.'

---

[4] The *Nishān Sāhib* of *pīrī* is considered higher than that of *mīrī*. Although *pīrī* and *mīrī* go together in Sikhism, precedence rests with *pīrī*.

[5] Many *Nihaṅgs* decorate their *domālā* (high turban) with this symbol carved in steel. During the time of the Sikh *misls* (principalities) wearing this symbol on the turban had become a prevalent practice with the Sikhs.

'I will then hold it with my teeth.'
'What are you going to do if your head is also chopped off ?'
'My duty stays so long as I am alive. If you cut-off my head, then he whose flag it is shall himself take it over.'

The Mughal commander became so disturbed by this reply that he disregarded the tradition of sparing the standard-bearer and attacked him with his sword, chopping off his head. It is said that before the flag could fall down, Bābā Ajīt Siṅgh jumped in and took over the flag, simultaneously putting the *faujdār* to death.

Such then is the spirit behind praying for it in the *ardās.* It is a prayer for its eternal survival.

BUṄGĀS

Buṅgā (Persian: *Buṅgāh* = shelter) connotes a living quarter. A secondary meaning is 'an institution'. In the Sikh parlance, *buṅgās* are living quarters attached to *gurdwārās* where arrangements exist for the stay of pilgrims; or they may be institutions that have been set-up to impart instructions for the upkeep of the religio-cultural traditions of the Sikhs.

In Amritsar, the Sikh cultural centre, six types of *Buṅgās* had been established. These were:

1. *Buṅgās* of *Giānīs* that had been set-up for the study of *gurbāṇī.* Arrangement had been made in these for the training of *graṅthīs* so that well-trained scholars with high moral character could be produced.
2. *Buṅgās* of *rāgīs* in which training in *kīrtan* was provided.
3. *Buṅgās* of *Akālīs,* wherein martial training in weaponry, etc., was provided.
4. Sectarian *buṅgās* established by such sects as *Nirmalās* and *Udāsīs.*
5. *Buṅgās* of *sardārs* set-up by chiefs of *misls* and other eminent *sardārs,* where visitors from their respective native territory could come and stay.
6. Religio-political *buṅgās* that included *Akāl Buṅgā, Jhaṅḍā Buṅgā, Kothaṛī Sāhib* and *Buṅgā Dukh Bhaṅjanī.*

These *buṅgās* made considerable contribution to the literary, cultural and educational life of the community. Most of these were established between 1765 and 1833. The Report of Srī Darbār Sāhib mentions eighty-four original *buṅgās*. Some of these merged, some disappeared due to neglect and the remaining ones, barring one, were purchased and dismantled by the Shiromani Gurdwara Prabandhak Committee in order to broaden the *parikarmā* (circumambulatory path) around the *sarovar*. The only exceptions were the *Akhāṛā Brahm Būṭā* of the *udāsīs* and the *Buṅgā Rāmgaṛhīān*. The former was destroyed during the pogrom of 1984. Hence the only *buṇgā* that survives today is the latter.

However, no alternate arrangement has yet been made to preserve the useful activities of the institutions that had been going on there. The plea for the perpetuation of *buṅgās* in the *ardās* is a plea for such institutions to survive/be revived.

CHAPTER 52

Hail Righteousness

In the *ardās,* supplication is made for the Sikh way of life, disciplined conduct and character, gifts of spiritual wisdom, conviction of faith, steadfast trust and the highest gift, that is, *Nām.* All these are sought so that there is *dharma kā jaikār,* i.e. righteousness be hailed.

What does *dharma kā jaikār* signify? Guru Gobiṅd Siṅgh declared that the motive of his coming to this world was *dharma chalāvan* (ensuring perpetuation of righteousness). It has two complementary aspects: *saṅt ubāran* (supporting the virtuous) and *dushṭ upāran* (uprooting the wicked).[1] That means hailing righteousness.

Gurbāṇī says that terrorizing others is atrocious but letting anyone terrorize you is cowardice.[2] For the Sikh, both are taboo. Valour without enmity is the Sikh creed. *Dharma kā jaikār* is the yearning for the victory of such *dharma.*

The above slogan is a declared resolve that righteousness shall not submit before any worldly power. A Sikh must uphold the flag of righteousness at all cost. This ideal he will cherish and make effort to realize it. In this struggle, he will 'assure his victory without any doubt'.[3] He does not look for material victory; but wants moral victory. If his faith remains unshaken until his last breath, and he has been able to defend his ideals, he has been victorious, even though victory may have cost him his life. That is *dharma kā jaikār.* That is *Wāheguru jī kī Fateh,* the Lord's victory.[4]

[1] *DG: Bacitra Nāṭak* 6.43.

[2] He who frightens none, nor lets anyone frighten him,
such a one, says Nānak, is an enlightened person.
—*Slok* m 9, p. 1427

[3] I should have no fear of the foe;
When engaged in a battle, convincingly turn victory to my side.
—*DG: Krishnāvtār* 231.1

[4] Nānak proclaims victory of the Lord .—*Bilāval* m 5, p. 829

Victory is not annexing territory or treasures but upholding *dharma* (righteousness). Even a political defeat may be a victory of righteousness. The Sikhs and their Gurus established this in their history. Gurū Gobiṅd Siṅgh lost his father, his four sons, his home and hearth and endured insufferable hardships; yet, even in that utterly deprived state, his moral victory was absolutely patent. His letter to the tyrant Emperor Auraṅgzeb, *Zafarnāmāh* (Epistle of Victory) stands testimony to this.

Dharma is not any particular creed. In reality, there is only one faith.

> There is only one *dharma*—holding fast to Truth.
>
> —*Basaṅt* m 1, p. 1188

Letting Truth percolate into one's life makes it real living.

Religion should be a part of life and not apart from it. The principle that *dharma* is cherished as the highest value in life is *dharma kā jaikār*. Sikh religion not only links man with God, it also links man with man. From this point of view, *dharma kā jaikār* is a declaration of blessing for the entire mankind.

Dharma kā jaikār is negating *adharma* (faithlessness), repudiating bigotry, discarding superstition, rejecting pretense, eschewing formalism, condemning invidious distinctions and nepotism and denouncing ritualism. In short, it is discarding all useless adnexa that often beset religion. It is declaring unblemished victory for Truth, i.e. *Wāhaguru jī kī Fateh.*

Dharma kā jaikār also means discharging the duty of the *jaikārā* (the martial cry): *Bole so Nihāl, Sat Srī Akāl.* This *jaikārā* has two connotations: the first is that 'whoever utters the Name of the Lord (the Eternal One) will be blessed with happiness', and the second is that 'wherever and whenever someone utters a call (for help), the *Khālsā* will come to his rescue'. Thus, it is a vow, and this vow is taken with a loud voice.

The slogan, *dharma kā jaikār* stands for religious tolerance, protection of the faithful and fighting to the end to defend these ideals.

Dharma kā jaikār is thus a phrase pregnant with multiple of nuances.

CHAPTER 53

Humble Mind and High Thinking

Our mundane mind (*man*) links us with the outside world through our sense organs and operates upon the environment through the organs of action. Evolved out of five elements,[1] our mind receives its light from *ātmā* (the Real Self). In fact, *man* is the product of coming together of conscious *ātmā* and the material body.

Haumai (the ego) stands at centre of man. It links all of our activity with 'I'. It exclaims 'I saw', 'I thought', 'I understood', 'I decided', 'I took action', 'I achieved', etc. Whatever *man* thinks, yearns for, does or achieves is for the sake of the 'I'. This kind of thinking is *ahaṅmat* (egoistic intellection).

Inflated *haumai* becomes *ahaṅkār* (arrogance). An arrogant mind accepts no advice, becomes morally polluted and deteriorates. But if it mellows and practises humility, it opens its doors to good counsel from all quarters. It receives the precepts of the Guru and so sublimates its intellect and refines its actions. Then what happens is:

> One has intellect, but practices innocence,
> One has power but appears feeble,
> One has little, yet shares with others,
> How rare is such a devotee !
>
> —*Slok* Kabīr, p. 1384

In the Guru's house whoever humbles himself ranks high.[2] The meek are blessed. They receive spiritual joy. The proud only rot in their pride.[3] The humble win, the arrogant lose.

[1]The *man* is born of the elements five.—*Āsā* m 1, p. 417
These five elements are: earth, water, air, fire and space.

[2]One who considers himself low, shall be ranked as the highest.
—*Sukhmanī*, *Gauṛī* m 5, p. 266

[3]Happy are the meek, their self they have tamed.
The arrogant rot in their arrogance.—*Gauṛī* m 5, p. 278

In humility, heaven itself pervades. That is why a humble mind has celestial fragrance. In humility shines divine light, and a humble heart is ever resplendent. Its faith remains ever fresh.

However, one must beware of false humility. One may give up worldly pride but exchange that for the pride of his piety. Such humility would be counterfeit and hypocritical. It is demonstrative and aims only at enhancing one's personal image in the eyes of others. At times, even feelings of guilt may get transformed into a show of excessive (hypocritical) humility.[4]

HIGH THINKING

The counsel of the mundane mind (*man*) is egoistic; hence it is mean, unsteady and unclean. It thinks low. Contrasted with it is high thinking that provides both sublime and profound counsel. It is called *bibek* (discriminating wisdom). The Guru's counsel is such counsel *par excellence.*

The egoistic counsel is worldly wise, but the Guru's counsel is heavenly wise. The former entrenches us in *dhāt* (worldly rat race) characterized by covetousness and envy, while the latter drenches us with *liv* (loving contemplation).

High thinking is not attained by scholarly pursuits nor through logical argumentation. It comes through faith, trust and love. It blossoms through divine grace.

Unless constantly protected by divine grace, even a sublime intellect might sink and become egoistic, infirm and unreliable. Hence, even high thinking and sublime intellect must seek divine protection.

[4]Like the deer-hunter, the guilty bow twice as low.—*Vār Āsā* m 1, p. 470

CHAPTER 54

From Which the *Panth* has been Separated

The life of Punjab centres around the memory of the Gurus. 'Punjab survives by the Gurus' name', said Pūran Singh. This holy land, however, was bifurcated in AD 1947 when the predominantly Muslim Pakistan separated from the predominantly Hindu India. The Sikhs, relying on promises given by Mahatma Gandhi and Jawaharlal Nehru, decided to side with the Hindu India. So, they were forcibly thrown by Muslims out of Pakistan. With that, the political misfortune of the Sikhs set in. The promises they had been given were meant to be forgotten. That undermined the desire of an independent entity of that simple nation. The grief of this tragedy was enormous but an even greater tragedy was the one for having been deprived of free access to their holy places that were located in the land from which they had been exiled. There were many *gurdwārās* of historical importance there.

GURDWĀRĀS IN NANKĀṆĀ SĀHIB

These holy places of which the Sikhs were deprived include the birthplace of Guru Nānak, from whom the town itself derives its name. The residents of that town still hold Guru Nānak as the owner of the land there and themselves as his lessees.

During Guru Nānak's time, Rāe Bulār was the chief of that town. His descendants who still live there continue to look after the Nānak's lands with great reverence.

Every Sikh longs to pay a visit now and then to that holy place. But they are no longer in a position to look after even their founder Guru's birthplace.

Besides it, there are several other shrines in Nankāṇā Sāhib that have been consecrated by the Guru's touch. These include: Gurdwārā Bāl Līlā, where the Guru used to play with his peers during his childhood; Gurdwārā Paṭṭī Sāhib, the school where the

Guru learnt his alphabet and wrote his *paṭṭī* (tablet); Gurdwārā Māljī Sāhib where he grazed his cattle; Gurdwārā Kiārā Sāhib, where the Guru blessed the ruined harvest back to lush life; Gurdwārā Sachā Saudā, where the Guru fed hungry *sādhus* and considered this a profitable bargain; and Gurdwārā Tambū Sāhib where the Guru, during his childhood, hid himself fearing his father's wrath.

During the early twentieth century, the management of these *gurdwārās* was wrested from the hands of a corrupt *mahaṅt*, Naraiṇ Dās, at the cost of several Sikh lives who participated in the agitation. The memory of how they were tied to trees and set on fire still haunts the Sikhs.

PAṄJĀ SĀHIB

Apart from Nankāṇā Sāhib, several other holy places had been lost to the Sikhs. Prominent among these is Paṅjā Sāhib where Guru Nānak demolished the arrogance of Valī Qaṅdhārī who declined to let Mardānā, the Guru's companion, take water from his spring. The other spring that the Guru opened for Mardānā is still alive.

GURDWĀRĀS IN LĀHORE

Ḍerā Sāhib, where Guru Arjan Dev was martyred is an important *gurdwārā* there. It used to be thronged by Sikhs everyday. It was left in Lahore, where also stands Shahīd Gaṅj that commemorates several martyrs who gave up their lives for the sake of their faith in Mīr Mannū's captivity. There Sikh women, children and even infants also suffered indescribable torture.

The other *gurdwārās* in Lahore are the birthplace of Guru Rām Dās in Cūnā Maṅḍī, *gurdwārā* commemorating Guru Hargobiṅd in Mozang, and the martyrdom site of Bhāī Tārū Siṅgh, who was descalped.

NON-HISTORIC *GURDWĀRĀS*

Apart from the above-mentioned important historic *gurdwārās* there were thousands of other *gurdwārās* of which the *Paṅth* has been deprived.

The intolerable pain that this deprivation produced resulted in the issuance of a *hukamnāmā* fom the *Akāl Takht* advising the Sikhs wherever they may be to include the following prayer in their daily congregational *ardās:*

O Supreme Giver, who has always taken care of the *Khālsā Panth*, pray, grant the boon to the *Khālsā Panth* of having free access to, and to take care of Nankāṇā Sāhib and other *gurdwārās* from which the *Panth* has been deprived.

This prayerful plea has since been repeated in our congregational *ardās* daily in all *gurdwārās.*

CHAPTER 55

The Will of the Lord Prevails

The *ardās* is the entreaty of humankind before God. In it functions Divine Will and Divine Power. Man is an utter weakling[1] incapable of accomplishing anything on his own.

All that happens, and all that will happen, is by His Will.
If we could do anything by ourselves, we would.
By ourselves, we can do nothing.
As it pleases the Lord, us He keeps.
My Dear Lord, everything is in Your power.
We have no power to do anything.
Grant us to live by Your Pleasure.

—*Sūhī* m 4, p. 736

Man is unwilling to acknowledge his weakness. He cannot give up his cleverness and presumes that nothing would happen if he did not put in his effort. He believes that only he causes whatever happens. He does not consider anyone more powerful than himself. Yet, the Guru has a different advice to offer:

One may call oneself a hero,
But without God's Power what can he do?
—*Gauṛī* m 5, p. 282

The power of God prevails in every way. He alone is Omnipotent; He can wield every power, every art, all devices and all prowess. He works in innumerable ways.[2]

He created the entire universe, put heaven in its place, created fire and concealed it in firewood. He arranged for all beings their fare even before He created them. He can create as well as destroy, and His Power alone can protect us, sustain us and help

[1] What is the human being? What power has he?
—*Gauṛī Guārerī* m 5, p. 178

[2] The Lord of the universe plays in a million ways.
—*Bhairoṅ* Kabīr, p. 1163.

us whenever we are in need.[3] If He were to imbue even an ant with His power, it would be able to vanquish even the mightiest of armies.[4] Interestingly, His power works secretly. His art is artless. It is not artificial; it is real, effortless and spontaneous. It requires no technology to make it function. It has been invoked under the name *Bhagautī* in the beginning of the *ardās*. Its assistance has also been invoked in the middle of the *ardās*. Towards the end of the *ardās* it is invoked as *kalā*. This *kalā* is the power of *dharma* that binds the whole of universe in its control.[5] Through this power, the creator has hypnotized the whole universe.[6]

No one can block this power, interfere with it or eradicate it.[7] Every faculty of ours, physical, mental or intellectual rests on God's *Dharma Kalā* (Power of *Dharma*). Upon it rests all dignity and honour.[8] Let us keep it in mind that in our mortal life we

> Do not play such a game,
> that we come to grief in the Court of God.
> —*Vār Āsā* m 1, p. 469

We must admit that 'the Lord's Will prevails', for in His Will lies the happiness and well-being of all.

Through the *ardās* we acknowledge this Power believing that in reliance on it lies our protection. Praying for it, we confess our helplessness and yearn the help we need from the Omnipotent Lord.

[3]He created His power and infused it into the earth.
He suspends the heavens from the feet of His Command.
The Lord who created fire and locked it into firewood,
He protects all, O Brother.
He gives no punishment to any of His creatures.
Himself the all-powerful Creator, He is the Cause of causes.
In an instant, He can establish and disestablish;
He alone is your help and support. —*Mārū* m 5, p. 1071

[4]Should He infuse His Power into a tiny ant;
It would reduce the armies of millions to ashes.
—*Sukhmanī, Gauṛī* m 5, p. 285

[5]This is Lord's Power of the *Dharma* that firmly binds the Creation.
—*Āsā* m 5, p. 396

[6]Manifesting His power, He ensnares the entire world.
—*Sukhmanī, Gauṛī* m 5, p. 287

[7] God's craft cannot be erased.—*Bhairoṅ* Kabīr, p. 1159

[8]The five bulls (the senses) drag the wagon of the body around.
By the Lord's power, one's honour is preserved.—*Rāmkalī* m 1, p. 879

CHAPTER 56

Through *Nām* is Attained Resplendent Spirit

Caṛhdī kalā is a difficult term to translate. It has many layers of meanings. Though we have tentatively translated it as 'Resplendent Spirit' which is possibly its closest connotation, its other nuances will emerge as we proceed in our discussion.

The hermeneutical lexicon of *Srī Gurū Granth Sāhib* (*nirukt*) explains *caṛhdī kalā* as follows:

> *Caṛhdī kalā* is an unblemished state of mind which denotes high spirits characteristic of the Sikh faith. In it, there is relentless festivity, inspired cheerfulness and exultation before which every bit of sinfulness, wickedness, oppression and brutality simply disappear. It cannot see anyone alone in suffering and is ever inspired for the well-being of all. This is what *Nām* does. This kind of state is not possible to attain with words alone, one has to mould one's actions accordingly. One has to let it be witnessed in one's field of action; so that the world can see how in the dark night the resplendent spirit of *Nām* spreads the radiance of its luminosity. It also progresses to fructify as the welfare of all.

Caṛhdī kalā is the sublime state of consciousness in which there is boundless joy. Fear and animosity are entirely absent, and self-respect and reliance on oneself sprout effortlessly. In this state of mind, one perceives comfort even in suffering. Such confidence stands out in relief when it is put to trial. The unwilting spirit of the *K͟hālsā* during genocidal vicissitudes that beset them is ample proof of their *caṛhdī kalā*.

Caṛhdi kalā does not depend on circumstances; rather, it challenges circumstance. Smiling patience and genial contentment shape its countenance and add sparkle to its spirit. The future finds it in tremendously joyful readiness and sublime inspiration[1] to

[1] Look ahead; turn not your face backwards.
Settle your account this time, lest you be born again.
—*Vār Mārū Dakhṇe* m 5, p. 1096

act. Even when abandoned by everyone, its courage and forbearance abandons no one. True confidence, not mere hope, is its citadel. Even in worldly defeat, it feels crowned with moral victory and reckons no obstacle as insurmountable. Remaining entirely undisturbed, it makes short work of obstacles and stays in rare steadiness. The future does not slip out of its hands, nor does it pass into the hands of adversaries. Jesting with life, it colours the future with his own favourite hues. It does not get dejected over the cowardice of comrades. This it always overlooks and is always ready to forgive. It even jests with death, because one who practices it believes that

> I shall not die, though the rest of the world dies,
> for now I have met the life-giving Lord.
> —*Gauṛī Guāreṛī* Kabīr, p. 325

It is a carefree state, indifferent to deprivation of all kinds, and unaffected by hardship and suffering. In it one is continually ready to fight for a righteous cause. Courage, valour, enthusiasm and joy throb in one's breast. Ardour, delight and perennial afflorescence deck one's brow.

How is the state of *caṛhdi kalā* achieved? It is the achievement of the rare individuals who perpetually rely on the Lord.

> Many speak and talk about God.
> Very rare is the humble servant
> who understands the essence of (true) Yoga.
> He has no pain—but is at peace.
> He beholds only the One (Lord).
> He sees no evil—for him all is good.
> Never suffers he defeat—he is ever victorious.
> He suffers no sorrow, is always happy;
> He neither discards nor does he grasp.
> Says Nānak, such a servant is the Lord himself,
> He neither comes, nor ever does he depart.
> —*Kānṛā* m 5, p. 1302

There is no room in *caṛhdi kalā* for any feeling of inferiority. It is resplendent with unlimited joy. Grief and sorrow have no place in it.

> Where there is infinite joy; no sorrow or duality.
> With that home the Guru has blessed Nānak.
> —*Gauṛī* m 5, p. 186

It is a state of 'truth, beauty and eternal joy'.[2]

The only person that can achieve such a celestial state of mind is a person imbued with the mellifluous *Nām*. Internal beauty, internal joy and internal state of *caṛhdī kalā* all derive support from *Nām*—from the Truth of *Nām, Satnām!*

> If I am blessed with the *Nām*, says Nānak,
> I really live, and my body and mind blossom forth.
> —*Mundāvṇī* m 5, p. 1429

The life of Guru Arjan Dev is a wonderful example of *caṛhdī kalā*. Earlier also we have noted that a time came in his life when Prithī Caṅd, with the help of his paid agents, had blocked all the ways and thus succeeded in enticing pilgrims away from Guru Arjan Dev. As a result the congregation with him thinned down, and the offering was so diminished that all the provisions got depleted and the Gurus' *laṅgar* became *mastānā* (depleted). Indeed, the Guru and his wife had to eat three-day stale food. Even in that state, the Guru was singing:

> With only dry crusts of bread, and a hard floor to sleep on,
> O sisters, I live happily with my Beloved.
> —*Kanṛā* m 5, p. 1306

This very Guru, while sitting on a red hot iron plate, was singing:

> Whatever You do, seems so sweet to me,
> Nānak begs only for the treasure of Your *Nām*.
> —*Āsā* m 5, p. 394

One who can consider adversity as God's gift is one whose soul is drenched in *Nām* of the Lord and is perpetually in a state of *caṛhdī kalā*. His morale never sinks. Who can conquer him or frighten him[3] when his morale does not droop? Examples of such *caṛhdī kalā* may be identified in the lives of many Sikhs. In December 1710, an imperial edict was issued by the Mughal government of Delhi that, 'Wherever worshippers of Nānak are

[2] *Jap(u)*, p. 4.

[3] My mind was not shaken; why should my body be afraid?
My consciousness remained fixed on the Lord's Lotus Feet
—*Bhairoṅ* Kabīr, p. 1162

found, they be sentenced to death'.[4] This order was in force for the next fifty years, and Sikhs spied anywhere were executed. At home, the Mughal government was their enemy, and from abroad, Ahmad Shāh Abdālī was mounting invasion after invasion on Puṅjāb. Under such unfortunate circumstances, survivors were in exile. In the eyes of the rulers, they were 'terrorists', so they were blown up to pieces. Their heads strung on spears were carried as exhibits. Those who survived hid in forests tormented by hunger and thirst for days. Even then, they called themselves the 'pampered army of the Lord' and were in the state of *caṛhdī kalā.* One who went hungry described himself as 'mad with prosperity'. Death was considered an *expedition* to the next world. While onions were called 'silver pieces', rupees were called 'pebbles'. If they had only parched grams to eat, they would declare, 'we are eating almonds'. A blind man was referred to as *sūrmā* (a brave warrior). A deaf one was referred to as a 'resident of the upper storey'. Such phrases testified to their *caṛhdī kalā.* For the officials of the rulers, they had coined despicable names. A cock was 'Qāzī' and a dog was 'Qutab-ud-dīn'. A police officer was called a 'donkey'. For them, these officials meant trifles or even less. These are only a few examples out of a vast vocabulary reflecting their *caṛhdī kalā.*

When Nādir Shāh came to Lahore, he asked Zakarīā K͟hān, the governor of Puṅjāb, 'Who are these people who have been shattering my defenses repeatedly? Let me know where they live so that I can exterminate their tribe completely.' Zakarīā answered, 'What should I tell you about them? They live in deep forests. Their homes are the saddles of their horses. They have a very unusual way of living. Their vocabulary is equally unusual.' Then he gave Nādir some examples of what he called 'their slang'.[5] Hearing all that, Nādir remarked *azīṅ qoum būe salltnat mī āmad* (I smell the prospect of a kingdom for this tribe).

Their high spirit of *caṛhdi kalā* was based on their dedication to *Nām.* Even while shifting their abodes in the jungles, they would carry with them a volume of *Guru Graṅth Sāhib.* Wherever they had a couple of peaceful days, they would try to complete a full

[4] *Akhbār Darbār-e-muallā.*

[5] Some examples have already been discussed earlier.

recitation of the holy book by relay reading. From that started the tradition of *akhaṅḍ pāṭh* (uninterrupted reading of the holy book). Even while astride their horses, they chanted the *Nām* with every breath they took. Bringing the fearless Lord to their minds, they rose above fear and terror of all kinds. Thus undaunted, they continually stayed in high spirit. They would joke with their own selves, make fun of their sufferings. They finally, kept their date with the Lord, 'mounting an expedition' to the other world:

> During their lifetime, they served the Lord,
> and while departing,
> kept Him enshrined in their heart.
> —*Mārū* m 5, p. 1000

CHAPTER 57

May all Prosper by Your Grace

'May all prosper by your grace' is the concluding line of the *ardās* in which universal benevolence affirms itself along with self-surrender to the Lord's Will as also to His grace. Both these go together in a mystical relationship. If we surrender ourselves before His Will, then it becomes natural to pray for 'well-being of all', because that inheres in His Will. It is on this count that *ardās* in its climax, spontaneously begins to sense that

> Whatever pleases You is good;
> True is the Pleasure of Your Will.
> —*Vār Gauṛī* m 5, p. 318

In His Will rests His Grace, full of love for His Creation. His eternal pleasure lies in the salvation of all.

True Love never breaks; throughout the ages, it remains steady.[1] Enshrining His Will into one's heart is an essential mode of Sikh worship.[2] When one begins to enjoy the *ras* (the relish) of the Lord's pleasure, then duality disappears, doubts and delusions vanish and one feels affinity for one and all.[3] Thus springs up the faith that:

> We have One Father; we all are His children,
> (and O Master) You are our Guru.[4]

His Pleasure, His Command and His Will are three aspects

[1]Whatever pleases You is good, O Beloved; Eternal is Your benevolence.
—*Birhaṛe Āsā* m 5, p. 432.

[2]Whatever pleases the True Lord is devotional worship;
His Will abides in the mind. —*Rāmkalī* m 3, p. 910

[3]Those who experienced the essence of God's Will
Their doubt vanishes from within.
O Nānak, know Him as the True Guru, who unites all with the Lord.
—*Srīrāg* m 1, p. 72

[4]*Soraṭh* m 5, p. 611.

of the same celestial Truth. His Pleasure is His delight; when it awakens, it becomes His Will, and when His Will comes into action Command follows. Thus, His Command is the embodiment of His Pleasure. His *Razā* (Pleasure) has twin connotations—on the one hand it signifies His assent, on the other it signifies His gladness. Hence, obediently carrying out His commands is tantamount to receiving His delightful benevolence. Thus one recognizes His Will while carrying out His Command. One then realizes that

> His Command pervades everywhere,
> and all come together under His Command.
> —*Basant* m 1, p. 1188

His *Hukam* (Command) is His pervasive discipline; the entire universe is in whose control.[5] *Hukam* is not different from His *Bhāṇā* (Pleasure).[6] The same Truth is being described from two different angles. From the Divine point of view it is His pleasure (*Bhāṇā*); from the point of view of the creation, it is Command (*Hukam*). These terms connote the different hues of the primordial consciousness. Inherent within it is the well-being and welfare of all. To surrender before Divine *Bhāṇā* is to hold the hem of His pleasure and to take it as our guide. One who accepts the Lord's Will cannot think of asserting his own petty will.[7] The disappearance of one's egoistical will denotes the summit of the *ardās.* In that state, one comes to identify with the Lord's Will so that one becomes that Will. It is then, that one can see none as alien or as an adversary.[8] He sees the entire universe populated with his own kin. The desire of the welfare of all spontaneously wells up from within him and cries out:

[5] The entire creation is strung on Your thread.
—*Sukhmanī, Gauṛī* m 5, p. 268

[6] The Hukam is the pleasure of Your Will.
To say anything else is far beyond anyone's reach.
—*Srīrāg* m 1, p. 17

[7] The river flows in whatever direction the Lord orders.
—*Slok* Farīd, p. 1382

[8] No one is my enemy, and no one is a stranger.
I get along well with everyone.
—*Kanṛā* m 5, p. 1299

In Your Mercy Lord, You take care of all Your creatures.
—*Vār Sāraṅg* m 4 *slok* m 5, p. 1251

When such a prayer emerges out of a devoted soul, one says:

The Great Giver heard my prayer, and comforted the world.
—*Vār Sāraṅg* m 5, p. 1251

The summit of the *ardās* is that one prays for the whole world and says:

The world is ablaze— shower it with Your Mercy, Lord!
Save it, through whichever portal You may!
—*Vār Bilāval* m 3, p. 853

How can one, who has become one with the Lord's Will, be an exclusivist? If one sincerely prays for the welfare of all, such a prayer is instantly accepted. Then, one can perceive the Merciful Lord's benevolence showering on all.

The Creator Lord issued His Command and the beautiful clouds began to rain.
Grain was produced in abundance; the world got cooled and comforted.
The mind and body got rejuvenated, in remembrance of the Inaccessible and Infinite Lord.
O True Creator Lord, pray, shower Your Mercy on us.
Do Whatever pleases You,
Nānak is ever a sacrifice unto You.
—*Vār Sāraṅg* m 5, p. 1251

When one who utters such an *ardās* finds it accepted before it was even uttered, how may he desist from feeling like sacrificing himself unto the Lord? When anyone makes such an *ardās* and bows before the Lord, before he raises his head, he finds

Look in whichever direction I may, Lord,
I find only You present there.
—*Vār Sāraṅg* m 4 *slok* m 1, p. 84

That is the climax of the *ardās*!

CHAPTER 58

The Traditional Way of Performing *Ardās*

According to the Sikh *maryādā* (the prescribed code), anyone may pray at any time anywhere. For performing the *ardās,* no priest is required. When it comes to communicating with your Lord and confiding in Him the longings of your soul, it is your own inviolable privilege and no intermediary is required for it. However, one also has the privilege of praying on behalf of others. In a congregation, anyone with the consent of the others may step forward and perform the *ardās* on their behalf. In fact, the Gurus have, for all times, freed their Sikhs from dependence on the priestly class.

If *Guru Granth Sāhib* is in session, the *ardās* must be said facing it. Otherwise, one may say the *ardās* facing any direction. The rest of the congregation also faces the holy book generally standing behind the *ardāsīā* or on the flanks.

Traditionally, the *ardās* is said in a standing posture with folded hands and complete concentration of the mind. If our attention is not there but we are standing with folded hands, the Guru would not approve of it; the same way he did not approve the *namāz* of the Qāzī whose mind was not in the prayer but had asked the Guru to join him. That is why while performing *ardās* the *ardāsīā* time and again invites us to 'say *Wāheguru* with full attention'. On five different occasions in the *ardās* this *jaikārā* (slogan) is raised and every individual in the congregation is supposed to respond to it by saying *Wāheguru* in a loud tone.

We have already affirmed that the *ardās* is the *bāṇī* (holy composition) of the *Guru Khālsā*. It can also be considered the national anthem of the *Khālsā*. It also inspires us to perpetuate our national traditions and institutions. It links us with 'the *Khālsā jī* wherever they are'. It also unites us with the entire humankind. Hence, it deserves our rapt attention.

While the *ardās* is being performed at the conclusion of a service in a *gurdwārā*, the entire *saṅgat* (congregation) remains standing. Even the person sitting in attendance on *Srī Guru Granth Sāhib* also stands up. Before starting the *ardās*, the following verse of *gurbāṇī* is recited by the entire congregation together:

> You, our Lord; to You, we pray.
> Body and soul are the gifts You gave.
> Parent You are; we Your offspring.
> On Your Grace, rests our well-being.
> No one knows Your extent, Lord.
> Master of Destiny, sublime You are,
> Strung on Your thread is existence all.
> Mortals ever obey your call.
> You only know Your limit, Your state
> Unto You is a sacrifice, Nānak Your slave.[1]

When the *ardās* is performed on behalf of the whole congregation, naturally the entire congregation stands. When, however, the *ardās* is performed on behalf of a single devotee or a group of devotees for their specified purpose, only the concerned individuals along with the *ardāsīā* stand while the rest of the congregation keeps sitting. On occasions such as name-giving, engagement, marriage, confession of having transgressed a taboo or seeking forgiveness for a wrong deed, only the concerned individual(s) would stand.

At the conclusion of the *ardās*, 'after the welfare of all' has been invoked, the concerned party or the entire *saṅgat*, as the case may be, bows low to touch the ground with their forehead. Then they return to the standing posture and loudly pronounce *Wāheguru jī kā Khālsā Wāheguru jī kī Fateh!* After that, the *saṅgat* chants a few traditionally chanted couplets. These couplets are not out of *gurbāṇī*, but have received general concurrence of the *Panth*. These are followed by the *jaikārā: Bole so Nihāl* to which the *saṅgat* responds by saying *Sat Srī Akāl* in a loud tone.

It is improper to add unapproved expressions of any type in the *ardās*. Such expressions as the invocation 'Bāī Vārs and Chaubīs Avatārs' or 'Chitra Gupt' or 'all sāhibzādas' are such

[1] *Sukhmanī, Gauṛī* m 5, p. 268.

objectionable expressions. Happily, these are fast disappearing.

By any account, the congregational *ardās* of the Sikhs has a beautiful literary form. Its diction has been chiselled by those who were spiritually advanced devotees and had mastery over folk expressions. Any expressions that were below par went out of vogue over time. What has been preserved is simply exquisite. Every phrase does not only effectively fit in its place, but also has appropriate cadence. Therefore, any perverse or profane addition to its perfect and sacred form would be sacrilegious. Shiromani Gurdwara Prabandhak Committee has accepted a form which has received considerable popularity with the Sikh congregations. That is the most suitable version to adopt because it has received wide concurrence of the *Panth.*

PART III

PRACTICE OF *ARDĀS*

CHAPTER 59

Ardās: Personal and Congregational

The *ardās* about which we have had an extensive discussion so far is our congregational *ardās*—the common prayer of the entire *Panth.* When a single person uses its text to say his prayer, he does so on behalf of the entire *Panth.* Even if he adds his personal supplications in it, he still says a joint *ardās.*

More often, however, we would long to talk to our God privately in the solitude of our soul. We might like to reveal our heart to Him, talk to Him about our sufferings and our joys, or invite Him into our own life. That would be our personal *ardās.*

Personal prayer has its own special significance and its own spiritual *ras* (relish). Whenever the fountain of faith springs up from a soul, it longs to speed Godward and waves of prayer emerge from within it spontaneously. Such personal prayer cannot arise without belief in the presence of God. Personal prayer may, at times, take us straight to the core of the mystical experience. Through its power, our soul may abide directly in the heart of Supreme Truth. Personal prayer can let us bathe in the pool of divine mystery.

Such prayer is generally speechless. If any words are employed, they merely attempt to harmonize our physical apparatus with that prayer. Such harmony cannot be attained through untrue words and insincere expressions. The words employed may be entirely our own or picked up from *gurbāṇī* due to their concurrence with our feelings. Their spontaneity and sincerity testify to their truth.

Gurbāṇī is by and large a continual *ardās.* Whatever we long to say we can find its expression in *gurbāṇī* in the most appropriate form. If we desire to supplicate God for anything—comforts, happiness, prosperity, success, benediction or salvation—*gurbāṇī* has prayers befitting the need. It offers prayers also for spiritual effort, *simran* and *sevā*. *Gurbāṇī* also incorporates prayers for the gift of *Wāheguru's Nām*, a glimpse of His visage, a longing for meeting Him and pangs of separation from Him. It has songs of laudation and hymns of thankfulness. It has invocations for His mercy and grace, benevolence and forgiveness.

Gurbāṇī reflects man's unworthiness and God's sublime worthiness; man's filthiness and God's holiness; man's ungratefulness and God's forgiveness; man's surrender before Him and God's loving protection. In it, there can be the experience of God's cosmic pervasiveness, His presence close at hand and the recognition of Him within one's bosom.

It contains supplication for protection from sins, removal of doubts and freedom from ignorance. In it, there is petition for the ability to accept God's Will; also for sublime wisdom and enlightenment of the mind. There is no mental state for which appropriate expression in *gurbāṇī* is not available. When lovers of *gurbāṇī* prepare for prayer, verses from *gurbāṇī* spontaneously emerge from their lips representing their inner intent.

If behind verbal expression there is attentive disposition and brimming love, then He to whom the prayer is addressed easily comes to be known.[1] With this, a change takes place in one's life. If, when we rise from the *ardās*, we find ourselves improved, this is evidence of *ardās* having been heard. *Ardās* inspires us to good action. A prayer that concludes without a vow for doing some good, has not been perfected yet.

Through prayer, we invite God's grace to bless our actions. He is always prepared to forgive us, but we have to have the longing to be forgiven. He remains ready to reveal Himself, but it is we who have to turn our face toward Him.

The emotive aspect of the *ardās* is a mix of gratitude, reverence and awe. Gratitude is not merely for His gifts and continual sustenance that He provides us, but also for His mystery and His transcendent love. Reverence is caused by the spontaneous feeling of one's triviality in front of His sacred presence. Awe is caused

[1] When there is focus in meditation, God comes to be known therein;
The *Gurmukh* tells this untellable tale. —*Rāmkalī*, m 1, p. 879

by having come into the grip of a sublime greatness that creates pleasant vibrations through one's being.

Close attentivity is essential while saying our *ardās*. While praying, we ought to be aware of the transcendent Power that surrounds and supports us. We should also feel the same Power inside ourselves. *Ardās* is the recognition at once of that great Power as also of our self-surrender before it. It is presenting ourselves and our honest feelings and yearnings unto Him and seeking to be under His benevolent eye. It is a servile request before Him to grant us His protection.

In prayer we must not try to settle accounts with our Master. How can we be forgiven on the basis of accounts? Let us give up accounting and declare bankruptcy. When we are left with nothing, we have the right to beg. However, we only get the right to beg, not the right to His Love because of our sins. Yet, He loves us, forgives us and showers His largesse on us. We, ungrateful ones, never even thank Him. He still loves us, the ungrateful ones.

Ardās, even if performed only for one's own welfare, is auspicious; if it is for someone else, it is more auspicious; if it is for the *Panth*, then it is still more auspicious; if it is for the whole mankind, it is most auspicious. If we pray for ourselves, it ought to be in utter humility; if it is for someone else, it should be flooded with love. When we pray for the whole *Panth*, we lovingly yearn for the welfare of the entire *gurmukh* fraternity and seek protection and favour for every member thereof. When we pray for all mankind, we long to see a profound spiritual atmosphere pervading everyone and everywhere. God's grace rains down so generously that all the souls are drenched with it and the entire universe becomes an extended heaven.

CHAPTER 60

Psychological Difficulties

Everyone has the right to pray, but few are attracted to it. This in part is because of the psychological difficulties that arise from attitudes that weaken our prayers. They prevent the prayer from having its full effect. One thus tends to turn away from prayer itself not realizing that our own mind is deceiving us. We need to know what these impediments are and take care of them so that our prayers may fructify.

DISBELIEF AND LACK OF FAITH

Lack of faith is one of the major hindrances to prayer. How can prayer take place if one doesn't have faith? An individual without faith cannot turn his face towards God; how can he pray? If perchance he does, he makes only empty pleas, because faith is absent.

Faith has suffered a great setback in the present age. Man is unwilling to accept anything on pure belief. Rationalism has taken the place of faith. Science has become man's God. He does not realize, however, that the realm of science is different from the realm of religion. There is no real conflict between them; there is only an assumed one. While science has hitherto sworn by the methods of objective absolutism and experimentation, religion employs faith and trust. If objective knowledge and logical analysis are the instruments of science, introspection and mystical experience are the tools of religion. Their realms are distinct—just as the realms of the eye and the ear are different. For the ear, the world of vision is a myth, and for the eye, the realm of sound is fabulous. How can one indict the other? In fact, just as one needs both eyes and ears to enjoy the comprehensive mystery around us, one needs both scientific and spiritual knowledge to appreciate the fulsome mystery of life. Unfortunately, in the present age, only materialistic values are being accepted, and faith has been pushed into an eclipse. Modern man has lost his faith but has not been able to shed his credibility. He appears to be hung like *trishaṅku* between heaven and earth. In his confusion, he looks for a substitute for religion. This is because having discarded religion, he finds a vacuum in his life. Marxism, humanism and scientism appear to be some of his attempts to find such a substitute. However, they neither provide the warmth nor the spiritual experience of religion. That is why they have not been able to replace religion; they have only enhanced disbelief.

Many people think that religion can be dispensed with. They think that instead of uniting mankind, it has divided them into conflicting factions. That has resulted in such atrocious hostilities as pogroms, genocides and crusades. They consider religion to be a danger for mankind. This also has undermined faith.

The above are the outstanding reasons for the decline of faith. Some people hold that a 'philosophy of life' may be able to replace religion, but no philosophy of any kind has been able to satisfy mankind.

The truth is that man is still groping for faith. This has rendered him incapable of repairing his life with the help of prayer. For faith, one has to pray, and for prayer, one has to beg. The misfortune is that man today is unable to do that. Thus, he has entangled himself in his own net.

Recently, two things have happened. One, nuclear science—especially that of sub-atomic particles—has cast doubt on the objectivity of science. Two, religious scholars have begun to understand that the claim of exclusivism by any religion is untenable. The combined effect of these two developments is likely to regenerate faith even though it may not sustain the extant religions. For prayer, faith is required, not necessarily an organized religion.

DOUBT

Doubt is a state of mental uncertainty. When we can't decide between real and unreal, we are in doubt. Doubt muddles us and makes it hard for us to turn to prayer.

A doubting mind may sometimes turn to prayer when it finds no other remedy, but even then its belief remains divided. It might say something like this,

O God, I have never seen you. I have only heard about you from some orthodox people. However, I am in great trouble, and my intellect has found no solution. So God, if you really exist, please come to my help. Still, I doubt if you really exist; if you do, pray help me. I am not sure that you even have the power to solve my problems, but since I don't find any other way, I have turned to you. Maybe my prayer helps.

How can this type of doubt be dispelled? Doubt dissolves through the grace of the Guru who tells us:

> The soul is polluted by doubt; how can it be cleansed?
> Wash your mind by attaching it to the *Shabad* (Word)
> and keep your consciousness focused on the Lord.
> —*Anand, Rāmkalī* m 3, p. 919

The state of *sahaj*[1] can only be attained through the Guru's grace. Grace alone dispels doubt and skepticism: Says Nānak,

> By the Guru's Grace, is *sahaj* attained, and doubt dispelled.
> —*Anand, Rāmkalī* m 3, p. 919

DISAPPOINTMENT

Disappointment arises if we suffer misfortune, failure, loss, obstacles or misery. If one is not careful, on such occasions one can easily lose hope, become thankless and quarrel with God.

As long as God fulfils our desires, we are happy with Him, but should He not do so, we call Him unjust and even cruel. It is important to know that both pleasure and pain are important for the moral control of the individual. Pain may be even more important than pleasure since suffering strengthens moral discipline. It teaches us what not to do. However, we generally consider prayer as petition for happiness only. If we feel pain, we get ready to sue God. However,

> None can command the Lord; one may only offer prayers.
> —*Vār Āsā* m 2, p. 474

[1] *Sahaj* is the state of perfect peace and equanimity. It is without any tension and hurry; the state of liberation and bliss.

However, in our helplessness, we may lose our balance and, like spoilt children, say unkind things to God.

Our major disappointments arise when we think that our prayers have not been heard. This might lead to unbelief. Instead, if we reflect on why our prayers have not been answered, we might gain moral benefit. It is possible that through analysis we might notice moral weaknesses in our prayers. We might even be able to see that we prayed without faith, that our prayers were entirely selfish or that we intended to deprive someone else of his right. Discovering such moral infirmities in ourselves serves to reform our intent and unite us to the real motive of the *ardās,* and thus strengthen our prayers.

Maybe we were unsure of the real motive of our prayer, and so we feel that it was not heard. Maybe our prayers were inimical to attaining better spiritual heights.

It is also possible that we have not learned how to pray. The purpose of *ardās* is not to provide God with a list of our needs. He knows our needs already. The real purpose of *ardās* is to open our bosom unto our God. If we have not bared our feelings before Him, we have not prayed at all. That is why we were disappointed.

At times of loss of hope, we must invoke help from our God. Hope on others will only yield despair.[2] At such times of despair we need to try praying with greater mindfulness and bare all our feelings before God. We should then invite His infiniteness into our finitude and wait to see what miracle happens.

[2] Says Kabīr, place your hope only in the Lord,
Other hopes lead but to despair.—*Slok* Kabīr, p. 1369

CHAPTER 61

Philosophical Problems

A seeker might face some philosophical questions during the practice of prayer. We consider some of these:

1. *If the experience of prayer is not amenable to intellect, how can it be proven?*

Human intellect can only analyse and distinguish relationships based on sensory data. That is the field in which it functions. It is of use to us only in carrying out our day-to-day, mundane activities. It has no place in the supernatural realm. Only spiritual experience reigns there.

An example makes this point clear. Eyes are required to see colour. A blind man simply cannot. Should he ask, 'What is the proof of what you call colour?' You are likely to say, 'One needs eyes to see colour.' Likewise, spiritual experience is required to perceive noumena. A blind man is likely to accept the evidence of those with eyes, but intellect hesitates accepting the evidence of those who have had spiritual experience. That is because intellect has the delusion not only of being self-illumined, but also of being omnipotent. Regarding colours, the blind man may argue, 'If I have four sense organs, others may be having a fifth one.' But, intellect cannot accept any other source of knowledge apart from itself because that would threaten its belief of self-illumination and omnipotence.

There is another aspect to consider. The congenitally blind who have never experienced colour do not find it easy to accept the presence of colour. Even if they do, they cannot understand to what use it can be put. They may say. 'All right, there might be colour, but what is the point of dyeing your garments in it?' The same way, those who have never had any spiritual experience might accept the evidence of those who have had it but would not be able to understand its utility in life. Only the people who have dyed their cloak understand the beauty, fullness and pleasure colour imparts to life. Likewise, those who have dyed their soul with spiritual experience are likely to say:

> O dear, those whose cloaks are dyed crimson,
> their Husband Lord is always with them.
> Bless me with the dust of their feet; this is my prayer.
> —*Tilaṅg* m 1, p. 722

2. *If God knows everything, what is the use of praying ?*

The real purpose of *ardās* is not telling God our needs and asking Him for gifts. He knows our needs without us begging for them.

> When He knows everything without being told,
> Unto whom should we offer our *ardās* ?
> —*Slok* m 3, p. 1420

He squanders His gifts on us without being asked. Good people as well as evil; the just as well as the unjust, all receive His concern. He does not wait for our prayers but showers His Love unconditionally. Those who do not pray for his gifts still receive them.

The real purpose of the *ardās* is not to beg but to attain proximity to our Lord. Prayer is the means of baring our heart before Him. When we tell Him our needs, it is not to give Him suggestions for His gifts, but only to find an occasion to talk to Him. Such an occasion arises out of our needs and our powerlessness. By making use of such occasions for initiating a dialogue with God, we can attain nearness to Him.

3. *If Divine Will cannot be changed, how then can* ardās *alter it?*

On the one hand it is said that everything can be attained by prayer; on the other, it is affirmed that everything is happening as per unchangeable Divine Will. How can these contradictory proclamations be reconciled? We have to first understand what 'Divine Will' is and then to see what relation it has with prayer.

Everything was created through 'Divine Will'—the entire universe, its mysteries, time and space, all the creatures, everything God has both created the entire creation and pervades it. As per His Will, actions good and bad come to be. According to the kind of his actions, man transmigrates from one living body to another. Pleasure and pain have been created by Him in order to enforce His discipline. Bondage and liberation are also under His Will.

> As long as man does not understand His Will,
> he remains miserable.
> Meeting the Guru, he comes to recognize His Will,
> and then becomes happy.
>
> —*Asā kāfi* m 5, p. 400

Ardās is not meant to transgress or alter His Will. It is an attempt to understand it by discarding one's own cleverness and submitting to the Lord's Will.

> I offer my mind and body and soul to You;
> Keep me as it pleases You, Lord; this is my *ardās.*
>
> —*Prabhātī* m 1, p. 1345

Ardās, then, is not an attempt to persuade God to modify His Will, but to harmonize oneself with Him and to sing His glory.

4. *If one can obtain what one desires through prayer, then what is the purpose of effort?*

Prayer is misunderstood by some as a substitute for effort. Their prayer means something like this, 'Even though You have given me hands and feet, I don't want to use them. I am too lazy. Please do my work and save me from putting in my effort.' They are pleased to waste the gifts that God has given them already and expect further gifts from Him because they are lazy. Do they deserve them?

If we do not take care of the health of the body that God has given us, we are ungrateful. If we do not put the intellect given by Him to proper use, we are answerable. If our sense organs are allowed by us to rust, we owe Him an explanation. When we do not put to use the valuable gifts He has given us already, do we deserve to ask for more?

In Sikhism, one is required to earn a living by honest effort.

In this faith, the practice of serving others logically follows the practice of the presence of God. Hands that have never served others, the Guru considered them filthy.

Effort is required even for praying. How, then, can prayer be opposed to effort? Only fools believe that *ardās* is a magic button, by pushing which God's Power becomes available to do our tasks. Prayer is not a substitute for effort but is in addition to it. Putting in due effort shows that one is making adequate use of Divine gifts. After we have done that, we earn the right to request for more. Effort is the essential beginning. One who hasn't begun cannot expect to move further. If we have made a faithful effort, we can ask God to lend it His grace and make it fructify.

5. *If one has to reap the fruit of one's actions, then what is the use of prayer?*

According to Sikh thought, God is the basic cause of all action. It is He who engages all living beings in their pursuits. *Karma* is, therefore, ordained by God and is not the handicraft of human beings. Man engages himself in whatever is ordained by God. However, an ego-ridden man considers himself to be the doer.

Actions good and bad, God Himself has created
The beast, in egoism, ascribes them to himself;
O Nānak, without the Lord, what can anyone do?
—*Bāvan Akhrī, Gauṛī* m 5, p. 251

Even though God has created good and bad actions Himself, He has to some extent given man the freedom to make his choice out of them. Man's accountability does not exceed the limits of that choice. God has vested in man the power to discriminate between good and bad.[1] It is on account of this choice that man is considered responsible, and so answerable, for his *karma*. He cannot project this (limited) responsibility on God.

Why do you slander the Lord, O you ignorant foolish woman?.
Good and bad actions are your own (responsibility).
—*Dhanāsrī, Trilochan*, p. 895

[1]The Lord Himself dispenses the sense of distinction between dirty and clean deeds.—*Sūhī* m 1, p. 730

That is why we will be judged according to our actions.

A question now arises: If man is really free, then what do the scriptural verses such as the following mean?

> God Himself gets good and bad actions done.
> The Creation has no control whatever.
> —*Srīrāg* m 5, p. 77

Further than this, even the following has been asserted:

> O Brother, no one knowingly makes mistakes.
> He alone goes wrong, whom the Lord misleads.
> He alone understands, whom the Lord instructs.
> —*Prabhātī Dakhṇī* m 1, p. 1344

It is a matter of context. In the context of mundane life, man is accountable within the limits of the choice given him. But at the transcendent level, man is no longer considered the doer; the only doer at that level is God. The mundane world is His game. Hence, everything in it is governed by His rules. In the game, one has to obey the rules. One who plays foul is answerable. There are few who understand that Divine game.

> The Creator Himself stages all the plays;
> How rare are those who realize this.
> —*Mārū* m 3, p. 993

The *karma* philosophy antedating Sikhism is mechanically rigid. Invariably, one has to reap the fruit of one's actions. However, in Sikhism, one who takes refuge with the Guru and mends himself as instructed and surrenders before God is forgiven by the Lord for even past sins.

> A child, innocently makes thousands of mistakes
> but his father instructs him, as also scolds him many times,
> yet, he hugs him close to himself in his embrace.
> Likewise, God forgives even our past sins
> and directs us to His Path in the future.
> —*Soraṭh* m 5, p. 624

One merely has to pray to invoke the Lord's forgiveness:

> I make mistakes every moment.
> I cannot be saved if You call for my account.

You are the forgiving Lord; forgive me and ferry me across.
—*Bāvan Akhrī, Gauṛī* m 5, p. 261

Such a prayer melts His Loving Heart and He opens wide the portals of His forgiveness. In that way, prayer unshackles the restraints of *karma* and lets even a sinner attain salvation.

CHAPTER 62

Shortcomings in Practice

At times, one is inclined to think, 'What is the use of prayer? I have prayed many times, but I never benefitted from it.' Many people endure this skepticism, but the main reason for not benefitting from *ardās* is defective practice. Here we consider some of these defects.

BEING STUCK WITH WORDS

Whenever human helplessness soars up towards the Divine, prayer emerges. It may then assume verbal expression. However, words are merely its vesture and not the real prayer. They are, however, often mistaken for prayer. That is why people occasionally spend all their effort in shaping the words of their prayer. However, verbal cleverness never pleases God. *Ardās* is essentially a state of the spirit—sincere and humble. It appears before words and lasts after words have concluded. If the spirit is absent, no prayer has been said.

In fact, in *ardās*, it is more important to listen than to talk. When we open our hearts to God, words automatically emerge to interpret our thoughts. Words have no function beyond that. Then it is important to listen to Him to whom you have bared your heart. For listening, silence and focused attention are required. Remember that:

> By listening, even the blind can find the path.
> —*Jap(u)*, p. 2

MY DESIRE AND HIS POWER

Often, we pray only to invite God's power to fulfil our desires, and we expect that He would do so instantly. Our impatience outbids itself when we are facing a disaster. In our impatience, we tend to believe that our prayer has the right to be heard and that it is God's duty to answer it at once. However, things take their natural course, and we tend to believe that God has not answered our prayer. That breaks our heart and weakens our faith. The fact, however, is that the prayer was answered but we did not realize it. We wanted to hear the answer that we had suggested to God. We only wanted to hear that answer and no other. But God is not amenable to any will other than His own. He has reserved the right to provide whatever answer He wills.

He answered our prayer, but we failed to follow it. He said, 'My child! You had been given the prerogative of prayer not to transgress my Will, but to recognize it. Why are you misusing it?' But we neither perceive His answer, nor do we want to accept it.

Our concept of 'benefit' is also coarse. We only look for material gain, worldly honour or status. God only smiles over us, saying, 'My child, you asked me for wealth and I gave it to you. But you became proud of the wealth and began to treat the less fortunate ones poorly. When you asked me for wealth, it only exposed the triviality of your desire. You didn't think of anything better.'

Those who know how to beg properly, do not ask for inferior things. Ansari, a Sūfi *dervish* of Herat, begged this of God, 'I have come to beg of You, what all the monarchs put together cannot have. They all come to You for fulfilment of their needs. I have come to You to beg of You Your own Self. Pray, give me that.' The Guru also tells us what to beg:

> To ask for anything other than You, Lord, yields utmost misery.
> Please bless me with Your *Nām* that yields content;
> so that the hunger of my mind is satiated.
>
> —*Rāmkalī* m 5, p. 958

STRUGGLING IN PRAYER

Sometimes we debate with God—not at the verbal but at the mental level—as if our desires are quarrelling with God's Will. We may not say it, but inwardly we feel, 'O God, what I have demanded from you is really hard, but if You do it in a particular way it can become possible.' For example, a student prays before his examination. Verbally he says, 'O God give me success'. But inwardly and silently he says, 'I know it is not easy, but if You arrange that the four questions that I prepared this morning appear during the exam, You will have done Your job'. This is fighting faith and wrestling with God.

In prayer, there should be no such struggling and wrestling with God; one must, instead, be struggling against oneself. One must fight inclinations such as laziness that make us neglect praying.

PRAYING FOR IMPROPER PURPOSES

In utter selfishness we may ask God to keep our evil actions masked. Even worse, we might pray for causing harm to our adversaries. Such supplications are impermissible in prayer, for they contravene basic moral values.

IGNORING GOD'S MERCY.

A mother pushes away the hand of her child if he were about to put it in fire. Similarly, God pushes the hand of the lost man away when he puts his hand into the fire of sin. The jerk that God gives him might appear as His wrath, but it is, in fact, His Mercy. In this way, God acts like a loving parent. Instead of recognizing His Mercy and being thankful to Him we go into tantrums like foolish children and may even get annoyed with God.

At such times, *ardās* can save us from becoming thankless. It behoves us on such occasions to hold fast the sacred hem of the Lord and pray ardently. Even if, at times, we might go astray, we shall get back on the right track if we keep praying.

CHAPTER 63

The Stages of *Ardās*

This way, we climb the ladder rung by rung
and come to merge with the One Lord.

—*Jap(u)*, p. 7

Ardās is in and of itself a perfect means of attaining God. Even though the beginning of the *ardās* is from our material needs and deprivations, if we continue on its path, it releases us from these and makes us realize our God. Starting with prayer for comforts, it proceeds to exuberant love for the Lord. The more this love increases, the more the Lord moves towards us. When one's impatience reaches its summit, the Lord takes the writhing soul into His embrace.

Taking me by the arm, the Lord has made me His own
not considering my merits or demerits.

—*Jaitsarī*, m 5, p. 704

The stage of spiritual advancement an individual has reached is apparent from his prayers. The greater the distance from our Lord, the more would be supplication for material needs in our *ardās*. As the distance diminishes, so does our supplication for such needs. Towards the summit, the desireless mind becomes an uninterrupted *ardās*. The prayer of every seeker evolves through a number of stages. Only those who have personally experienced the stages know what they are. The seekers who are still struggling at the level of material needs cannot say anything about the higher stages. Notwithstanding, no discussion on the *ardās* is complete without at least a cursory mention of these stages. What follows is a treatment of the experiences of a number of accomplished souls. However, they naturally felt hampered by the ineffability regarding much of their experience. This attempt at describing essentially indescribable experiences is guided by the hope that those who are at the preliminary stages will be aided by some indication of the coming scenario. Of course, those who have passed through all the stages do not need any further information.

STAGE I: *ARDĀS* OF PETITION

The first stage of *ardās* is marked by petitioning or supplicating the Lord for the fulfilment of our needs. A deprived person naturally makes this kind of prayer. Even in such a prayer, there is a glimmer of sweet love. God is pleased if we unhesitatingly approach Him with full confidence and tell him our needs—just as our children come to us and tell us their needs. We cannot do much for our children, but God can do everything. So why hesitate to ask Him who is able to fulfil all our needs:

> The Lord is the Fulfiller of desires, the Giver of all comfort;
> who owns the wish-fulfilling cow.
> So meditate on such a Lord, O my soul.
> so that you obtain total peace.
>
> —*Dhanāsrī* m 4, p. 669

If we trust our Lord fully, how can we beg from another person at all? Won't that be shameful for us?

> O imprudent being, don't you feel ashamed?
> Having forsaken the Lord, where will you now go?
> Unto whom will you turn?
> One whose Lord is the most exalted —
> Is it proper for him to go to the house of someone else?
>
> —*Gauṛī-Soraṭh* Kabīr, p. 330

If we beg unhesitatingly from our Lord, maybe we make inappropriate demands. But children also make wrong demands from their parents, and parents have the right to accept or reject those demands. If, in ignorance, we make a silly demand from our Lord, even if that demand is not fulfilled, we at least achieve nearness to the Lord. Why let this benefit go? Let us beg with full freedom just as Bhagat Dhannā did. Here is how he petitioned:

> O Lord of the world, this is Your lamp-lit worship service.
> Those who perform Your worship, you set their affairs right.
> Lentils, flour and ghee I beg of You.

These things would ever please my mind.
I beg of You shoes, fine clothes, and grain of seven kinds,
A milch cow, a water-buffalo,
and a fine horse from Turkestan.
Finally, a good wife to take care of my home.
Your servant Dhannā begs of You all these.
—*Dhanāsrī* Dhannā, p. 695

Whether we have material privations or mental problems, we have none else apart from our Lord to approach. If we are beset by a fear, we must supplicate God for His protection. Here is how a petition has been inscribed in a verse that is a part of our *nit nem.*

With Your hand, protect me Sire,
And fulfil my heart's desire.
Close to Your Feet, Lord, let me dwell.
Make me Yours, protect me well.
Smite my enemies one and all,
Keep me safe, and make them fall.
Let my kin in peace abide,
My votaries and serfs, beside.
—*DG, Benatī Caupaī* 1,2

When through such petitions, we attain proximity to the Lord, our values begin to change and privations begin to appear frivolous. The concept of 'comfort' changes. The desire for material things begins to appear insignificant. We start to feel the triviality of our demands.

What should I ask of You? Nothing lasts.
—*Āsā* Kabīr, p. 481

At that point our prayers begin to transcend our material needs and our requests take a new form:

Eating, drinking, playing and laughing,
I wandered through countless incarnations.
Pray, lift me out of the terrifying world-ocean,
Nānak seeks Your Support, O Lord.
—*Bāvan Akhrī, Gauṛī* m 5, p. 261

Then the seeker begins to feel that his own mind is an obstacle in the way of his spiritual progress, as it pushes him into the mundane rat race. His instincts keep him on tenterhooks. Surging waves of lust, blazing fire of wrath, covetousness for things and power, fragile attachments with relatives and friends, and the proud, intoxicated ego, all break on the raft of his life. He wishes to escape from the throes of these adversaries and prays:

> Five vicious thieves are assaulting poor me;
> save me, O Saviour Lord!
>
> —*Gauṛī* m 5, p. 206

Whether man asks for physical comforts, mental felicity or spiritual progress, he is essentially begging. As his *ardās* evolves, his prayers become more subtle and he begins to soar into higher states.

STAGE II: PRAYER OF THANKFULNESS

It is easy to beg, but it is not so easy to thank. After receiving gifts, it should be natural to thank, but it seldom is. Even in everyday life, we see that it is natural for a child to request the parents for his/her needs, but the child has to be taught how to thank them. When we receive gifts from God, we consider it His essential obligation. Often, we consider the gift the result of our own effort, but we don't consider who has enabled us to make that effort.[1]

When we have to beg for some gifts, our face is invariably towards God; after we have received the gift, we turn our back on Him. How unthankful![2] The ungrateful ones have been described as burden on Earth. They are considered worse than the worst human beings.[3] Thankfulness is the sign of being civilized; thanklessness is an indication of being uncivilized.

Thankfulness is an important aspect of prayer. However, some of us are likely to think that since God is so great, what difference does our thanking make to Him. It surely makes no difference to

[1] I have not appreciated what You have done for me, Lord;
You alone have made me worthy.—*Muṅdāvaṇī* sl. m 5, p. 1429

[2] You bless us with everything through Your Mercy;
But we are such ungrateful wretches!—*Bilāval* m 5, p. 809

[3] The ungrateful are the heaviest burden on the earth—
They are easily the worst of the worst beings.
—Bhāī Gurdās *Vār*, 35.8

Him, it only makes a difference to us. If a child does not thank his father, it makes little difference to his father; however, a child who thanks his father is appreciated by his father. To thank *Wāheguru* is to sing His praise. He gives what we beg of Him, and even what we have never begged for.

Thankfulness makes the *ardās* even easier. We can then supplicate with greater confidence and greater freedom.

In fact, thanking God is little more than our desperation. For how many of His gifts can we thank Him? He has provided us with far more than what we have ever asked of Him. In reality, we do not even know our needs. We also don't know how to make *ardās* properly even for our own needs. Yet, we get everything—more than we could ever ask for. However, our ungratefulness remains absolutely patent.[4]

When the shame of our ungratefulness arises from within, we become aware of other transgressions that we make and also of the negligence of our duties. This feeling becomes even more intense when one is really thankful. Repentance then wells up and penitent tears begin to flow. One then seeks refuge with God and implores His forgiveness. The forgiving Lord

> Forgives the past actions,
> and places one on His path for the future.
> —*Soraṭh* m 5, p. 624

STAGE III: PRAYER OF ADULATION

Gratitude and adulation are related sentiments. Both glorify the Lord. When we thank Him, we laud Him for His gifts. When we praise Him, we glorify His Being. Adulation is a higher state of mind than that of gratitude. Gratitude is oriented toward needs, adulation is oriented towards God. Anyone who has absorbed himself in the adulation of God knows how inadequate we are for that. We would feel:

[4] I have hardly appreciated what You have done for me,
Lord, I grasp even what is forbidden.
What face shall I show You, Lord? I am but a wicked thief.
—*Srīrāg* m 1, p. 24

Which of Your Glorious Virtues should I recount and sing?
You, my Lord, are the treasure of excellence.
I hardly can express Your Glorious Praises.
You are my Master, lofty and supreme.

—*Sūhī* m 4, p. 735

Just as a river falling into the ocean cannot know the depth of the ocean, likewise, those who laud the Lord have no idea of His greatness.[5] Whatever little we know of His grandeur, it is on account of His grace or His gifts.

When someone tunes his mind to laud the Lord, he realizes that the entire universe is singing His praises. Guru Nānak's composition *Sodar* affirms such an experience. He found even the earth, the sky, the sun and the moon, the stars and the galaxies all singing the Lord's *ārtī*, the lamp-lit worship service.[6]

We describe God as the greatest of the great, but do we really have an expression commensurate with His greatness? Can our best words even begin to sing His fulsome praise? When we become aware of our inability to praise Him adequately, our humble clay feels ashamed and embarrassed. It humbly supplicates before the Lord, 'O Lord, enable me to praise you. On my own, I am utterly incapable'. Whenever, through His grace, God harnesses someone to His praise, the heart of that individual automatically begins to sing. The subtle music of these songs is His *kīrtan*. The souls that are dyed in His praise eventually become

[5]The praisers praise the Lord, but cannot assess His enormity.
Like the streams and rivers that flow into the ocean,
But do not know its vastness. —*Jap(u)*, m 1, p. 5

[6]Upon that cosmic platter of the sky, the sun and the moon are the lamps.
The stars and their orbs are the studded pearls.
The fragrance of sandalwood is the temple incense, the wind is the whisk.
All the flora makes the altar flowers for the offering to You, O Luminous Lord.
What a beautiful *Ārtī* (lamp-lit worship), this is!
O Destroyer of Fear, this is Your Ceremony of Light.
The Unstruck Sound-current is vibration of the drums.

—*Sohilā, Dhanāsrī* m 1, p. 13

indistinguishable from Him. At that point they don't have to beg from Him anymore. They transcend all needs; they know the mystery of pleasure and pain and thereafter find pleasure in pain and satiety in hunger. They forever abide in an unending peaceful state. This tranquil state is the state of *Sahaj*.

STAGE IV: DIALOGUE IN PRAYER

A tranquil soul rests in the love-lap of God like a satiated infant in the lap of his mother. A satisfied child chuckles in his mother's lap with joy. A satisfied soul in a state of transcendent ecstasy is in dialogue with the Master. The language of the soul is the *ardās* while God's language is *bhāo apār* (infinite love).[7]

When we talk to God through *ardās*—like the chuckling of the child—then the Lord in His infinite grace responds to us—like the smile of the mother. What God communicates to the squirming soul becomes the *anāhat nād* (unstruck music)—the music of silence—and His love percolates into every pore of the devotee.[8]

The Lord who has given us the right to pray never grows tired of our supplications. If we talk to Him, He becomes only more fond of us. If we seek His counsel, He becomes only more benevolent to us. He knows what is in our mind, and He never turns His face away from us.[9]

Who can be better from whom to seek advice than the omniscient and omnipotent Lord?[10] The Lord, who is all love, is keen to let us be His partners in dialogue. Practitioners of *ardās*

[7]True is the Master, True is His *Nām*;
His language is infinite love.—*Jap(u)*, m 1, p. 2

[8]The Sound-current of His Word fills my ears;
my body settles down into the Lap of my Beloved.
—*Sārang* m 5, p. 1210

[9]My conversation is with the One Lord alone;
He neither frowns, nor turns His face away.
He always knows the state of my soul;
And never ignores my love at all.—*Vār Rāmkalī* m 5, p. 958

[10]My only counsellor is He who is all-powerful for He alone destroys and creates. —*Vār Rāmkalī* m 5, p. 958

seek His counsel for everything because He alone can support us.[11] He remains ready to participate in even our pettiest undertakings. He is more than eager to assist us, and He does not leave us alone even in our everyday work:

> The Lord hurries to be wherever the affairs of His servants are.
> He appears near at hand to His servant.
> Whatever the servant asks for, that comes to pass instantly.
> —*Āsā* m 5, p. 403

This experience of the Lord's nearness to us makes our being full to the brim. When God is with you, you do not need to depend on anyone else. A silent joy fills your soul and a pervasive intimacy sprouts from within. There is no alienation anywhere. Only friendship abides everywhere, within as well as without. When He becomes your friend, you seem to live in a world that is all friendliness.

STAGE V: SPEECHLESS PRAYER

Ardās is basically a spiritual experience not dependent on words. Even when it appears in words, its wordless form comes into being before any words get uttered. Even when the echo of words subsides, its subtle presence continues to flicker in the praying soul.

We are always happy to talk to one who we love, but when love touches its summit, words drop down altogether. Then, the presence of one another is enjoyed through reciprocal love-glances. Likewise, when our love for the Lord touches its peak, then words simply drop away from *ardās*, and our entire being becomes an unending *ardās*. In our life, there are cravings, relations and experiences of so subtle a nature that they defy being couched in words. Speaking of such experiences is utterly in vain.[12] There are many skirmishes of the soul which cannot be stated. It is not necessary to talk to God when we experience Him;

[11] I talk with the Lord, I also seek His counsel,
His *Nām* always takes care of me.—*Vār Vadhaṅs* m 4, p. 592

[12] O friend, for realizing Truth, talking is in vain
—*Vār Mārū Dakhṇe* m 5, p. 1100

we can just let our fatigued soul rest in the solitude of His all-loving lap. Where else can we rest our soul when we have become sick of our life? When a love-sick soul rests there, it does not need to talk at all. Its eloquent silence says, 'I have reached here after a very long journey; I am dead tired. Can I rest in your loving presence? I don't want to go anywhere else now. I only want to rest. Don't separate me from You even for a moment.'

A heart engaged in silent *ardās* brims with the pleasant illumination of the Lord, and the entire universe seems full of indescribable beauty. Life becomes fragrant, and one's being appears intoxicated.

At times, divine luminosity speeds inside like lightning. In this state, even spiritual wonderment leaves us not only utterly speechless, but also unaware of ourselves. When all suffering disappears, what is left to supplicate for?

> Seeing God, His minstrel is rid of pain and hunger;
> now he can't think what to ask .
>
> —*Vār Mārū Dakhṇe* m 5, p. 1097

When there remains nothing to beg and nothing to say, the praying devotee becomes a living *ardās* himself.

Bibliography

Ādi Srī Guru Granth jī Sāhib (Puṅjābī): ed. Giani Badan Siṅgh, Patiala, Punjab Languages Department, 1989, 4th Edn.

Attar Siṅgh: *Sākhī Pothī,* Amritsar, Office K͟hālsā Samācār, 1968.

Besant, Annie: *The Ancient Wisdom,* London, Theosophical Publishing House, 1897.

Bhagat Singh: *Gur Bilās Pātshāhī Chevīṅ* (Puṅjābī), ed. Gurmukh Siṅgh Patiala, Publication Bureau, Punjabi University, 1997.

Bhāī Bālā: *Janam Sākhī* (Puṅjābī), Amritsar, Bh. Jawāhar Siṅgh Kirpāl Siṅgh & Co., 1962.

Bhaṅgū, Rattan Siṅgh: *Prācīn Paṅth Prakāsh* (Puṅjābī), ed. Bhāī Vīr Siṅgh, New Delhi, Bhāī Vīr Siṅgh Sāhitya Sadan, 1993 (rpt.).

Bible, The New Testament, The Gideons, Paulo Alto, National Publishing House, 1969.

Bowker, John: *The Oxford Dictionary of World Religions,* Oxford, Oxford University Press, 1997.

Caupa Siṅgh: *Rahit Nāmā* quoted in Padam, Piara Singh, *Rahit Nāme* q.v. below.

Cohen, Arthur A. and Paul Mendes-Flohr: *Contemporary Jewish Religious Thought,* London, Collier Macmillan Publishers, 1972.

Dasam Granth—Randhīr Siṅgh, Bhāī q.v. below.

Dilgeer, Harjiṅder Siṅgh: *The Sikh Reference Book,* Edmonton Alb., University of Alberta Postal Outlet.

Euripides: *The Phoenician Women (c.411-409 BC),* tr. Elizabeth Wycoff.

Ganda Siṅgh, ed.: *Hukam Nāme Guru Sāhibān, Mātā Sāhibān, Baṅdā Siṅgh te K͟hālsā jī,* Patiala, Punjabi University, 1963.

Garjā Siṅgh, ed.: *Shahīd Bilās,* Ludhiānā, Punjabī Sāhit Academy, 1961.

Gianī Giān Siṅgh: *Paṅth Prakāsh,* 1880.

Glasse, Cyril: *The Concise Encyclopaedia of Islam,* London, Stacey International, 1989.

Gopal Siṅgh: *Sri Guru Graṅth Sāhib* (English Version), Delhi, Gurdas Kapur & Sons, 1960.

Greenlees, Duncan: *The Gospel of Guru Graṅth Sāhib,* Adiyar (Madras, India) The Theosophical Publishing House, 1952.

Grewal, J.S.: *A Study of Guru Granth Sahib,* Amritsar, Singh Brothers, 2009.

Grewal, J.S. and Irfan Habib: *Sikh History from Persian Sources,* New Delhi, Tulika, 2001.

Gurdas, Bhāī: *Vāraṅ,* Text, Transliteration and Translation by Jodh Singh, Patiala, New Delhi, Vision & Venture, 1998.

Harbans Singh, ed.: *Encyclopedia of Sikhism,* Patiala, Punjabi University, 1992.

Harī Siṅgh, Gurmukh Bābā: *Rāh Numāe Dīdār e Haq* (Urdu), Lahore, Divan Printing Press, 1935.

Holy Qur'an (Arabic), English Translation by Maulawi Sher 'Ali Qadian, Qadian, Mirza Wasim Ahmad Nazir Dawat-o-Tabligh, 1965.

Homer: *Iliad,* tr. Samuel Butler.

Jagat Singh, Major: *Kes Mahatta* (Punjabi), Patiala, Guru Nanak Dev Mission, 1968.

Joshi, S.S., Mukhtiar Singh: *Punjabi-English Dictionary,* Patiala, Publication Bureau, Punjabi University, 1994.

Khafi Khan: *Muntakhib Lubāb* (Persian) MS.

Koer Siṅgh: *Gurbilās Patshāhī 10* (Punjabi), ed. Shamsher Singh, Patiala, Punjabi University, 1980.

Manī Siṅgh, Bhāī: *Sikhāṅ di Bhagat Mālā* (Punjabi), New Delhi, Bhāī Vīr Siṅgh Sāhitya Sadan, 2007 (also titled *Giān Ratnāvalī*).

Maslow, Abraham: *The Further Reaches of Human Nature,* London, Viking Press, 1971.

McLeod, W.H.: *Guru Nanak and the Sikh Religion,* Delhi, Oxford University Press, 1976.

———: *The Evolution of the Sikh Community,* Delhi, Oxford University Press, 1975.

———: *The Chaupa Singh Rehat Nama,* Duniden, University of Otago Press, 1987.

Mobad: *Dabistān-e-Mazāhib* (Persian) quoted in Grewal and Irfan q.v. above.

Monier, Monier-Williams: *A Sanskrit-English Dictionary,* Motilal Banarsidass, 1999.

Nabha, Kahn Singh: *Mahān Kosh* (Punjabi), Delhi, National Book Shop, 1992.

Narang, Gokul Chand: *The Transformation of Sikhism,* New Delhi, Kalyan Publishers, 5th edn., 1989.

Neki, Jaswant Singh: *Ardās, Darshan Rūp te Abhiās* (Punjabi), Amritsar, Singh Brothers, 2004.

———: *Spiritual Heritage of the Punjab,* Amritsar, Guru Nanak Dev University, 2000.

———: *Basking in the Divine Presence,* Amritsar, Singh Brothers, 2008.

Nietzsche, Friedrich: *Thus Spake Zarathustra,* Cambridge, Cambridge University Press, 2006.

Oberoi, Harjot: *The Construction of Religious Boundaries,* Delhi, Oxford University Press, 1994.

Padam, Piārā Siṅgh: *Rahit Nāme* (Punjabi), Amritsar, Singh Brothers, 1995.

Parkash Singh: *Community Kitchen of the Sikhs,* Amritsar, Singh Brothers, 1994.

Pritam Singh: *Sikh Vichār Dhārā* (Punjabi), Amritsar, Shiromani Gurdwara Prabandhak Committee, 1962.

Randhir Singh, Bhāī: *Shabdārath Dasam Graṅth Sāhib* (3 vols.), Patiālā, Publication Bureau, Punjabi University, 1985.

Rahner, Karl, ed.: *Encyclopedia of Theology,* London, Burn & Oates, 1981.

Rumi, Mevlana: *Masnavi.*

Saṅtokh Siṅgh, Bhāī: *Srī Gur Pratāp Sūraj,* Amritsar, Manager, Khalsa Samachar, 1955.

Sarna, Navjot: *Zafarnama,* New Delhi, Penguin, 2011.

Sevā Siṅgh: *Sarab Loh Graṅth,* Amritsar, Bhāī Catar Siṅgh & Co., 2000.

Srī Guru Graṅth Kosh (Punjabi), Amritsar, Shiromani Gurdwara Prabandhak Committee, 1899.

Shabdārath Srī Guru Graṅth Sāhib jī (Punjabi), Amritsar, Shiromani Gurdwara Prabandhak Committee, 1986.

Talib, Gurbachan Singh: *Sri Guru Granth Sahib* in English Translation, Patiala, Publication Bureau, Punjabi University, 1988.

Teja Singh: *Sikhs and Non-Violence,* Amritsar, Chief Khalsa Diwan 1968.

Tresidder, Jack: *The Hutchison Dictionary of Symbols,* Oxford, Helicon Publishing Ltd., 1997.

Vīr Siṅgh, Bhāī: *Saṅthyā Srī Guru Graṅth Sāhib jī* (vols. 1-7, Punjabi), New Delhi, Bhāī Vīr Siṅgh Sāhitya Sadan, 1997.

Index of Names

Abdālī, Ahmad Shah 190, 213, 233
Abdulla Ḍhāḍī 153
Adinā Beg 177
Ajīt Siṅgh, Bābā 101-2, 104, 219
Akbar, Emperor 123
Ālā Siṅgh 190
Ālā Siṅgh, Bhāī 218
Andrews, C.F. 134
Aṇī Rāe, Bābā 101
Ansārī 257
Atal Rāe, Bābā 101
Auraṅgzeb, Emperor 55, 131, 133, 144

Bābur, Emperor 51
Bādū, Bhāī 194
Bahādur Shah, Emperor 126
Bahilo, Bhāī 184
Baiṇī, Bhagat 24
Balvaṅḍ, Rāe 24, 171, 199
Baṅdā Siṅgh Bahādur 59, 122, 133, 136
Basāvā Siṅgh 106
Bhāg Bharī 95
Bhāg Siṅgh 105
Bhagvān Dās 108
Bhagvān Siṅgh 106
Bhaṅgā Siṅgh 105
Bhīkhā, Bhāī 87
Bhīkhaṇ, Sufi *fakir* 24
Bholā Siṅgh 105
Bidhī Caṅd, Bhāī 96fn, 138f
Bīrbal 125
Bishan Siṅgh 105
Brookes, Phillip 79fn
Bū Alī Qalaṅdar 205
Buḍḍhā, Bābā 213, 216
Buddhā, Lord 187
Būṛ Siṅgh 105

Caṅbā Siṅgh 105
Caṛhat Siṅgh 106
Caupa Siṅgh 55, 185
Cūhaṛ, Bhāī 184

Dalīp Siṅgh, Mahārājā 191
Damodar Siṅgh 106
Darbārā Siṅgh 105
Dāsū jī 100
Dātū jī 100
Dayālā, Bhāī 96fn, 144
Dayāl Siṅgh 105
Decker, Thomas 187
Desā Siṅgh Majīṭhīā 218
Devā Siṅgh 98
Dhannā Bhagat 24, 260
Dhannā Siṅgh 105
Dharam Siṅgh 105
Dharam Siṅgh, Bhāī 98
Dilbāgh Siṅgh 105, 141
Dīn Muhammad 118f
Dīp Siṅgh, Bābā 195
Durgā, goddess 78f

Farīd, Sheikh 23, 89
Farrukh Saīyar 116, 214
Fateh Siṅgh, Bābā 101-2
Fātimā Bībī 142

Gaṅgā Siṅgh 106
Gaṅḍā Siṅgh 106
Gāṅdhī, Mahātmā 205
Gharbārā Siṅgh 105
Gobiṅd, Bhāī 57
Gobiṅd Rāe, Srī 90, 101, 135
Gujrī, Mātā 102
Gulāb Siṅgh 106
Gurdās, Bhāī 86-7, 123, 207
Gurdās Siṅgh 106

Gurdit Siṅgh 106
Gurdittā, Bābā 101
Gurdittā, Bhāī 96
Guru Aṅgad Dev 23, 57, 99, 100, 122, 194, 195
Guru Amar Dās 23, 100, 199, 123, 184, 195, 217
Guru Arjan Dev 23, 58, 101, 109, 123, 125, 130, 171, 177, 186, 208, 211, 213
Guru Hargobiṅd 58, 101, 126, 127, 153, 184, 215, 217
Guru Harkrishan 101, 135
Guru Har Rāe 101, 123, 135, 156
Guru Gobiṅd Siṅgh 58, 94, 96, 99, 101, 105, 123, 125, 126, 127, 131, 136, 158, 163, 164, 168, 174, 177, 180, 188, 189, 195, 217, 221, 222
Guru Nānak Dev 23, 26, 51, 55, 57, 82, 96, 99, 100, 101, 115, 119, 122, 126, 137, 161, 179, 184, 188, 189, 194, 195, 217, 264
Guru Rām Dās 23, 58, 100, 111
Guru Tegh Bahādur 23, 101, 125, 129, 133, 135, 144, 177, 211, 213, 217

Haṅdāl 138fn
Har Bhagat 138
Hardās Siṅgh 106
Harī jī Sodhī 136
Hari Siṅgh 105
Harī Siṅgh, Gurmukh Bābā 112
Harkishan Siṅgh, Bāvā 195
Harsā Siṅgh 105
Himmat Siṅgh 98, 106

Jādo Siṅgh 105
Jagat Siṅgh, Major 188fn
Jahāṅgīr, Emperor 216
Jai Dev, Bhagat 24, 211
Jaimal Siṅgh 106
Jaitā, Bhāī 96fn, 125
Jaṅg Siṅgh 105
Jassā Siṅgh, Sardār 177
Jawāhar Siṅgh 106
Jawālā Siṅgh 106
Jeṭhā jī 96, 100
Jhaṅḍa Siṅgh 106
Jodhā, Bhāī 124
Jogā Siṅgh 105

Kabir, Bhagat 24
Kahna, Bhagat 112
Kalashār, Bhaṭṭ 200, 217
Kalhā Siṅgh 105
Kanhaīyā, Bhāī 109
Kapūr Siṅgh 142
Karam Siṅgh 105, 106
Karan Siṅgh 105
Kelman, Harold 192
Keso, Bhaṭṭ 87
Khāfī Khān 133
Khaṛag Siṅgh 106
Khīvī, Mātā 122
Khushāl Siṅgh 105
Khushvaqt Rāe 164
Kīrat Siṅgh 105
Kripāl Siṅgh 105
Kirpal Siṅgh 106

Lachmaṇ Siṅgh 105
Lakhmī Dās, Bābā 100
Laṅgāhā, Bhāī 96fn
Locan Dhūm 80

Macauliffe, M.A. 173
Mahādev, Srī 100, 101
Mahāṅ Siṅgh 105
Mahāṅ Siṅgh, Jathedār 105
Māī Dās 135
Maīyā Siṅgh 105
Manī Siṅgh 26, 135, 196
Mān Siṅgh 105
Mardānā, Bhāī 24, 122, 161, 188
Massā Raṅghaṛ 60, 213
Matāb Siṅgh 60, 106, 213
Matī Dās, Bhāī 96fn, 144
Mehkhāsur 81
Mīāṅ Miṭhā 208

Mīāṅ Mīr 211
Mīr Mannū 163, 214
Mohan, Bābā 86, 100
Mohiṅdar Siṅgh Rattan 195
Mohkam Siṅgh 106
Mohkam Siṅgh, Bhāī 98
Mohrī, Bābā 100
Mohsin Fānī 58
Moses, Prophet 31
Muhammad, Prophet 41, 142, 188, 206
Muīn-ud-Dīn Chishtī, Khwājā 208f

Nādar Shāh 238
Nāmdev, Bhagat 24
Naṅd Lāl, Bhāī 54-5, 119f
Narbud Bhaṭṭ 87
Nānakī, Bebe 57
Nārāyaṇ Dās, Mahaṅt 225
Nārāyaṇ Siṅgh 106
Nathā Ḍhāḍī 153
Nidhān Siṅgh 105
Nihāl Siṅgh 105
Nihāl Siṅgh 106
Nūr Dīn 125
Nūr Muhammad 144

Paiṛā 96fn
Paṅjāb Siṅgh 106
Parmānaṅd, Bhagat 24
Pāro Julkā 186
Phirmā Bhāī 96fn, 184
Phūlā Siṅgh, Akālī 60, 154
Pigārū, Bhaṭṭ 125
Pīlū 112
Pīpā, Bhagat 24
Prem Siṅgh 106
Prītam Dās, Bābā 217
Prithī Caṅd 100, 123, 130, 213
Pūran Siṅgh 122

Rāe Bulār 57, 225
Rāe Siṅgh 105
Rakt Bīj 77
Rāmānaṅd, Bhagat 24
Rām Rāe, Bābā 101
Raṇjīt Siṅgh 106
Raṅjīt Siṅgh, Mahārājā 50-1, 60, 61
Rattan Siṅgh 106
Rāvaṇa 110
Ravidās, Bhagat 24
Rumī, Mevlānā 31

Sadhnā, Bhagat 24
Sādhū Siṅgh 105
Sādū, Bhāī 194
Sahaj Siṅgh 106
Sāhib Devāṅ, Mātā 98, 158
Sāhib Siṅgh 106
Sāhib Siṅgh Bedī, Bābā 117f
Sāhib Siṅgh, Bhāī 98, 195
Sahjo Bāī 83
Sāhlo, Bhāī 184
Saiṇ, Bhagat 24
Sāmarth Rāmdās 126
Samīr Siṅgh 105
Saṅgat Siṅgh 160
Sāṅgo Siṅgh 106
Saṅtokh Dās, Bāvā 217
Saṅtokh Siṅgh, Bhāī 185
Saṅt Siṅgh 105, 106
Sardūl Siṅgh 105
Sarjā Siṅgh 105
Sarūp Siṅgh 106
Satī Dās, Bhāī 144
Sattā, Bhāī 24, 95
Sevā Siṅgh 105
Shāhbāz Siṅgh 141, 142
Shāh Hussain 112
Sher Siṅgh 105
Sher Siṅgh, Mahārājā 218
Sirī Caṅd, Bābā 100
Sobhā Siṅgh 105
Subeg Siṅgh 141, 142, 143
Suhel Siṅgh 105
Sujān Siṅgh 106
Sukhā Siṅgh 60
Sulhī Khān 37, 125
Sultān Siṅgh 105

Suṅdar, Bhāī 24
Suṅdrī, Mātā 88
Sūraj Mal, Bābā 101
Sūrdās, Bhagat 24

Ṭagore, Rabiṅdra Nāth 188
Tārā Bāī 122
Tārā Siṅgh, Bhāī 138, 189
Tejā Siṅgh, Principal 195
Ṭhākur Siṅgh 106
Tiāg Mal, Bābā 101, 125
Trilocan, Bhagat 24
Trilok Siṅgh 106

Udā, Bhāī 96fn

Vinobā Bhāve 188
Vīr Siṅgh, Bhāī 195
Vishnū Digambar 188

Wazīr Khān 102

Yāhyā Khān 142

Zakarīā Khān 123, 136, 139, 141, 233
Zarathustra 41
Zorāwar Siṅgh, Bābā 101, 102

Subject Index

Akāl (the Immortal) 31ff
  Bungā/Bungah (Hospice) 153
  Purakh (the Immortal Lord) 152
  Regiment 154
  Takht (Throne of the Immortal Lord) 153ff
Akhand Pāṭh (un-interrupted recitation of the holy Book) 234
All-Steel 165
  protection by 165, 176fn
Amrit (ambrosia; potion for initiating ceremony) 98
  -dhārī Sikh 189
  -sanskār (initiating ceremony of the *Khālsā*) 98
Amristar 211
  Harmandar Sāhib 167
Ardās (Prayer) 29-267
  in the Sikh faith 53ff
    as instrument of worship 53
    as vision of the *Khālsā* Commonwealth, 164
    bāṇi of Guru *Khālsā* 238
    congregational 53, 243ff
    in *Rahitnāmās* 54ff
    personal 243ff
      Gurbāṇī a collection of 244
    presides over every aspect of Sikh life 54
    unique literary form, of 65
    unites devotees with *Wāhegurū*, time and again 64
    what is? 31ff
  Etymology 32ff
    phonemic significance 33
  Evolution of 57ff
    collectively approved present form 69-70
    compilation of first version of current text by Bhāī Manī Singh 59
    with Guru Nānak 57
    with Guru Angad 57
    with Guru Rām Dās 58
    with Guru Arjan Dev 58
      addressed to *Pothī Sāhib* 58
    with Guru Gobind Singh 58ff
      a manuscript of Ardas during Guru Gobind Singh's time 59
      ardās in the presence of the *Panj Piāre* 59
    with *Khālsā Panth* 60ff
      ever-evolving *bāṇī* of the *Panth* 61
Form of 67ff
  linguistic form 34
  structure of 75ff
Functions of
  a way of worship 33
  declaration of collective pledge 63
  declaration of faith 63
  declaration of 'ever-readiness i.e. *tiār bar tiār*' 64
  declaration of victory 63
  inspiring faith and martyrdom 63
  metaphysical considerations 29ff
  vehicle for the unity of the Sikhs 63
Maryādā of *ardās* (conventional way of performing) 238
  declares uncompromised monotheism at the outset 62

recited facing *Srī Guru Granth Sāhib* 238
standing posture with hands folded 238
touching forehead to the ground at its conclusion 239
Practice 241ff
with faith and devotion 243
with full attention 238
problems of 244ff
Philosophical impediments 250ff
Can *ardās* alter the fruit of Karma? 253
Can *ardās* change Divine Will? 251
Effort vs *ardās* 252
God omniscient, then why *ardās*? 251
Proof of efficacy of *ardās* 250
Psychological problems 246ff
Disappointment 245
Disbelief 246
Doubt 247
Practical hurdles 256ff
Being stuck with words 256
Ignoring Divine Mercy 258
Improper purpose 258
impleading God's power for personal desire 256
struggling in *ardās* 257
Spirit of 35ff
, faith 37
, humility 36
, beware of false 37
true 37
self-surrender 38
Stages of 259ff
I. Petition 260
II. Thankfulness 262
III. Adulation 263
IV. Dialogue in Prayer 265
V. Speechless Prayer 266
Text of the congregational *ardās* 69-73
Original in *Gurmukhī* script 69
Translation into English 73
Transliteration into Roman script 71
Universality of 41-4
in Buddisnm 43
in Christianity 43
in Islam 42
in Judaism 43
with Parsees 42
in Sikh faith 43, 53ff
in Vedas 41
with Zarthustra 41
ardāsīā (one who leads *ardās*) 160

Bhagautī (The Divine Sword) 78ff
, the ballad of 78
, goddess Durgā 78, 79
, also vide 'the Divine Sword'
Bhāṇā (Divine Pleasure) same as 'Divine Will' q.v.
Bibek (discrimination; wisdom) 199ff
four aspects of 199
leads to spiritual enlightenment 201
Bird (reputation) 171ff
ki paij (dignity of) 171ff
Bol bāle (lofty utterance, may it prevail) 179ff
words of authority 179
Buṅgā (hospice) 63, 219ff
six types of 219

Caṛhdī Kalā (high spiritual morale) 160, 170, 230ff
achieved by relying on God 230
challenges circumstances 230
Nām as the basis of 232
Caukīs (choirs) 60, 63, 215ff
historical 216

of *Nitnem* 215
pilgram 216
Consciousness, states of 141

Dān (gift, charity) 182ff
of Amritsar *ke ishnān* (a dip in the pool of immortality) 211ff
of *bharosā* (trust) 204
of *bibek* (discrimination; wisdom) 119ff
lead to enlightenment 201
of *kes* (unshorn hair) 187ff
enhance dignity and vigour 188
mandatory for the *Khālsā* 189
preserved by the spiritually endowed people 188
symbolic of *bhaktī* and *shaktī* 188
of *Nām* (the holy Name), a super-gift 207
signifies spiritual cleanliness 192
of *rahit* (code of conduct) 198
of *Sikhī* (the Sikh faith) 184ff
of *visāh* (conviction) 202ff
Deg (cauldron, signifying Divine Benevolence) 166
as *kaṛāh prasad* 121
first served to *Pañj Piāre* 99
, introduced by Guru Nānak 122
, *laṅgar* as a form of 121
no discrimination in distribution of 124
symbolic of basic needs 121
symbolic of dignity of labour 168
Dharam/dharma (Righteousness)
ka jaikār (hail righteousness) 221ff
kalā (art of, power of *dharam*) 229
three-item- 115
Dharamsāl 155

Ethics
high moral courage 93
moral aspect of *ardās* 47ff

Faith 37, 149
as gift 184
four loci of 149
freedom of 133
upholding the dignity of 149ff
Fetch vide 'victory'

Grace, Divine 33, 52
, all prosper through 235ff
and *Hukam* 236
and Bhāṇā 236
Gurdwārā(s) 63, 155ff, 225ff
as *dharamsāl* 155
as *saṅgat* 155
, *dharamsāl/saṅgat* later designated as 156
, *laṅgar* as part of 156
, *gurmat paṭhshālā* as part of 156
, *graṅthī* as caretaker of 157
, left in Pakistan 225ff
Guru(s) 82ff
all have the same spiritual light 84, 86ff
are non-personal, i.e. supracorporeal 85
as disciple 99
established by Divine Grace 85
Graṇth Sāhib 88
coronated as perrenial living guru 88
Paṅth 93ff
, Word as 85
Graṅthī (caretaker of the *Guru Graṅth Sahib*) 157
Gurbāṇī (Guru's Word) 243ff
and *ardās* 243-4
Gurus' office 100ff
not hereditary 100ff
vested also in the *Pañj Piāre* 99
Gurmattā (resolution) 151fn

Gurmukhī (The script of *Guru Granth Sāhib*) 156

Haṭh (strong determination; obduracy) 107, 109ff
, *dharam-* (determination for righteous action) 130
karam (acts of) 110
, *man-* (self-willed obduracy) 110
taboo in *gurmat* 110
yoga (a yoga of self-imposed physical strain) 110
Haumai (Ego, the sense of self) 223
Hukam see 'Will, Divine'

Jaikāra (slogan of victory) 239
bole so nihāl (whoso utters it, shall be delighted)
Sat Srī Akāl (True is the Immortal Lord) 239
Jap, *Jāp* (repetition of God's Name or a holy text) 107
, devices of
Kālpnik 112
Lom jāp 112
Malom jāp 112
Praṇāyām 112
Praṇ saṅglī 112
, as *simran* 114
Japī (one regular in *jap*) 107
Jhaṅḍā (Flag), 63, 217ff
also called *Nishān Sāhib* 217
, white 217
, saffron 217
in front of *Akāl Takht* 217
in war, carried by standard-bearer 218
of *pīrī* and *mīrī* : carries inscription of a *chakra* butressed by two *kirpāns* and vertically crossed by a *khaṅḍā* 218

Ks, five 187ff, 197
Kes (sacred hair) 187ff, 197
, attacks on 189
dān 187
mandatory for *amritdhāris* 189
part of Divine design 187
symbol of *bhaktī* and *shaktī* 188
symbol of freedom 190
symbol of spiritual culture of India 187
Kirpān (the sacred sword) 197
different from *talvār* of tyrants 126
symbol of *mīrī* and *pīrī* 127
Kachehrā (shorts) 198
symbol of purity in sex 198
Kaṅghā (comb) 197
symbol of cleanliness 197
Kaṛā (steel bangle) 197
symbol of self-restraint 197
Kalā (power, skill, art) 229
, *dharam-* 229
Wāhegurū jī kī 229ff
Khālsā, the 158ff, 163ff
brotherhood 158
Commonwealth, a non-state nation 164
, protection and concession for 163ff
, *sarbat-* 158
, word given it by Guru Gobiṅd Siṅgh 95
Khaṅḍā (a special double-edged sword) 98, 127
as symbol of Divine creativity 121
Kirt (honest labour) 115, 167
Kīrtan (holy choir) 194

Laṅgar (free kitchen) 119
Akbar partakes of 123
as arena of *sevā* 167
belongs to the Guru 123
, equanimity in 168
related to *paṅgat* and *saṅgat* 123ff
run by devotees' offerings 123
, spiritual discipline in 168
Love 46
only gives 46
, revolution of 120

Loved ones, Five 96ff
as Guru 93ff, 150
as twice-born 158
tested on the sword 96-8

Man (mind) 223ff
nīvāṅ (lowly, humble) 223
Mat (clear intellect) 223
should think sublime 223
Miracles 107
an alien taste, taboo 107
through haṭh yoga 107
Muktā (the salvaged person), 104ff, 115
forty *muktās* of Camkaur 105
forty *muktās* of Muktsar 106
Muktī (salvation) 104
Mūlmaṅtra 81
Nām (the Name of God) 111ff
as creative state of *Brahm* 209
as *dān* (topmost divine gift) 207ff
as Divine Essence 115
basis for *caṛhdī kalā* 230
japnā 115
leads to *chaṛhdi kalā* (resplendent spirit) 230ff
pervasive in and support of everything 209
the Creator revealed through 111
they who chanted 111ff

Overlooking faults of others 128ff
and forgiveness 130

Pāhul (same as *Amrit*) 161, 196
, *charan-* 161fn
, *khaṅḍe dā* 161
Paṅth, the 93ff
as embodiment of Guru 93ff, 150
a spiritual community 150
kī jīt (victory of) 120, 160, 173ff
, unity of 159
, what is? 173

Rahit (code of conduct; discipline) 192ff
, collective 192
, daily liturgies 193
, external 196
, individual 192
, internal 192
of *Amrit* 196
of *Nitnem* (daily liturgy) 193
Rāhnumā-e-Dīdār-e-Haq 112

Sacrifice 174
never suffers defeat 174
Sāhibzādās 100ff
, four (of Guru Gobiṅd Siṅgh) 101ff
Samādhī (deep inner attentivity)
, intent-less 46, 111
of *sevā* 196
, *suṅn* 114
, *sukhmālaṅbanā* 113
Saṅgat (congregation) 158
baṛī 158
choṭī 158
pakkī 158
presided over by *Srī Guru Graṅth Sāhib* 194
Sharing 115ff
, *daswaṅdh* as 119
, *laṅgar* as institution of 119
Shabad (the Word) 85
, *anāhat* 113
, *anhad* 113
, *paṅc* 113
Shahīdī (martyrdom) 132ff, 151
for freedom of faith 133
, highest miracle of *dharma* 133
, zest for 133-4
Sikhī (Sikh way of life) 184ff
dān (gift) 184ff
defined 193
, five types of 185
Srī Sāhib (the holy Sword) 176ff
, only heroes can wield 177
to be employed as a last resort 177
, worship of 176
Sword, the Divine 78ff
in hand (of God) 168

, invocation of 78
of enlightenment 176
, those who wielded 125

Takhts 152ff
Abcalnagar/Huzūr Sāhib (at Nandeṛ) 154
, Akāl- (at Amritsar) 153ff
Damdamā Sāhib (at Sābo kī Talwaṅdī) 154
Harmaṅdar Sāhib (at Patna) 153, 154
Kesgaṛh Sāhib (at Ānaṅdpur) 96, 153, 154
Tap (austerity, penance) 107
of *sevā* 109
, Sikh concept of 109
Tapī 109
, Guru Arjan Dev as supreme example of 109
Teg (Sword) 125ff
and *Ahimsā* 168
for the protection of the tyrrannized 127
worshipped 168

Vaṅd Chakṇā vide 'Sharing'
Victory 170
belongs to *Wāhegūrū* 125
ensured by weapons and rations 166ff
of *deg-teg* 170
of *Paṅth* 170, 173ff
of *Wāhegurū* 125, 170
Vismād (ecstatic wonder) 161
, *sahaj* 114

Wāhegurū 90ff
gurmaṅtra 162
, *jāp* of 107, 114
jī kī fateh (victory of) 125
, utter ye with full attention 32, 90ff
Will, Divine 146
cheerful acceptance of 146ff
ever prevails 228ff

Yoga
, *haṭh-* 109
, *paṅcāṅga-* 46